Roots in the African Dust
Sustaining the Sub-Saharan Drylands

The image of Africa in the modern world has come to be shaped by perceptions of the drylands and their problems of poverty, drought, degradation and famine. Michael Mortimore offers an alternative and revisionist thesis, dismissing both on theoretical and empirical grounds the conventional view of runaway desertification, driven by population growth and inappropriate land use. In its place he suggests a more optimistic model of sustainable land use which is based on researched case studies from East and West Africa, where indigenous technological adaptation has put population growth and market opportunities to advantage. He also proposes a more appropriate set of policy priorities to support dryland peoples in their efforts to sustain land and livelihoods. The result is a remarkably clear synthesis of much of the best work that has emerged over the past decade, and a timely and useful study.

Michael Mortimore is a Senior Research Associate at the Department of Geography, Cambridge University and the Overseas Development Institute, London. He was Professor of Geography at Bayero University, Kano from 1979 to 1986. He is the author of *Adapting to Drought* (1989) and, with Mary Tiffen and Francis Gichuki, *More People, Less Erosion* (1994).

D0217322

Roots in the African Dust

Sustaining the Sub-Saharan Drylands

MICHAEL MORTIMORE

CAMBRIDGE
UNIVERSITY PRESS

PUBLISHED BY THE PRESS SYNDICATE OF THE UNIVERSITY OF CAMBRIDGE
The Pitt Building, Trumpington Street, Cambridge CB2 1RP, United Kingdom

CAMBRIDGE UNIVERSITY PRESS
The Edinburgh Building, Cambridge CB2 2RU, United Kingdom
http://www.cup.cam.ac.uk
40 West 20th Street, New York, NY 10011–4211, USA
http://www.cup.org
10 Stamford Road, Oakleigh, Melbourne 3166, Australia

First published 1998

Printed in the United Kingdom at the University Press, Cambridge

Typeset in Rotis and Adobe Garamond 10½/13   [SE]

A catalogue record for this book is available from the British Library

ISBN 0 521 45173 6 hardback
ISBN 0 521 45785 8 paperback

In memory of Hawuwa, who died at Dagaceri on 22 September, 1995, aged three months. One among many denied a life, even in poverty

Blessed are you who are in need; the Kingdom of God is yours
Luke 6:20(REB)

Contents

Figures

Plates

Tables

Preface

The title of this book is intended to communicate hope, which is the spiritual diet of farmers, and for none so much as those who live in the drylands. Smallholders are themselves like roots in the soil. They shoot in good times, but when times are hard, they search deeper (or wider) for the moisture and the nutrients they need to sustain themselves. They die back to the basics, and surprise us with their resilience when the rain returns. Small farmers and livestock producers are the roots of African economies, and the basis for their development.

For too long it has been the convention either to dismiss smallholders as anachronistic survivors, certain to disappear in the rush to modernisation, or as quite malignant in their treatment of the African environment. This condescension, as is now recognised, was more a product of ignorance than any rational understanding. Only now, when so many foreign transplants have wilted or died in the hard earth of Africa, is the value of indigenous resources openly acknowledged. Given an enabling policy environment and unobstructed access to new ideas or markets, the resources of dryland communities can be mobilised in sustainable systems for managing natural resources.

The evidence for these assertions is found in a heterogeneous corpus of field-based studies whose published reports are widely distributed. I am more aware than any of my readers that I have been selective in choosing material for this study; and furthermore, my selectivity is the result of ignorance as well as design. Those whose work is not used must forgive me for trying to build a coherent case on what I know best, recognising that other selections might either strengthen, or bring into question, my arguments. However I believe that the multiplication of unco-ordinated, and sometimes duplicative, parallel case studies has gone far enough. There seems to me to be a need for research and debate driven by the search for a unifying theory of environmental management in drylands, encompassing their natural and human resources. I would like to think that if this root, which I am trying to nurture, perishes in the dust, a stronger one will take its place.

Acknowledgements

Some of the work reported in this study was supported (in Kenya) by the Economic and Social Research Programme of the Department for International Development (DfID, formerly Overseas Development Administration) of the United Kingdom Government, the Rockefeller Foundation, and the World Bank, and (in Nigeria) by the Global Environmental Change Programme of the Economic and Social Research Council, the Natural Resources Systems Programme of the DfID (Project No EMC X0265), and the World Bank. These agencies can accept no responsibility for the information provided or views expressed. The Kenya study has been published in greater detail elsewhere. The Nigeria studies are being prepared for publication, and I am indebted to my colleagues for their agreement for me to use selected material.

I am grateful for the institutional support and encouragement that has enabled me to pursue my interest in drylands research in Africa over many years: Ahmadu Bello University, Zaria, and Bayero University, Kano (both in Nigeria); and the Centre of West African Studies of the University of Birmingham, the Overseas Development Institute, and the Department of Geography at the University of Cambridge (in the United Kingdom), whose third year students of the Geography of Africa in 1993/94 suffered an earlier exposure to, and hopefully questioned, these ideas.

In tilling this soil I have learnt from so many people that it is impossible to mention them all. In their contributions to this project, as it grew from seed bed to flower garden, the following friends joined me: through wrestling with theory and design, Bill Adams, Michael Chisholm and Mary Tiffen; through shared labours in the field, Afolabi Falola, Francis Gichuki, Ahmed Ibrahim, Alhaji Chiroma, Aminu Shehu, Donald Thomas, Maharazu Yusuf, Salisu Mohammed; with tutorials on soil science, Frances Harris; with cartographic ornamentals, John Antwi; by commenting on the vista, Bill Adams, David Anderson, Frances Harris, Mary Tiffen and an anonymous referee; for killing many weeds and cheerily challenging my presuppositions, Beryl Turner.

To the villagers of dryland Africa it is impossible to compose a *gracias* adequate for the acceptance, willing co-operation, hospitality and above all, friendship with which I have always been blessed on my researches. Living on the margin of the global economy, Sahelians are notable exponents of courtesy.

1   Introduction

Sub-Saharan Africa is poor.

> Sub-Saharan Africa is on a knife-edge. For more than a decade the region has been locked in a downward spiral of economic and social decline . . . On current trends, the ranks of the 218 million Africans already living in poverty will increase to 300 million – equal to half the region's population – by the end of the decade. (OXFAM 1993)

The drylands contain most of the poorest countries in sub-Saharan Africa. Of the world's twenty most disadvantaged countries, according to the UNDP's Human Development Index, twelve are in dryland Africa (UNDP 1991: 16). This area

Plate 1 An advancing Sahara? Moving dunes versus annual grasses at Maiburin in the Manga Grasslands, northern Nigeria (August, 1993).

1

(which is defined in chapter 2) comprises a vast tract that crosses Africa from west to east and from north to south (Fig. 1.1).

Africa is believed to be degrading.

It is commonplace to find statements that the drylands, in particular, are subject to wind and water erosion, the loss of forest and woodland, the degradation of natural grasslands, declining soil fertility and salinization. According to the United Nations Environment Programme (UNEP), of 800 million Africans in 1990, 41 per cent lived in areas susceptible to such degradation (UNEP 1992). This population will double by the year 2025 if current projections are correct.

> Throughout Africa, land resources are deteriorating at an accelerating pace . . . A complex matrix of factors has produced the current crisis. The interaction between uncontrollable external factors, such as drought, and human abuse prevents formerly effective productive systems from satisfying the needs of the population. Increased pressure on the land has led to overgrazed range areas, reduced fallow periods in cropped areas, diminished soil fertility, a deteriorated soil structure, lowered rainfall infiltration, and increased erosion. With land becoming less productive, new land must be exploited to maintain total output. If new land is not available, then greater pressure must be exerted on existing land. Added to this cycle are the effects of excessive tree cutting, uncertainties about land use rights, inadequate price incentives, and migration patterns that provide temporary relief for one area, while, as is often the case, exporting inappropriate and destructive land use practices to other areas. Desertification can be accelerated by uncontrolled bushfire, by new anarchic settlements, and by the encroachment of agricultural land use onto fragile pastoral rangeland. (Falloux and Mukendi 1988)

A linkage between the growth of the population and the state of the environment has existed since the origins of technology and social organisation in Africa, perhaps four millennia ago. But the numbers and the rates of growth experienced in recent decades are unprecedented. This linkage is complex and indirect, as most studies show. However, one view, widely believed and energetically propagated, states that inappropriate technologies and management of natural resources are driven directly by population growth. Through overgrazing, overcultivation, overcutting of woodlands and deforestation, they have led (or will lead) remorselessly to environmental degradation (or *desertification*). There are two logical outcomes of such a model. One is that inappropriate technologies and land use systems need transformation: indigenous management of natural resources is myopic and destructive. The other is that population numbers require limitation, in the name of 'saving the environment' for future generations.

But is such a doomsday scenario accurate, either in a predictive or an explanatory sense? If not, what are the consequences of a misdiagnosis? Is there an alternative paradigm? Is the growth of population really out of control, decoupled

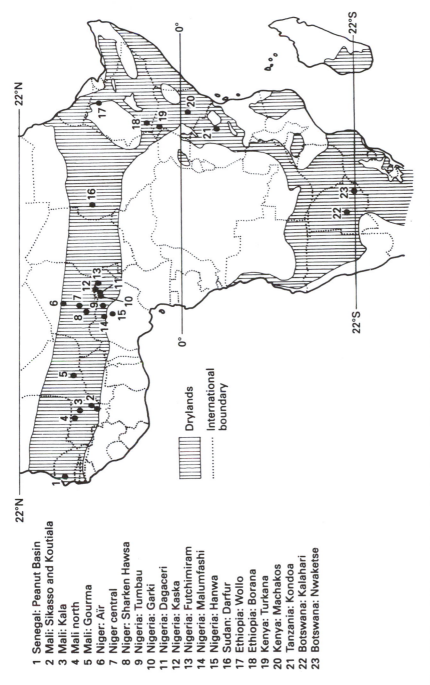

1 Senegal: Peanut Basin
2 Mali: Sikasso and Koutiala
3 Mali: Kala
4 Mali north
5 Mali: Gourma
6 Niger: Aïr
7 Niger central
8 Niger: Sharken Hawsa
9 Nigeria: Tumbau
10 Nigeria: Garki
11 Nigeria: Dagaceri
12 Nigeria: Kaska
13 Nigeria: Futchimiram
14 Nigeria: Malumfashi
15 Nigeria: Hanwa
16 Sudan: Darfur
17 Ethiopia: Wollo
18 Ethiopia: Borana
19 Kenya: Turkana
20 Kenya: Machakos
21 Tanzania: Kondoa
22 Botswana: Kalahari
23 Botswana: Nwaketse

Figure 1.1 The sub-Saharan drylands, showing the countries and case studies referred to in this study.

from the growth of productivity? Are existing technologies and land use systems – as practised by the majority of African small farmers and livestock producers – really obsolete and in urgent need of transformation? Do appropriate and viable alternatives exist? These are questions relating to internal or endogenous factors. Others relate to external or exogenous forces. What are the effects on environmental management of world markets, global economic recession and the impoverishment of African governments through debt repayments, diminishing revenues, inefficiency, corruption and war?

In the light of these endogenous and exogenous factors, what resources can be located within the drylands communities themselves to provide a basis for sustainable management, better policies and appropriate interventions?

Dryland ecosystems are relatively low in productive potential on account of their meagre and variable rainfall, short growing seasons and scarcity of nutrients in the soil. On the other hand, high solar radiation gives them productive potential where water and nutrients are not limiting. They border (taxonomically if not geographically) the unproductive systems of the desert. Risk, emanating from low and variable rainfall, compels adaptive behaviour both in the natural ecosystems and in the livelihood systems that, through human ingenuity, have developed over the centuries. Aridity – whether seasonal, inter-annual, or permanent – governs almost every level of biological existence. These characteristics ensure that dryland management poses a specific set of problems, which differ from those in other biomes, both for the local communities, and for development agents who seek to intervene.

The downward spiral predicted for the African drylands (Fig. 1.2) differs both in intensity and in its specifics, from the generalised African predicament whose nature, however, is commonly represented in similar deterministic terms (as the quotation above illustrates). Like much conventional wisdom on the subject, it shows an equilibrium, disturbed – perhaps irrevocably – by linkages between population growth and environmental degradation. There are, however, good reasons for questioning whether the equilibrial assumption is always appropriate for understanding the drylands. This question, which has radical implications, is taken up in this study.

Like other scenarios this is a diagnostic and predictive model, dependent for its usefulness on the accuracy of its data base and the soundness of its premises. However, its data base, by common consent, is less than satisfactory. Much uncertainty exists concerning the rate, the magnitude, the significance and the causes of processes of environmental change in the drylands (Warren and Khogali 1992). This has prevented the kind of numerical elaboration that has been possible, for example, in global models of climate change and its effects on agriculture and land cover change (IPCC 1994; Rosenzweig et al. 1993; Rosenzweig and Parry 1994; Hulme 1994b; Meyer and Turner 1994).

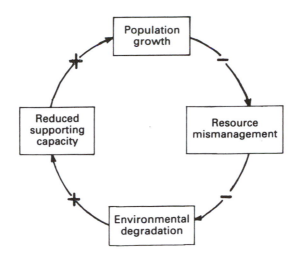

Figure 1.2 The 'Malthusian' spiral for dryland Africa.

A model it is, nevertheless. Ness (1994) concludes from a review of models that there is no direct relationship between population and environment; technology and social organisation always mediate between them. Complexity therefore seems to be inevitable. Cleaver and Schreiber (1994), in reviewing linkages between population, agriculture and environment in Africa, conclude that population growth is only one of several possible causes of environmental degradation and has its place in a socio-economic 'nexus'. Complexity undermines the simplistic assumptions of the 'doomsday' model and reopens theoretical debate on the nature of the linkages supposed. The debate is not an idle one, as productivity is at the heart of policy for governments and international agencies concerned with strategies for economic and resource management. The difficulties of obtaining accurate and reliable data do not help resolve these uncertainties.

Neither data deficiencies, nor uncertainties about the linkages, facilitate prediction. A fundamental reason for caution in predicting the future is that uncertainties, or methodological qualifications, even if admitted by their progenitors, are quickly forgotten when predictions are taken up in public or policy debates. There is a tension between treating models of environmental change 'as heuristics or truth machines': a tension which is easily lost sight of when science enters the public domain (Wynne and Sackley 1994). This is exemplified in the doomsday scenario for dryland Africa, where self-reinforcing repetition of claims, backed by governments or international institutions, easily obscures the evidence and thereby suppresses critical debate.

Thus desertification, as represented by the UNEP in policy statements, publications and international fora for two decades after the United Nations Conference on Desertification in 1977, has acquired the status of 'institutional fact' in advance of the settlement of scientific uncertainties about its claims (Swift 1996). This scepticism was not reflected in the formulation of the International Convention to Combat Desertification, which was an outcome of the Rio 'Earth Summit' of 1992. The Convention became binding on its signatories on 26 December, 1996. Yet objective support for the UNEP's claims that 21 million hectares of valuable land are being lost every year, and that 900 million people are at risk from desertification, is hard to come by. Even while this controversial concept is passing into negotiated international policy, a rearguard action is being fought to defend it against its many critics (Stiles 1995; Thomas and Middleton 1994).

A further reason for scepticism with regard to predictions of environmental change is that they prejudge the abilities of human communities to develop adaptive responses to processes in which they are already deeply immersed as participants. Scenario constructors rarely extend their investigations to the complex economic and social adjustments that embody the everyday decisions of ordinary people. Yet they have good reason for using their natural resources responsibly. There is an epistemological gulf fixed between 'scientific' and 'indigenous' knowledge systems (Richards 1983) in managing natural resources. This gulf is linked in many cases to one of scale (Lambin 1993). The doomsday scenario for the African drylands is partly dependent on a global perspective, making use of monitoring and predictive techniques that depend on extensive data sets. Micro-scale studies of natural resource management, on the other hand, are more likely to reflect indigenous perceptions, to be holistic and specific to place and community. It is not surprising that the outcomes of such divergent systems of thought are often difficult to unify: yet this challenge must be taken up.

The purpose of this book is to question the value of the doomsday scenario for dryland Africa and lay some foundations for an alternative paradigm. This is not a new enterprise. The literature contains numerous studies that call into question one or more aspects of conventional wisdom, whose inertia needs to be better understood (Leach and Mearns 1996). The orientation adopted here is that of the smallholder producer, whose perception of change and risk is apt to be incongruent with that of scientific expertise. Why is this so?

The contradictions are reduced to general terms in the form of five paradoxes which can be stated as follows:

(1) Why has the 'advancing Sahara', the subject of scientific claims for nearly a century, failed to eliminate the Sahel and its peoples; and why does the concept of desertification, after two decades of promotion, remain controversial?

(2) If overgrazing affects vast areas of the drylands (61 per cent, according to UNEP 1992: 5), and has done so for several decades at least, why has the livestock economy not collapsed?

(3) If cultivated land is degrading, and has been doing so for several decades, how do increasing numbers of people support themselves? If indigenous technologies are conservative, inappropriate and destructive, why do they continue to be preferred?

(4) If overcutting is 'mining' the woodlands, why has a scarcity of wood fuel not led to the collapse of rural energy systems, even in the most densely populated areas?

(5) Why do human fertility rates remain relatively high in the face of such powerful environmental constraints? If markets undermine local food sufficiency, why is increased participation in markets desired by dryland smallholders? If risk threatens the viability of primary production in the drylands, why is permanent out-migration not more extensive than it is? These and other paradoxes concerning the household will be touched on in chapter 6.

The dichotomy referred to above, which separates global- from local-scale studies of the African drylands, has implications for the method used in this book. Doomsday scenarios are usually based on global perspectives and emphasise the need to measure, map and predict environmental change in large areas (continental or sub-continental). Local-level studies (at the village or district level) often appear much more optimistic. So far, the concept of desertification owes most to the first viewpoint, and the attempts that have been made to generate a paradigm from local or micro-scale studies have been incomplete. The vantage point of this book (except in chapter 2) is the local scale. But the use that I can make of the numerous studies of dryland Africa's many thousands of village systems is selective and incomplete. The locations of the case studies on which I have drawn are shown in Fig. 1.1. In view of the limitations of my field experience, I have decided to make sustained use of the northern Nigerian and Kenyan cases. These I believe to be exceptionally important, on account of the depth of work achieved and the theoretical terms in which the results have been presented, to the current debate on management of the drylands.

2 Global perspectives on Africa's drylands

Characterising the drylands

The African continent spans a huge range of climates, from equatorial to tropical, desert, and sub-tropical, on both sides of the equator. It has coastal plains, partly inundated by the ocean, wet and humid, and at the other extreme, land-locked plateaux whose rivers end in inland seas, whose waters are lost in evaporation and seepage in arid climates. Between them are vast uplands of forest or savanna, and mountains whose climates range through temperate to sub-arctic. A little of this breathtaking diversity is captured in the maps of mean annual rainfall and of vegetation classes (Fig. 2.1). Much of Africa – 36 or 43 per cent,

Plate 2 Degraders or custodians of a natural heritage? Dagaceri, northern Nigeria.

depending on the definition used – is dryland, receiving less than 1000 mm of rainfall a year in less than 180 days, the remaining months being relatively or absolutely dry. High temperatures during the tropical rainy season cause much of the rainfall to be lost in evaporation; and the high intensity of storms ensures that much of it runs off in floods. For securing human livelihoods, the two dominant characteristics of the dryland climates are (1) aridity and (2) variability.

Aridity

The drylands of tropical Africa normally have little or no rain for six months of the year or more. This calls for ecosystems adapted to drought stress, in which the production of biomass is sharply concentrated into the wet seasons, and there are long quiescent periods when annual plants die and perennials produce little growth. The faunal populations, especially the larger animals, are limited by the supply of edible biomass and surface water during the dry seasons, unless moisture is available in rivers, lakes or depressions. Insects and small animals with short reproductive cycles multiply rapidly when the rains return. Domestic animals undergo weight loss and (in drier years) starvation. They must be watered from wells, consuming much labour. Crop production is restricted to the short, wet seasons. Farming activity is therefore episodic, with periods of intense and exhausting work separated by periods of relative inactivity.

The exceptions to the foregoing statements are the wetlands (such as the *fadamas* of northern Nigeria, or the *dambos* of Zambia and Zimbabwe, the flood plains of rivers or the margins of lakes), which offer dry season grazing, flood-recession farming, or irrigation opportunities. The value of the wetlands is a function of their scarcity (generally less than 10 per cent of the drylands).

The first thing to appreciate about Africa's drylands is that their definition is not a straightforward matter. Two classifications of aridity are available (Table 2.1). The first is the FAO's typology of agroclimatic zones based on the length of the growing period in days, which was used for the global study, *Potential population-supporting capacities of the developing countries* (Higgins *et al.* 1982). The three zones, arid, dry semi-arid and moist semi-arid define the drylands for our purposes. The second scheme is preferred by the UNEP in its *World atlas of desertification* (1992). This also has three zones: arid, semi-arid and dry sub-humid. Although they are obviously subsumed under the term 'drylands', the hyper-arid deserts (where there is no recognisable rainfall regime and long periods without precipitation) are excluded for present purposes, as they have few inhabitants and their management presents entirely different problems. The FAO and the UNEP schemes produce significantly different estimates of the areas. When

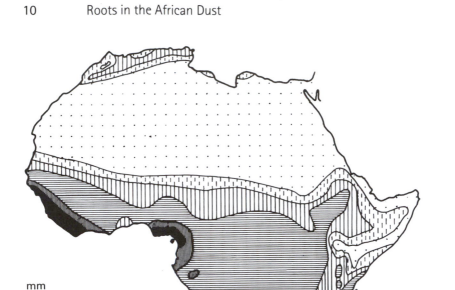

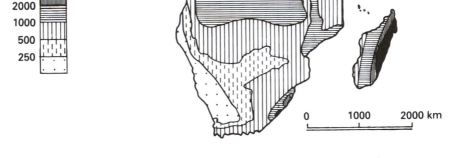

Figure 2.1 Mean annual rainfall (left) and vegetation classes (right). (*The University Atlas*, Philip, 1978).

mapped, their distribution also differs in detail (Fig. 2.2). More than 90 per cent of the drylands have tropical climates.

As we shall be concerned in this study with agricultural systems (crop and live-stock production), the agroclimatic zones of the FAO are preferred. The severity of dryland environments is thus measured, for present purposes, in terms of the length of the growing period (LGP) for annual plants. The heart of the drylands is the semi-arid zone, where crops and livestock are of equal importance and where high human and livestock densities are found. This zone is subdivided into two sub-zones – dry (75–119 days) and moist (120–179 days). Thus defined, it occupies 19 per cent of the African continent, with 24 per cent of those areas

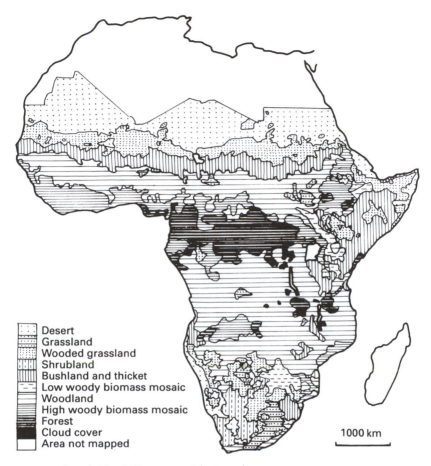

Desert
Grassland
Wooded grassland
Shrubland
Bushland and thicket
Low woody biomass mosaic
Woodland
High woody biomass mosaic
Forest
Cloud cover
Area not mapped

1000 km

Figure 2.1 (*cont.*). After Millington *et al.* (1994: 17).

having a tropical temperature regime (FAO 1982). It contains about one third of the human and cattle populations of tropical Africa and a quarter of its sheep and goats (Jahnke 1982). The average population density in 1975 was estimated to range from forty to seventy-four persons per square km (FAO 1982: 193).

The arid zone (with an average growing period from one to seventy-four days) cannot, apart from irrigation, normally support crop production, and livestock must be kept at lower densities. There is also an important distinction to be made between unimodal regimes (where all rainfall normally falls in a single season) and bimodal regimes (where there may be two short rainy periods each year).

Table 2.1 *Alternative classifications of aridity for the African drylands.*

Authority:	FAO			UNEP		
Basis of classification:	Length of growing period			Aridity index		
Zones:	Days LGP (a)	million ha	per cent Africa	P/PET (b)	million ha	per cent Africa
arid	1–74	488	17	0.05–0.20	503	17
dry semi-arid	75–119	232	8	0.20–0.50	514	17
moist semi-arid*	120–179	313	11	0.50–0.65	269	9
Total		1,033	36		1,286	43

Notes:
* or dry sub-humid (UNEP)
(a) LGP is defined as the duration when both water and temperature permit crop growth, i.e. when moisture supply is half or more than half of potential evapotranspiration (FAO 1984: 107).
(b) Aridity index is defined as precipitation over potential evapotranspiration.
Sources: Higgins *et al.* 1982: 109; UNEP 1992.

Variability

Rainfall is not only sharply seasonal but it is also variable: both between years and during seasons (for an example – Niger – see Sivakumar *et al.* 1993). For the ecosystem, both wild and domestic animals and also the human populations, the variability of the rainfall introduces an element of risk into almost all life-supporting activity. For example, seed germination must adapt to the possibility that the rain may be insufficient for the completion of a growth cycle – whence will the next generation of seed come? This problem is solved by variations in seed coatings which ensure that only a proportion germinate at once. Some fauna – especially insects – have mechanisms for surviving long periods of food scarcity and multiplying rapidly when food is available. Others diversify their food sources, or starve. Domestic animals, when other food sources fail, may have to be kept alive on the foliage of trees, which are brought down for them with some effort. Human populations must store food grains from season to season and, if possible, guard against partial or complete crop failures, which can occur in several seasons running.

Since the average growing period in the drylands ranges from 179 days to less than seventy-five, the effect of rainfall variability increases with aridity. This can be understood if rainfall is conceived in terms of rain events rather than in milli-metres. Under tropical conditions the greater part of rainfall occurs in short epi-sodes of high intensity, 50 mm, for example, falling in half an hour. The number of such events required to supply a seasonal rainfall of 250 mm (which is typical

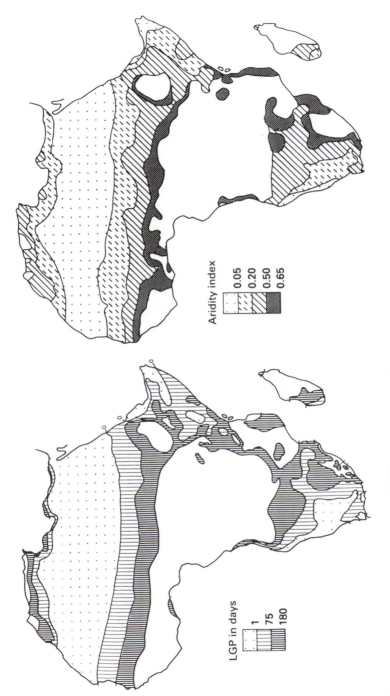

LGP in days

1
75
180

Aridity index

0.05
0.20
0.50
0.65

Figure 2.2 The length of the growing period (LGP), according to the FAO (left) and aridity index, according to UNEP (right) for the African drylands. After FAO (1982) and UNEP (1992).

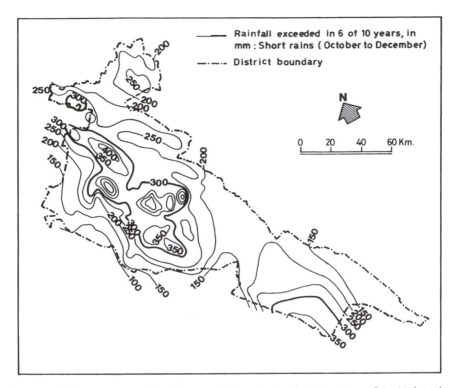

Figure 2.3 Rainfall probability in Machakos District, Kenya. After Jaetzold and Schmidt (1983). The isohyets show the rainfall exceeded in six of ten years (mm), for the Short Rains (October–December).

of the border between the semi-arid and arid zones of West Africa, or in the bimodal semi-arid areas of East Africa) is small, and a reduction of one or two rain events can make the difference between a bumper crop and a catastrophe. The variability of rainfall is normally expressed in terms of probabilities. Thus it can be stated that, in a certain area, there is a 60 per cent probability of the seasonal rainfall exceeding 250 mm (Fig. 2.3). Unfortunately, while such a statement enables an assessment of risk and returns in agriculture, it provides no basis for predicting the time or intensity of drought events.

But what is a drought? It can be defined in several different ways. We assume it means less than the expected amount of rainfall, but how do we define expected and how do we define less? A *meteorological drought* is an abstract statistical index usually based on deviation from the mean rainfall. But why should that have any particular importance? An *agricultural drought* is a deficiency defined in relation to a particular crop and its requirements, and as we know how much rain cowpea, or sorghum, needs, we can state rainfall deficiency precisely (Agnew 1989). In the

Table 2.2 *Seasonal drought probabilities in Machakos District, Kenya, using a drought index (average of seven stations).*

Type of drought	Percentage of years	
	Long rains (Mar–May)	Short rains (Oct–Dec)
Light drought or worse ($\leq$ −0.2)	44	57
Moderate drought or worse ($\leq$ −0.5)	40	35
Severe drought ($\leq$ −0.8)	29	10

Notes:
Average number of years in series: 48.
Drought index: seasonal rainfall − long-term average divided by seasonal standard deviation (Downing *et al.* 1987).
Source: Mutiso *et al.* (1991).

drylands, however, there are several crops in a farming system and their requirements are not the same (indeed this is a deliberate strategy to reduce risk). Furthermore, some soils retain moisture better than others, so it is difficult to use the concept of agricultural drought in a general sense. Then there is *hydrological drought*, which states a deficiency in ground or surface water conditions, often linked only indirectly with rainfall deficiency owing to interregional transfers by rivers and subsurface flow, and storage in lakes, swamps or deltas. *Ecological drought* means insufficient rainfall to support normal growth in the natural vegetation. Here it is necessary to differentiate between trees, on the one hand, and the grass and herb vegetation on the other. Meteorological drought indices are therefore at best a rough guide to agricultural performance, still less to the social and economic impact of a drought.

Table 2.2 shows the computed frequencies of light, moderate, or severe droughts in the rainfall records of seven stations in Machakos District, Kenya, from 1894 to 1988. These were defined meteorologically, using a drought index (for details, see Mutiso *et al.* 1991). In 40 per cent of years, there was a moderate or severe drought in the long rains, and in 35 per cent of years in the short rains. Sometimes droughts occurred in several consecutive seasons, even as many as four. Farmers and livestock breeders cannot count on receiving the *average* rainfall; to think in terms of probabilities is more realistic.

Diversity in the drylands

It is common to hear highly generalised statements concerning areas of Africa which are subject to aridity or variable rainfall. Yet the African drylands are far from homogeneous. A brief outline of their diversity is necessary in order to show how production systems need to respond to the specific properties of many different environments.

Natural diversity

The use of the length of growing period for defining the drylands necessarily ignores other climatic variables. Three tropical and three sub-tropical thermal regimes (warm, moderately cool and cool) are represented in the semi-arid zone. Both unimodal and bimodal rainfall regimes are found: the first mainly in northern and western areas, and the second in eastern areas (Leroux 1983). Bimodal regimes usually have two distinct rainy seasons in the year. This property has a significance for farming systems second only to that of the growing period. In either regime, the monthly pattern of rainfall varies according to latitude, and (especially in eastern Africa) altitude. All these variables have a bearing on bioproductivity, but moisture (expressed in the length of growing period) is the most critical.

The semi-arid zone alone encompasses a wide range of soil and vegetational conditions. Some seventeen major soil classes occur, sixteen major species dominate the grassland communities and eleven major vegetational classes are recognised (FAO 1960; FAO/UNESCO 1977; UNESCO/AETFAT/UNSO 1981). The reason so many soil classes are found is that soils are primarily dependent on parent materials, and only secondarily on climate. Parent materials are themselves sometimes the result of past climates, as in the former desert sands found along the southern side of the Sahara, but elsewhere they are more closely related to the underlying geology. Vegetation, on the other hand, is more responsive to present climates and less to soil classes. The semi-arid zone is associated predominantly with savannas, the density and size of trees diminishing with increasing aridity. In the arid zone, the grasslands are classified as steppes, but the dominant species of the grasslands are quite variable. Owing to clearance for cultivation, grazing, and burning, the natural vegetation communities of the semi-arid zone have been transformed under millennia of human occupance into mosaics, consisting of farmland, fallow, rangeland, residual woodland and eroded or degraded land.

The severity of soil degradation in the semi-arid zone is considered to vary from low to very high (UNEP 1992). Because the intensity of use is greater in this zone, the risk of degradation is probably higher than in the arid zone. Degradation risk also varies with the properties of the soil in question.

Co-variance among such parameters is the exception rather than the norm. Locally, natural conditions may be relatively homogeneous; but on the continental scale, generalisations have little value. For example, the semi-arid zone of tropical Africa and Madagascar can be divided into eighty-three distinct environ-mental units (ranging from 10,000 to 285,000 square kilometres in size), based on combinations of dominant soils, vegetation classes, degradation risk, tsetse risk and livestock and population densities (Mortimore and Turner 1991). This vari-ability has practical significance for the formulation of technical recommenda-tions for managing natural resources.

Social diversity

The drylands contain a few of the most densely populated areas of tropical Africa (300–500 per square km) and also some of the emptiest (<5), as shown in Fig. 2.4. There is a weak relationship between aridity and population density. While high densities are rare in the arid zone, the higher ones are found not in the moist, but in the dry semi-arid zone. This has major implications for theory and policy which will be discussed in later chapters. The variability of population density in the drylands confounds all attempts to establish a simplis-tic relationship between density and degradation (though it has not discouraged some writers from trying to do so).

When other social and economic parameters are taken into account, the natural and demographic diversity of the semi-arid zone is multiplied. There are hundreds of ethnic groups, each operating one or more production systems based on crops, livestock, sometimes fish and occasionally wild animals or plants. These systems are differentiated in terms of their social organisation, population mobil-ity (migration and circulation), the conditions of land and other resource tenure, land use, technology, economic specialisation (especially between crops and live-stock) and other variables. Such diversity, therefore, should counsel caution to those wishing to find simple, generalised prescriptions for better management of the natural resources (such as high-yielding crops, inorganic fertilisers, family planning, the banning of fires, or land use regulation). The need for agricultural research to be orientated to specific eco-regions and systems is now recognised, for example by the international research institutes working in Africa, though its implications have yet to be fully understood.

The supreme example of how a generalised perception has confused under-standing of natural resource management in the drylands is the idea of desertification. It is instructive to review its history and critique.

The idea of desertification

Under a different name, the idea of desertification[1] was already abroad in West Africa by the second decade of colonial rule, when the French

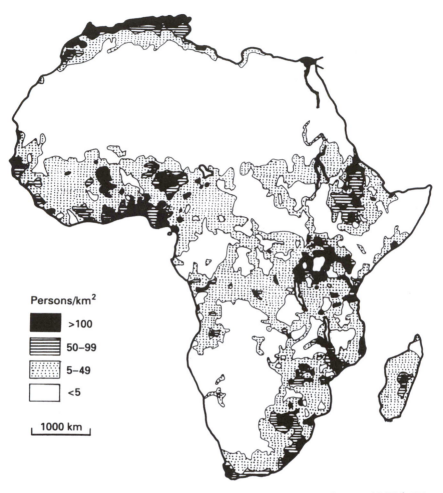

Figure 2.4 Estimated population densities in sub-Saharan Africa,1990. Sources: UNEP (1992: 38), for central, East and southern Africa; OECD Club du Sahel (1994), for West Africa.

Comité d'Etudes commissioned a study of *dessèchement progressif* (Hubert 1920). Drawing on thirty-one reports relating mainly to locations in modern Mali, Mauritania and Senegal, the study considered the evidence for *dessèchement* to be irrefutable. Fossils and archaeological remains of human activity had been found in desert areas, and water-loving animals and fish had been isolated by the retreat of surface water. But the evidence for contemporary *dessèchement,* it was believed, was in moving sand on vegetated or fixed dunes, especially in Mauritania and Senegal; and the rainfall, recorded over a few decades, was claimed to be diminishing in Senegal. Though the fixed dunes had been previously understood (correctly) to show that the desert had retreated northwards, Hubert noted that there were ripple marks in the sand, and argued that they were *forming* under vegetation.

Following Hubert, Bovill (1921) cited diminishing rainfall and well water levels in Sokoto, Nigeria as evidence of what he called the 'encroachment of the Sahara on the Sudan', but his inferences could not be substantiated from the rainfall records then available. He claimed that some crops could no longer grow, pastures were depleted and there was migration to the south. However, alternative explanations were available to account for these observations (Raeburn 1928; Prothero 1962).

It is probable that these early views were influenced by the low rainfall which was recorded in several years between 1905 and 1920, especially in 1913, when famine caused heavy human mortality in many areas of West Africa. It is striking that after a relatively short acquaintance with interior West Africa, a number of European observers were so soon convinced of the reality of ecological degradation. Generalising on the region as a whole, Renner (1926: 587) reported that 'there is a general belief that aridity is increasing in the Sudan'. There is, however, no evidence that this conviction reflected indigenous perceptions.

Theories of climatic change were being promoted at this time by Huntingdon (1915), who linked them with the historic decline of civilisations in the old world; Bovill, at least, acknowledged the influence of these ideas. At the other end of the continent, persistent drought was threatening to ruin farmers in the dry areas of South Africa, and provoked an anxious study by the government (Union of South Africa 1923). In East Africa, there had been five major droughts between 1898 and 1918, though by 1929 the government of Kenya was more concerned with soil erosion than with drought (Thomas 1991).

The climate was soon to lose pride of place. Stebbing (1935, 1937, 1953), a forester with Indian experience, visited West Africa and became the most energetic proponent of the 'encroaching Sahara' hypothesis.

> And the desert is advancing, how far or how fast I am yet to learn. People are living on the edge, not of a volcano, but of a desert, whose power is incalculable and whose silent and almost inevitable approach must be difficult to estimate. But the end is obvious, total annihilation of vegetation and the disappearance of man and beast. (Stebbing 1935)

He even extended himself to predicting the rate of advance of the Sahara (1935: 10) – in which he was mistaken, having mislocated the boundary near Maradi in Niger. Had he been correct, much of northern Nigeria would by now have been swallowed up.

Why were Stebbing's claims misled? Visiting West Africa in the *dry season*, he interpreted his observations of extensive burning, cutting and clearing as a process that was transforming the Sudan savanna woodland (a 'mixed deciduous forest') into a man-made savanna (a 'scattered thorn bush'). The savanna in turn was being downgraded into desert. Hubert (1920: 422) had noted earlier that vegetation destroyed by woodcutters (whether African or European) was usually succeeded by a type characteristic of a drier regime. Although Stebbing gave a role in this process to 'intermittent rainfall' (increasing length and severity of dry periods), man with his 'misutilisation of the soils' was the culprit: 'over-utilisation of the vegetable covering of the soils . . . commences the reduction of water supplies and the lowering of the water table in the soils' (1953: 120); and erosion was bringing intermittent rainfall in its train. Thus anticipating the feedback theories, linking land use with rainfall, that were formally stated more than two decades later (Charney and Stone 1975; Macleod 1976; Walker and Rowntree 1977), Stebbing nevertheless failed to spell out clearly the mechanisms he proposed.

Stebbing wrote when the soil conservation movement was sweeping the USA and, by extension, several colonial administrations in Africa (Anderson 1984). The new prominence given to 'inappropriate' land use practices and to engineering solutions (terraces, dams and other structures) by the US Department of Agriculture, the new US Soil Conservation Service (established in 1933), and in derivative texts (Bennett 1939), was exported to Africa as colonial agricultural officers were sent for training and later carried back their expertise. Conservation became a preoccupation of colonial policy in some countries; and a review of soil conservation in all British territories was carried out (Hailey 1938). Local studies were commissioned in Kenya, for example, where, in the paternalistic ethos engendered by white settlement, it was even advocated that 'the troops' should be used to impose conservation practice upon native farmers (Huxley 1937): the government was criticised by the conservation lobby for not being urgent enough.

Stebbing's views were not accepted without criticism (Jones 1938; Stamp 1940). In 1937 the governments of Nigeria and the Niger Colony appointed an Anglo–French Forestry Commission to tour both sides of the border separating the two countries (in the dry season). Its main conclusion (1937: 8) was that 'there is no obviously apparent danger of desiccation' (a natural increase of arid conditions), but:

> There is unquestionably an impoverishment of the sylvan conditions of the country. This impoverishment is due almost entirely to uncontrolled expansion of shifting cultivation as a result of the security afforded by European administration . . . Consequently a large part of the natural woodland which covered the country has been so seriously degraded in quality that it is of very little use and it has not been replaced, except in very few localities, by farmland of real value.

This hostility to shifting cultivation, which was very different in character from the intensive European farming familiar to colonial officials, reflected an inadequate understanding of the land and labour ratios of African agriculture, and ignored its cyclical pattern of cultivation and fallows. However, the Commission's view was tempered by two of its members (Collier and Dundas 1937: 192), who pointed out:

> Shifting cultivation, wasteful though it may be, can do no permanent harm to the soil provided that there is an adequate 'bush fallow' period for recuperation. But once the demand for land becomes such that the recuperative period allowable is insufficient, the only hope of maintaining fertility lies in replacing the bush fallow by manure; a requirement that is realised in the fine, well-timbered farmlands of Kano.

In drawing attention to the permanently cultivated Kano Close-Settled Zone (a term introduced to the literature by Buchanan and Pugh (1955)), they followed Morel (1911: 234) and Temple (1918: 147), who more than twenty years earlier had written of the productivity and sustainability of this farming system.

Aubréville (1949), also a forester, introduced the term *désertification* to describe degradation by burning, clearing and erosion in the forest and savanna zones of West Africa, graphically illustrating his thesis with cross-sectional models of the latitudinal vegetation zones, before and after human impact. Like Stebbing, he was quick to convert a spatial ordering (of vegetation zones) into a sequential hypothesis (or progressive degradation). With a broad brush, he painted a vivid picture of the destruction of Africa:

> The closed forests are shrinking and disappearing, like evaporating spots. The trees of the open forests and savannas become more and more spaced out. On all sides the bare skin of Africa appears as its thin green veil of savanna burns releasing a grey fog of dust into the atmosphere. Arable land is carried away by the yellow waters of rivers in flood. Slabs of sterile truncated soil, bearing tufts of grass around uprooted bushes, recall a kind of leprosy that is spreading over the face of Africa; elsewhere great slabs of ferruginous or blackish rock abound. Great banks of sand are deposited in the beds of streams and rivers around which small threads of water meander in the dry season. Billions and billions of small red or grey particles multiply evenly over the soil; these are the great termitaria whose populations share out the debris of the wasting forest vegetation or search out the relative coolness of its sap. The mountains are magnificently bare, their erosion gullies, their fractures, etched in sharp lines, their structure clearly visible. Above, the atmosphere vibrates with intense heat. Alluvial soils, sands and valleys are cultivated intensively; in the dry season winds carry away clouds of dust. In the thorn steppes, whose disappearance marks the beginning of the desert, the shrubs become more and more spaced out, no longer reproducing; the rains have ceased or appear only irregularly, the winds that bring the summer rain are no longer humid enough. Elsewhere broad-leaved trees dry up one by one and die; they are not replaced by young individuals but, instead, thorn trees gather as if favoured by a dry season that has become longer and more arid . . . During the dry season, the whole of Africa burns, lines of fire running everywhere, chased by the dry

winds, no portion left undamaged . . . Thus we see how tropical Africa would be transformed if the 'savanisation' towards which she is fast proceeding were some day to be accomplished. (Aubréville 1949: 341)

By dwelling on the *dry season*, asserting irreversible changes where little careful study had been done and castigating the apparently destructive force of fire, Aubréville manipulated his readers towards a pessimistic conclusion that has not been borne out by events. The boundaries of the rain forest, where they have been carefully studied, have been found to be stable: in Nigeria (Morgan and Moss 1965), and in Guinea (Fairhead and Leach 1996). Fifty years on, vast areas of the savanna have been transformed from natural woodland into settled farms and villages with a canopy of economic trees.

The momentum was maintained by Chevalier (1952), who repeated the dreary litany, by then very familiar, of *dessèchement progressif*: remobilised sand dunes in the north, laterites in the south; soil erosion and degradation; disappearing surface water and falling well levels; dying perennial rivers and disappearing gallery woodlands. The unanimity of the colonial forestry school is thus impressive.

The idea of desert encroachment was not confined to the borders of the Sahara. In South Africa, it was the subject of government concern. A Drought Investigation Commission and a Desert Encroachment Committee reported in 1923 and 1951 respectively (Union of South Africa 1923, 1951). They lent official weight to an orthodox view of degradation, as a result of overstocking, which extended as far back as the eighteenth century (Beinart 1996). According to this view, the grassveld was being transformed into degraded karoo shrubland and the southwestern desert was on the move towards Pretoria.

The wetter years of the 1950s, the arrival of independence and (perhaps) of aid to the agricultural sector distracted attention from environmental degradation, but not for long. Even before the Sahelian drought had reached its peak, the USAID (1972) claimed that several studies of the Sahara (which were not cited) had 'concluded that there had been a net advance in some places, along a 2,000 mile southern front of as much as 30 miles per year'. This interpretation seemed to be borne out when the Sahelian drought peaked in 1972–74; the desiccated landscapes appeared even more degraded, and few observers attempted to distinguish between the episodic effects of drought and the longer-term processes of desertification.

In the Sudan, in a report of 1975 (Lamprey 1988), it was estimated from air transects that the boundary of the desert had shifted southward by 90–100 km in seventeen years since the ecological boundaries were previously mapped. There was evidence of drifting sand, mortality among the gum-producing trees, *Acacia senegal*, and of abandoned farmlands.

It was generally understood by the natural resources specialists on the reconnaissance teams that the ecological degradation taking place in the northern Sudan
is largely due to past and present land use practices but is accelerated during
periods of drought. It must be stated, however, that the sand encroachment
problem cannot be attributed only to recent mistakes but is the result of several
thousand years of abuse of the fragile ecosystems which formerly existed in the
Sahara and Nubian areas. (Lamprey 1988)

However, using satellite imagery, air photography and ground data, Hellden
(1988) and his colleagues were unable to verify a systematic encroachment either
of the boundary of the Sahara, or of major sand dunes. 'There was no creation of
long lasting desert-like conditions during the 1962–79 period in the area corresponding to the magnitude described by many authors' (1988: 11). A study of the
Sahara between 1980 and 1990 (Tucker *et al.* 1991) obtained a close correlation
of annual rainfall with an index of vegetation derived from earth satellite data.
The study showed that the desert boundary (which was taken to be the 200 mm
annual rainfall isohyet) oscillated north and south across the Sahel by as much as
three degrees of latitude between extremes, and 110 km in a single year
(1984–85). Given such interannual variations, no long-term expansion or
contraction of the Sahara desert could be determined from only ten years' data.

A conception of desertification as a linear encroachment of desert conditions
(popularised by Eckholm and Brown 1977: 9) is misleading. Bernus (1977: 92,
1979) demonstrated that in the arid zone of Niger, 'desertification happens at particular points; it is patchy, not linear'. More elaborate distinctions were suggested
between linear extension, extension at points near wells and extensions in rings
around villages (Mainguet 1980), but Hellden was unable to confirm such forms
of desertification in the Sudan. Another study in that country had claimed that
declining millet yields – according to official statistics – and the mobilisation of
dust in the atmosphere were related to the extension of cultivation in marginal
areas (Ibrahim 1978, 1984). However, the variations in crop yields were found to
be better explained by rainfall variations (Olsson 1985), and the major impact on
the biological productivity of the land was that of climatic controls (Ahlcrona
1988). Similar inadequacies in the concept of linear desertification in South
Africa have emerged from recent research (Beinart 1996).

Even before the Sahelian drought, pessimistic assessments of degradation were
being made (Dregne 1970), but it was that event which popularised the issue
(Eckholm 1976). It provoked a veritable sandstorm of literature surrounding the
United Nations Conference on Desertification in 1977. The human dimensions
were the primary focus of interest (e.g., Johnson 1977; Biswas and Biswas 1980),
and human agency was uppermost in the official understanding of desertification.
The Conference concluded by approving a Plan of Action to Combat

Desertification (PACD), which was co-ordinated by the Desertification Branch of the UNEP, as the basis for national plans. Not superseded (in UNEP) until 1992, the definition approved at that Conference had much influence on subsequent debate and controversy:

> Desertification is the diminution or destruction of the biological potential of the land, and can lead ultimately to desert-like conditions . . . Overexploitation gives rise to degradation of vegetation, soil and water . . . In exceptionally fragile ecosystems, such as those on the desert margins, the loss of biological productivity through the degradation of plant, animal, soil and water resources can easily become irreversible, and permanently reduce their capacity to support human life. Desertification is a self-accelerating process, feeding on itself, and as it advances, rehabilitation costs rise exponentially. (UNEP 1977a: 3)

Setting aside the difficulties of defining 'biological potential', 'desert-like conditions' and 'irreversible', the emphasis placed on human 'over-exploitation' (Dregne, 1983) prejudged the issue of natural versus anthropogenic causes. Like the concept of biological potential, over-exploitation (over-grazing, over-cultivation, over-cutting) can be defined only in relation to an optimal level of exploitation – carrying capacity, critical population density, sustained yield – whose specification depends in turn on numerous assumptions concerning management, macro- and micro-economic determinants and the possibilities for change. The low profile given to climatic controls, whether rainfall decline or interannual variability, side-stepped the serious question of understanding the linkages between climate and desertification.

In response to these and other criticisms (Gorse and Steeds 1987; Nelson 1988), the UNEP redefined its definition of desertification for the Earth Summit in 1992 (Cardy 1993; Darkoh 1995; UNEP 1993) as follows:

> Desertification means land degradation in arid, semi-arid and sub-humid areas resulting from various factors, including climatic variations and human activities.

In other official publications, however, it was still insisted that desertification (or dryland degradation) is 'resulting mainly from adverse human impact'(Dregne *et al.* 1991; UNEP 1992: vii). Warren and Khogali (1991: 6) wanted to restrict the term 'dryland degradation' to degradation 'brought about mainly by inappropriate land use under delicate environmental conditions', reserving the word 'desiccation' for natural drying out over decades. So the debate about definitions has yet to be finally settled.

Desertification was not given a high profile at the Rio Earth Summit in 1992, but afterwards became the subject of negotiations for an international convention, adding a new political interest to the UNEP's struggle to demonstrate its seriousness for the world community. Desertification is used to justify strong planning, policies or interventions by central governments in smallholders' systems of natural resource management; more resources for centralised forestry activities; spending by aid donors and development agencies; and politically appropriate responses to drought and famine crises. Yet the PACD, after its approval in 1977, persistently failed to receive the support expected. 'Many governments did not recognise the enormity of the desertification threat, or appreciate the costs or complex processes of desertification' (Buonajuti 1991: 31; Odingo 1992). Africa, 'the bedeviled continent' (Kassas *et al.* 1991: 20), continued to attract the greatest attention, if not the necessary funds. Endless repetition of time-hallowed associations between population growth, over-exploitation and degradation continued to substitute for research; and global assessments continued to make extensive use of approximations and assumptions (Dregne *et al.* 1991). The inclusion, in the *definition* of desertification, of human agency or management means that its *causes* must be understood (or assumed) before any area of the world can be said to be subject to desertification. Yet these causes are commonly little investigated, or controversial.

The old idea that the desert is advancing out of the Sahara still has enormous popular appeal because it is something that everybody understands, or imagines that they understand. Though it is good for mobilising concern, it is far from accurate. Mainguet, in a comprehensive review (1994), considers that while the myth of an advancing desert has been laid to rest, the continuing plurality of definitions is far from satisfactory. Yet, rather than the less ambiguous term dryland degradation, desertification has been preferred in international environmental negotiations leading to the International Convention for Combating Desertification (ICCD). Throughout the history of the debate on desertification, it is fair to say that the case has rested, to an undesirable extent, on fragmentary evidence, unsystematic field observation and hypothetical arguments; and scepticism has not been lacking. The ICCD has since developed an institutional dynamic of its own, with the preparation of national action plans in signatory countries, and the possibility of international donor assistance.

Assessing degradation

Searching for indicators

Much effort has been committed to mapping worldwide desertification. A brief review of these efforts is instructive. Aridity zones based on an index (precipitation over potential evapotranspiration) were mapped (UNESCO 1979). Aridity, however, may provide an indication of the potential for degradation but not its actual extent or severity, which depend on climate change, rainfall variability and human agency. Some additional parameters were therefore superimposed on the bioclimatic (aridity) zones to produce a map of desertification. These were 'high human and animal pressure', geomorphic vulnerability to some desertification processes, and 'degree of desertification hazard' (UNEP 1977b). The inclusion of such parameters necessarily introduced a subjective element. Their combination into an index was worse. Desertification hazard was mapped in three generalised classes, moderate, high and very high, which reflected problems of subjectivity, scientific uncertainty and ambiguities in definition – there were over 100 definitions in use in the literature according to Glantz and Orlovsky (1983).

In order to map desertification, objective indicators were needed. It is not difficult to identify indicators of ecological degradation, and their monitoring presents few technical problems. A suitable list might include the following (Reining 1978; Dregne 1983): soil characteristics (depth, organic matter, crusts, salt or alkali content and dust deposits); water (depth to groundwater, quality, extent of surface water and status of drainage systems); and vegetation (ground cover, reflectance, biomass above the ground and species composition). However, difficulties arose when attempts were made to identify social indicators of desertification. Among those that were first proposed (Reining 1978) were certain characteristics of land and water use, settlement patterns, demography and social processes. However, these may be either *cause* or *effect* of degradation, or indeed, *both* or *neither*. The selection of such an indicator necessarily appropriated an explanatory hypothesis. Indeed, descriptive and explanatory modes were frequently confused in discussing desertification.

There is little agreement as to how such indicators should be selected, weighted and manipulated in order to achieve an integrated index of desertification. The theoretical basis of combining such disparate parameters, and the essential differences between the social and the natural indicators, received insufficient attention. The approach is open to the objection that there is too much interdependence among the indicators (Olsson 1993). Nevertheless, these objections have not stopped the search for indicators, which was revived by the UNDP after the Earth Summit of 1992. If the attempt to generate an integrated index of desertification is abandoned, as it must be, the conclusion is implicit that the components of desertification need to be understood separately, and that each requires appropriate policy and action.

An official consensus

Since 1986, the claim has been made that 'Currently each year some 21 million hectares are reduced to a state of near or complete uselessness' (Tolba 1986); and to this UNEP added the statement that 'As many as 900 million people in 100 countries are at risk from desertification' (Mabbutt 1985). Ten years after, the UNCOD's analysis of the desertification problem had taken on more strident tones:

> When I presented the GAP [General Assessment of Progress] report to UNEP's twelfth Governing Council, the three horsemen of 'desertification', 'population growth' and 'underdevelopment' were joined by the fourth of the apocalypse – 'famine'. Millions of people were threatened by starvation in over 20 African countries in 1984. Desertification destroys the productive capacity of the land and, when drought strikes, the weakened land collapses. (Tolba 1987)

However, if the old meaning of desert encroachment is agreed to be inaccurate and misleading, what does the concept of desertification now stand for? There are four main components. First is soil erosion, either by water or by wind. Second is the degradation of the chemical or physical properties of the soil. Third is the degradation of natural vegetation on the rangelands. Fourth is deforestation, or the destruction of the woody vegetation. The estimates of the Global Assessment of Human-induced Soil Degradation, which form the basis of the *World atlas of desertification* (UNEP 1992) are given for the drylands of sub-Saharan Africa in Table 2.3 and Fig. 2.5.

More than one type of degradation affects many susceptible drylands, according to this assessment. Wind and water erosion are the most important, but chemical and physical deterioration are also very significant. The first of these includes the loss of nutrients on cultivated land and salinisation in irrigated areas. The second includes compaction, sealing, crusting, waterlogging and soil desiccation.

Reasons for scepticism

The practical difficulties of identifying, mapping and assessing desertification do not encourage confidence in global estimates. It has already been observed that an insistence on human agency removes objectivity from an assessment of desertification, since there are very real difficulties in distinguishing in the field between natural and man-made changes. The estimates in Table 2.3 are not based on measurements but on the informed judgements of scientists and technicians, and are on a broad scale (Warren and Khogali 1991: 21). The necessity of relying on such a form of assessment, after a decade of activity in defining, measuring and mapping desertification, is itself a commentary on the provisional status of 'desertification science' in Africa. There is 'a discouraging scarcity of hard data about land degradation' (*ibid*: 5). This problem will now be reviewed in relation to each of the four major components of desertification.

Estimating soil loss through water erosion is notoriously difficult for large areas; reliable measurements are only available for small erosion plots or of river sedi-

Table 2.3 *'Human induced' soil degradation in the African drylands (millions of hectares), according to the Global Assessment of Soil Degradation.*

Type		Northern sub-Saharan Africa	Southern Africa	Total
Water erosion	(light)	97.5	2.0	99.5
	(moderate)	24.7	12.5	37.2
	(strong or extreme)	20.4	30.9	51.3
Wind erosion	(light)	156.2	5.7	161.9
	(moderate)	99.5	16.1	115.6
	(strong or extreme)	5.7	4.1	9.8
Chemical deterioration	(light)	25.6	2.2	27.8
	(moderate)	8.8	0.3	9.1
	(strong or extreme)	5.0	0.1	5.1
Physical deterioration	(light)	18.7	1.2	19.9
	(moderate)	8.7	1.1	9.8
	(strong or extreme)	3.1	4.1	7.2
Degraded areas		473.9	80.3	554.2
Susceptible drylands		802.4	295.0	1097.4

Notes:
Water erosion: sheet wash, rills, gullies, underground piping
Wind erosion: deflation, abrasion, deposition, dust clouds
Chemical deterioration: nutrient depletion, salinization
Physical deterioration: compaction, sealing, crusting; sodication; waterlogging; aridification; subsidence
Susceptible drylands: arid, semi-arid and dry sub-humid zones according to UNEP's scheme (see Chap. 2)
Source: UNEP (1992), 29–33

ment loads; and soil is rarely lost in an absolute sense, but rather redistributed through the agency of water to other locations, in deltas or flood plains for example (Stocking 1996). At least two estimating equations are available (the Universal Soil Loss Equation, or USLE, based on values derived in the USA, and the Soil Loss Estimating Model for Southern Africa, or SLEMSA). To use such equations, it is necessary to specify certain parameters, such as land use. This tends to restrict their usefulness to small sites. More realistic assessments take account of soil renewal through natural weathering and deposition, in order to arrive at 'soil budgets'. Such a budget may be put into an economic context to estimate the productive life of a soil under a given management regime. However, a simple budget may not take adequate account of the different nutrient values of soil hori-

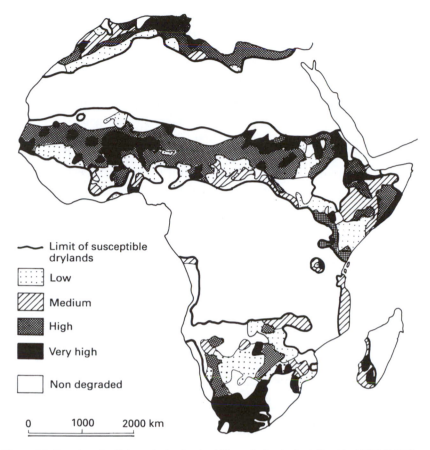

Figure 2.5 Severity of soil degradation in the African drylands. As defined by UNEP (1992).

zons, the uppermost being both the richest and most vulnerable to erosion (Stocking and Pain 1983; Warren and Khogali 1991). An application of the SLEMSA model in northern Nigeria concluded that physical soil life is adequate for many years to come; but the loss of fertility is a more immediate danger (Olofin 1992).

Estimating soil loss through wind erosion is even more difficult, since the eroded material is mobilised and redistributed by air. Deposited in dunes, it may look barren, but can be recolonised by vegetation and even support crops, given rain. Some dryland soils have little profile development, having themselves been moving dunes a few thousand years ago; so the economic loss when material is blown from the top few centimetres is difficult to assess.

A budgeting approach has also been taken to estimating soil nutrient balances.

At the crudest level, nutrient inputs (via fertilisers) can be compared with outputs (via crops exported). This method misses nutrients supplied by soil renewal processes, nitrogen fixation and dust deposition. Estimates have been offered on a continental scale and for certain countries (Smaling 1993), but the risk of error on such scales is very high. Or budgets can be computed for individual crops. Groundnut exports from Senegal, for example, were blamed for the impoverishment of soils in the 'peanut basin', as fertilisers failed to make good the nutrients exported to Europe in the crop (Franke and Chasin 1980); but it is implicit in such a thesis that, without adequate replenishment from outside the area, the cropping system must ultimately collapse, and it has not done so. In southern Mali, a nutrient budgeting study concluded that 'soil mining' is depleting the natural capital (van der Pol 1992). But budget or accounting approaches based on crop production necessarily ignore the dynamics of nutrient cycling, both on uncultivated land (which is usually a large proportion of the whole) and on the farm, which in subsistence-orientated systems involves flows of greater magnitude than exports or imports (Harris 1994, 1996). The potential for error is large and the explanatory power of this approach weak, except on the scale of very small units, where budgets can be linked to soil management.

Savanna soils are characteristically poor in nitrogen and phosphorus (Jones and Wild 1975), and the impact of cultivation regimes on nutrient levels is critically important for the future of smallholder farming systems (Pieri 1989). Soil properties can be monitored at intervals. Under chemically intensive farming this type of assessment is open to the objection that nutrient levels are largely maintained by inputs, administered from crop to crop, and little would be learnt from the exercise. However, in subsistence-orientated systems in the drylands of Africa, where inorganic fertiliser inputs are usually low or non-existent, soil monitoring can tell us the health of the soil under cultivation. Very few studies have been made because of the absence of baseline data for known sites.[2]

Not only nutrients are important. Monitoring can also tell us what is happening to the physical properties of soils under cultivation, for example the clay fraction, which is important for retaining moisture. Some dryland soils are prone to surface compaction, which is the more likely when vegetation is sparse, and this accelerates erosion while impeding seed germination. However, bare soil may have functional value in concentrating scarce water where it is most needed, as recent work suggests in the *brousse tigré* of West Africa (in which strips of woodland or scrubland occur in a pattern unrelated to slope. Wallace *et al.* 1994).

According to the UNEP (1992: 35), overgrazing is responsible for 58 per cent of soil degradation in the drylands of sub-Saharan Africa. Behind this bland statistic there lies a large area of scientific controversy and technical uncertainty. In the Sahelian drylands, in South Africa and elsewhere, grassland vegetation responds sensitively to variations in the rainfall, both spatially and temporally, to the extent that rainfall is a strong predictor of biomass (le Houérou 1985: 177). For this reason, it is difficult to estimate the impact of grazing management apart from the rainfall, especially where herds are moved around in response to feed supply. Until recently, an almost unquestioned orthodoxy held that most arid and semi-arid rangelands are over-grazed. The incongruity of this claim with the known resilience of the plant communities, and with an historical tendency for livestock populations to increase between droughts, went unobserved. The Sahelian drought was seen, in this light, as the natural outcome of excessive stocking, and the significance of the rapid recovery of many herds afterwards (Bonfiglioni 1985) was not sought.

Research in the arid zone has demonstrated that grassland communities are not normally damaged by grazing because before this can occur, animal numbers have fallen through mortality or migration. The controlling factor is the dry season biomass. When the rain returns, there are insufficient animals to threaten the recovery of the grassland (Ellis and Swift 1988; Hiernaux 1994). Apart from being incapable of inflicting permanent damage on the range, grazing has some positive effects: promoting green shoots and tillering, for example. It is now known that some kinds of environmental disturbance help to maintain the diversity and adaptability of ecosystems, though little is known of the limits of such ability to cope with stress (Williams and Balling 1995). Overgrazing effects around wells have been exaggerated (Warren and Khogali 1991: 42). The Eghazer and Azawak areas of Niger, which were the subject of a study in 1977, were revisited in 1983 and found to be less affected by grazing than by rainfall (Bernus 1977; Warren and Khogali 1992: 43).

In the Kalahari too, an interpretation of environmental deterioration – 'which nobody denies exists' – rested on the introduction of large cattle herds by commercial ranchers using boreholes (Cooke 1985). This interpretation received support from studies of satellite imagery (Ringrose and Matheson 1991), but has been since challenged (Dougill and Cox 1995).

The situation may be different where stockraising and farming share the same environment, and farmland expands at the expense of natural rangeland. However, the issue may be complicated – at least in the Sahelian region – by an increasing supply of crop residues from the farmland and even, in some systems (such as the Akamba system in Kenya), of cultivated fodder crops (van Raay and de Leeuw 1976; Tiffen *et al.* 1994). This may counterbalance the loss of natural grazing, and, together with a switch from cattle to small ruminants, make it possible for livestock populations to increase even where rangeland has been eliminated by permanent fields (Hendy 1977; Bourn and Wint 1994).

Objective indicators of overgrazing are hard to find, and assessments depend to an undesirable extent on the impressions of scientists in the field. 'Obviously, only experienced range scientists can make reasonably reliable estimates of the productivity of the present plant community compared to what is possible using the best management practices' (FAO/UNEP, n.d.: 24). Changes in plant density, the ratio of woody to grassland species and in the species composition of the grassland, can be brought about by selective grazing, by burning, by rainfall change, or by changes to the surface soils induced by erosion, desiccation or trampling. Exemplifying such ambiguities, the substitution of annual for perennial grasses in areas of the Sahel after the droughts of the 1970s and 1980s was influenced by rainfall rather than by grazing pressure. The annual grasses are liked by cattle and support herds throughout the year; their nutritive value is at least equal to that of the perennials they replaced (de Wispelaere and Peyre de Fabregues 1986; Mortimore 1989a).

Deforestation or domestic over-exploitation for woodfuel or other uses are blamed for 26 per cent of soil degradation in the drylands of sub-Saharan Africa (UNEP 1992: 35), almost all of it in the Sahel region. Conventional wisdom has it that 'intense fuelwood cutting causes the severest forms of dryland degradation near urban areas' (Eckholm and Brown 1977; Warren and Khogali 1991: 44). Yet one of the largest of dryland Africa's cities, Kano in Nigeria, is surrounded by a dense farmed parkland that maintained or increased its woodstock through two major drought cycles in the 1970s and 1980s (Cline-Cole *et al.* 1990). This is not unique, for settlements are associated with increased densities of trees throughout West Africa (Pullan 1974).

Changes in woody vegetation are hard to measure because exploitation may take the form of using deadwood, harvesting branches, pollarding, coppicing or felling, and it is a highly selective activity depending on the ownership, growth status, fuel and other use value of trees. This applies both to trees on farmland and those in woodland. Earth satellite data have been used to survey the present status of vegetation, including woodland, in Africa (Millington *et al.* 1994). The monitoring of change is another matter, since what determines timber volume is the balance between offtake and increment, or natural regeneration, over a period of time. There are large differences between species. Rates of regeneration for woodland communities are at best the subject of informed guesses. The hypothesis of woodland degradation is confused by the revolution in management which takes place wherever farmland expands and becomes more permanent under individual tenure. Whereas the government's gazetted forest reserves, and woodlands under common access come under intensified pressure (especially from urban woodfuel suppliers), and may degrade, the trees on private farmland may increase in number and size as their value is enhanced.

The replacement of the idea of desertification with the concept of dryland degradation facilitates the disaggregation of its components and the identification of appropriate monitoring procedures. The 'social aspects of desertification' can more clearly be recognised as either causes or effects of degradation, but the uncertainties cannot be so easily disposed of. Dryland degradation is not like ozone depletion or global warming. The many variables that require measurement have been inadequately observed over time; the reconstruction of baselines in the past is fraught with difficulties; and the search for accuracy appears to be vulnerable to generalisation, over-simplification and distortion for political or funding purposes.

Dilemmas of desertification

This review highlights two dilemmas facing the 'science of desertification', the first relating to substance and the second to application. Enough has been written to show that the conceptualisation of desertification created operational difficulties, which can best be solved by decoupling causal factors from its identification and measurement. However, if we redefine it as 'dryland degradation', irrespective of whether its causes are human or natural, data scarcity is still a problem. A recent study of the links between desertification and climate (Williams and Balling 1995) concluded that:

> The single biggest impediment to quantifying the interactions between desertification and climate stems from the variable quality of the data relating to the extent, severity and trends of the various forms of dryland degradation collectively contained within the general term desertification.

What of climate trends? As we have already noted, the decline (real or supposed) of the rainfall was given a prominent role in early analyses of *dessèchement* and desert encroachment. However, 'inappropriate land use' and its progenitor, population growth, were given a much higher profile in the debates surrounding the world conference on desertification in 1977. Only when the evidence of rainfall decline in northern sub-Saharan Africa acquired statistical weight with the passage of years did the agency of desiccation gain more credence. In eastern Africa, however, there is no evidence of decline and, in southern Africa, the evidence for it is less conclusive (Fig. 2.6).

Therefore we may say that, at least in the Sahel, a secular decline in the rainfall – of a significant order of magnitude – must have contributed materially to the desiccation of soils and vegetation, and that everywhere in dryland Africa, unpredictable and sometimes severe or prolonged droughts administer shocks to the natural and managed ecosystems.

Are these trends and shocks related in any way to global warming? Recent

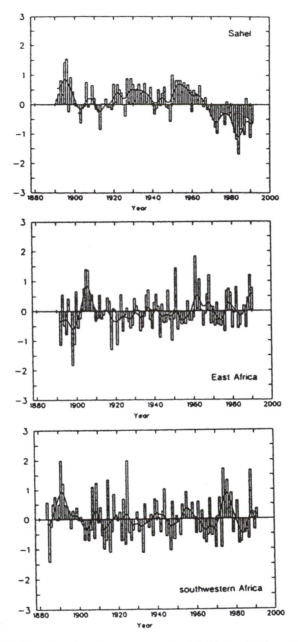

Figure 2.6 Departures from the mean annual rainfall in the Sahel, equatorial East and southwestern Africa (smoothed with a ten-year statistical filter). After Hulme (1992). The top two time-series show annual anomalies using January–December totals, the lower series using July–June. The smooth curves are 10-point Gaussian filters fitted through the data, which suppress variations on time-scales of less than a decade.

warming has dominated the dryland areas globally, and the Hadley Centre's model predicts a rise of from 1 to 2 degrees celsius throughout most of Africa by the year 2040. But no statistically significant changes in precipitation have been established in the world's drylands as a whole (Williams and Balling 1995). The models which predict precipitation vary widely in their regional predictions, so little confidence can yet be placed in them as a guide to future rainfall patterns in particular areas (Hulme and Kelly 1993). Nevertheless, climate change scenarios have been used to suggest that cereal producing areas in the tropics and sub-tropics will be more vulnerable than those in the developed nations (Rosenzweig *et al.* 1993; Rosenzweig and Parry 1994). Increased vulnerability has been predicted for the inhabitants of semi-arid areas in Kenya, Senegal and Zimbabwe (Downing 1992).[3]

The second, less obvious dilemma concerns the policy outcome of diagnostic and prescriptive studies of dryland degradation. The implication of the traditional view of desertification is that 'mismanagement' of natural resources is responsible:

> Desertification is caused almost entirely by the human misuse of the environment . . . This misuse, which is not necessarily the result of ignorance, takes the form of felling trees to provide fuel, overgrazing by domestic animals, and harmful agricultural practices. (Cloudsley-Thompson 1984)

And:

> People are the producers of desertification. Why has there been the temptation to maximize the natural causes and to minimize the human responsibilities? (Mainguet 1994: vii)

Since the drylands are occupied predominantly by African smallholders it follows that indigenous technologies and systems of natural resource management are deemed inappropriate in expert judgement – at current population densities. What are the policy implications of such a stance? There are two.

The first is that indigenous technologies and systems require transformation or replacement by better ones. This not unfamiliar theme was formerly justified on the grounds that technological transformation was necessary in African farming and pastoral systems in order to support improved incomes and living standards, and narrow the gap between rich and poor, north and south. Adoption was usually (but not always) voluntary, and the search to explain why African smallholders were often reluctant to embrace the new technologies and systems looked for economic or cultural bottlenecks. Latterly, however, inappropriate land use is believed to be setting up irreversible trends of degradation. On this diagnosis, choices can no longer be left to the smallholder. Top-down, centralised, expert-led modes of intervention (whether presented in a participatory guise or not) are unavoidable.

The second implication is that interventions designed to 'combat' desertification are likely to be ill-equipped to evaluate the rationales of indigenous land use systems, or to identify technical and managerial resources within the existing systems. Yet these systems embody all the practical experience that is specific to the environments in question; by comparison, the experience of experts is superficial in the extreme. Further: based as they are on social communities, rather than on isolated production units, the indigenous systems utilise pooled knowledge and menus of technical options or economic strategies. This type of experience is thus broader and more adequately contextual than that of the professional, and because individuals farm or graze particular resources (sometimes many of them) they are familiar with the ecosystem at the micro-scale, in all its spatial and temporal diversity.

In truth, the paradigm of desertification as a one-way regression from pristine nature to man-made sterility is inappropriate. It has been influenced to an undue extent by a Western conception of the *drylands as wilderness* – a safari or culture park (suitable for tourism perhaps) quite unlike the landscapes of transformation created by capital for market production in western Europe or north America. This conception now needs to be questioned, in the light of new research which shows with increasing clarity that an economic and social rationale also informs the management of *dryland landscapes under transformation*, even at very low population densities.

For these reasons, the debate on dryland management must come to grips with the perspective of smallholders. For they it is who must continue to manage most of the drylands, as the financial resources for top-down solutions become difficult to obtain, the competence of some agencies to implement centralised interventions is being called into question, and the political environment favours economic autonomy rather than authoritarian government. What can we learn from such a perspective?[4]

1 Generally credited to Aubréville (1949), the term desertification, since its adoption by the United Nations Conference on Desertification (UNEP 1977a) has swallowed up a number of related terms found in earlier literature, including desert encroachment, 'the advancing Sahara', desiccation, desertization (sic) and the French *dessèchement*. Notwithstanding attempts to replace it with the word 'degradation', which many consider to be more exact, the term was rescued at the Rio Earth Summit in 1992, and is now enshrined in the International Convention on Desertification.

2 Mortimore (1993b) used longitudinal soil monitoring to show that the soils of the Kano Close-Settled Zone in Nigeria had not deteriorated significantly under annual cultivation for thirteen years; and Mbuvi (1991) compared cultivated and

uncultivated sites in Machakos, Kenya, to evaluate the impact of cultivation over several decades.

3 Scenarios of climate change and its consequences for food production suggest, in some cases, a reversal of trends observed in recent decades. For example, some models predict contradictory trends in rainfall in the eastern and western Sahel. Records show decline since about 1960 (Fig. 2.6). Yet global warming has been with us for much longer. For global warming to cause declining cereal yields in semi-arid countries of Africa, a reversal of recent increases in cereal output, such as those recorded in the Sahel (Snrech *et al.* 1994) is necessary. Continuity between present and future trends would, however, be expected. At least the mechanisms whereby such reversals can occur need to be specified.

4 The discussion of rangeland management and dryland degradation will be resumed in chapters 4 and 7.

3 A smallholder's perspective

How does a smallholder's perspective on the management of natural resources differ from that of the global discourse outlined in chapter 2?

Given the differences shown in Table 3.1, the need to 'earth' the global discourse in the realities of dryland households' objectives is self-evident. With the exception of those areas controlled by large-scale, commercial farms and ranches (in Kenya, Zambia or Zimbabwe for example), everyday decisions about the management of natural resources are made by small-scale producers. Their livelihoods depend on individual, family or community rights of access to land, water and

Plate 3 Producers, reproducers or consumers? Family farming in northern Machakos, Kenya, 1990.

Table 3.1 *Global and smallholder perspectives on natural resource management.*

	Global perspective	Smallholder perspective
Spatial scale	global or regional	local or micro
Predictive time-scale	half-century or longer	generation
Planning horizon	government term; five-year plan; budget year	production year
Prioritisation	sustainable environment	livelihood security (social reproduction)
Type of authority	central direction	grassroot autonomy
Knowledge system	science and technology	indigenous knowledge
Nature of programme	generalised, inflexible	diverse, adaptive

trees. Their goals are defined in terms of the welfare and reproduction of the household, as well as individual profit. They work under severe constraints in labour, land and capital. While their decisions can be influenced by policies (on agricultural prices, or land and water rights, for example), they cannot be dictated, especially under conditions of the diminishing financial and technical resources of most governments. These limitations highlight the need, which was less apparent one or two decades ago, to mobilise private resources for investment and technical change (including those of smallholders themselves), directed towards sustaining productivity and conservation. If technical assessments of environmental change are ever to be turned into practical recommendations *and adopted by African smallholders,* their perspective must be understood (Richards 1983).

What are the essentials of a smallholder's perspective on managing natural resources? At some risk of over-simplification, these may be summarised in the form of twenty-four 'driving questions', arranged under seven headings (Table 3.2). On the answers to these or similar questions, strategic decisions at the individual and household level are based. On these decisions depend both the economic and the environmental sustainability of the system.

The first point to observe about this list is its diversity. There is nothing simple about surviving in the drylands. Although livestock specialists may not farm, and some farmers may not keep livestock, the range of 'driving questions' is wide for everybody because diversity is characteristic of dryland economies. A second observation is that the answers to many of these questions change every year, or even several times in a year. Thus decisions are made continuously. But a strong annual pattern is imposed by the seasonality of the growing period. A third point is that these questions relate directly to natural resources. Many more would need

Table 3.2 *Driving questions in managing natural resources.*

1 Labour
(1) How sufficient is adult family labour (males or females) to meet the needs of crop production or grazing, and how does farm work compare with other options open to it?
(2) What are the conditions of access to non-family labour (hiring, group, community)?
(3) How much child labour is available, subject to schooling?

2 Cultivated land
(4) Is there access to sufficient cultivated land for meeting subsistence needs and market opportunities?
(5) Are there land and labour for expanding cultivation; and if not, how can existing fields be fertilised?
(6) How does subdivision of landholdings between generations affect the viability of the landholding?

3 Livestock
(7) Can the family livestock provide sufficient milk, transport, traction, manure and income?
(8) What are the conditions of obtaining additional livestock (purchase, loan, management contract)?
(9) What are the risks (disease, starvation, robbery, sale) of losing animals, and what is the potential (reproductive females) for increasing their numbers?

4 Crops
(10) What choices are available of technically and economically appropriate food and market crops?
(11) How resistant are they to drought, low soil fertility, pests and diseases?
(12) How profitable are they, and how risky?

5 Fodder
(13) How accessible are rangeland, crop residues and browse in terms of distance and rights?
(14) How adequate is the available fodder, in quantity and quality?
(15) How does fodder supply vary between seasons and between years?

6 Trees
(16) Where is fuel available, and how much labour does it need to harvest it?
(17) What are the benefits of planting or protecting trees (food, fodder, medicine, materials)?
(18) What are the costs (labour, capital) of planting or protecting trees, and what are the risks (birds, animals, thieves)? Do they compete with crops for nutrients or water?

7 Water
(19) Where is water available, in terms of distance and rights of access?
(20) How much labour (female or male?) is necessary to raise and carry it?
(21) How much water is available at or near the surface (for livestock or irrigation), and for how many months of the year?

8 Technologies
(22) What technologies are available to increase the amount of cultivated land, or the number of livestock, that can be managed?
(23) What technologies are available to increase the productivity of land, or of livestock, and how reliable is the supply of inputs?
(24) How much capital can be found for new technologies, and how risky is investment?

Table 3.3 *Family labour in a sample of households (Futchimiram, Nigeria).*

	Type of household	Men	Women	Boys	Girls	Total	Land Quartile
1	Large, labour +, land +	2	1	4	0	7	1
2	Large, labour −, land +	1	1	1	2	5	1
3	Large, labour −, land −	1	1	1	2	5	4
4	Small, labour −, land −	1	1	0	0	2	4
5	Single, independent male	1	0	0	0	*1	4
6	Single, dependent female	0	1	0	0	1	4

Note:
Land quartile: size of landholding by quartile in the village (thirty-three households).

to be added in order to take account of off-farm activity. Thus, successful management of the dryland environment requires both complex and continuous decision-making.

Labour: people to do the work

The point to begin with is the household's chief resource, labour. The demographic endowment of a household defines its supply of family labour. A family well-endowed with adults (especially men) and boys is better off than one that is highly dependent on female, elderly or child labour. But the composition of the family is not the result of choice. Children are seen as the gift of God, rather than the products of decisions; fertility, health and mortality vary unpredictably from household to household. Table 3.3 illustrates six differently composed farming families from a village in northern Nigeria.

These six households are very differently endowed:

- with three adults (the family head, his wife and a grown son) and four boys, Household 1 is well endowed both in the present and for the future;
- with only two adults among five people, Households 2 and 3 are much less well endowed.
- Household 4, while having two adults available now, has no children yet for the future; will it be able to evolve like Household 1?
- Households 5 and 6 are single people living alone. The man in Household 5, however, can support himself, whereas the elderly woman in Household 6 cannot work and depends on relatives' help.

Under conditions of hand farming, the labour supply limits the amount of land that can be cultivated. We might expect, therefore, a simple relationship between the size of the family labour force and the size of landholding. In this village, where abundant land is available for cultivation, the families best endowed with labour appear in the top quartile of landholdings and the worst in the lowest quartile. In livestock producing households, labour is also limiting, as it is needed for lifting water from wells in the dry season, as well as for tending the animals. However, many factors intervene to complicate such a relationship.

In the first place, group labour still plays a part in many communities, though with diminished importance, or in adapted forms. Additional labour may be drawn from outside the family, from the labour markets which are becoming ever more pervasive. Labour hiring tends to differentiate between those who hire, and who own the capital to do so, and those who sell their labour, having insufficient resources – or income – to manage by themselves. However, this distinction is by no means rigid. The labour market is taking over, in some dryland countries, the role of community sharing institutions which reallocated labour amongst households according to need at different times of the year.

In some Muslim communities (for example in West Africa), married women should not participate in heavy farm work (such as weeding), and this makes the number of resident men more critical. In other societies, especially in eastern and southern Africa, women have always been mainly responsible for food crops, and take over the farms when their men are away. In such a situation, the key to success is having enough strong children. However, children are supposed to attend school, where it is available. A conflict therefore exists between the present value of children as workers and their value in future, as assured by school attendance, which, though it may eventually enhance their income opportunities, is likely to take them away from farming. The conflict may result, as in some Nigerian communities, in high rates of parentally sanctioned truancy, especially in the farming season. In others, such as in East Africa, education receives high priority.

For households having enough capital to change to a labour-saving technology, such as the ox-plough, the relationship between land and labour acquires a different order of magnitude. One person can perform certain operations on a much larger area in the same amount of time. If the plough is hired, together with its ploughman, capital rather than family labour becomes the limiting factor.

Cultivated land: securing the fruits of labour

Cultivated land is shared out in a bewildering variety of spatial patterns and social distributions. However, it must first be created by labour from woodland or grassland, whose clearance is achieved by cutting and burning, and

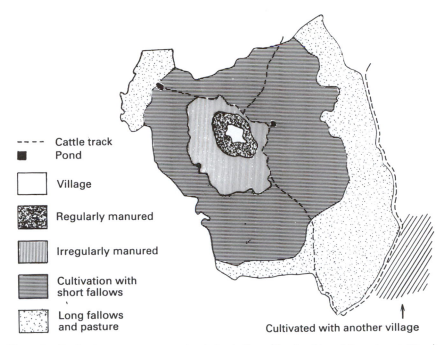

- - - - Cattle track
■ Pond

☐ Village

▨ Regularly manured

▥ Irregularly manured

▤ Cultivation with short fallows

⬚ Long fallows and pasture

Cultivated with another village

Figure 3.1 The land use pattern around a dryland village (Gourjae, Maradi Department, Niger) in 1978. After Grégoire (1980).

whose regeneration must be controlled by weeding and uprooting from year to year. The fields may also be enclosed by thorn fences to keep off livestock. When their natural fertility is exhausted, if they are not to be abandoned, they must be fertilised. All of these operations are investments, adding, through labour, to the productivity and value of the land.

Because labour-time spent on walking to fields is unproductive, cultivated land close to the house is preferred to that further off, creating the concentric rings of land use that characterise innumerable dryland villages (Fig. 3.1). As its natural fertility declines, the land close to the village becomes increasingly dependent on fertilisation from animal manure, village refuse and human waste, or purchased inorganic fertilisers (which also need to be carried to the fields). Further away, fallows are used to maintain fertility, and the more land available, the longer the fallow period may be. Thus the question, 'How much land is available?' breaks down into several classes of land. Access to each class depends on the rules of tenure obtaining, and on any restrictions imposed on cultivation (such as grazing reserves). As land becomes scarce, the concentric pattern of land use around the village breaks down and the cultivated areas of adjacent communities merge into one another. The pattern of settlement may become dispersed.

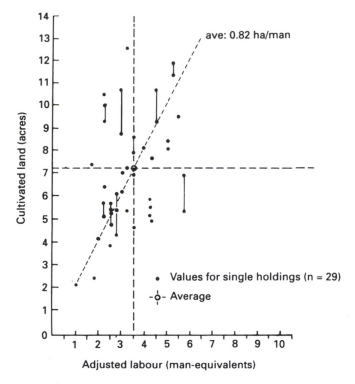

Figure 3.2 Land and labour in Takatuku, Sokoto State, Nigeria in 1967/68. The horizontal line shows average cultivated land (including fallow) per household (2.9 ha), and the vertical line shows the average family labour per household (3.56 man equivalents, where an adult man = 1; adult woman = 0.75; child aged 7–14 years = 0.5). The sloping line shows the land:labour ratio for the whole sample (0.82 ha per man). Households with some land fallow are shown with a vertical line: the upper dot shows the position of the household including fallow, and the lower dot its position excluding fallow. Constructed from data in Norman *et al.* (1976).

Where land is scarce, the amount of cultivated land a household uses cannot easily reflect its family labour supply. Economic inequality enables some to surmount the problem more successfully than others. Figure 3.2 shows the distribution of cultivated land and family labour among thirty-one households in a land-scarce community near Sokoto, Nigeria. Cultivated land included some parcels left fallow (perhaps for want of labour), and it ranged from less than one to five hectares per household. Family labour is given in man-equivalents, and it ranged from 0.75 to 9.75 per household. The average amount of land per man equivalent was 0.8 hectares. There were three groups of households, based on their land:labour ratios: those with more land and labour than average (top right quadrant) and with less land and labour than average (bottom left) – these households conformed approximately to the average land:labour ratio; those with more land than average and less labour (top left quadrant) – who were likely to need additional labour; and finally those with less land than average and more labour (bottom right quadrant) – who were relatively over-supplied with labour. It is notable than ten of the twelve households who had some fallow were relatively well-endowed with land (lying on or to the left of the sloping line).

A common cause for fallowing in land-scarce systems in Nigeria is a lack of labour or of capital with which to fertilise it. Fallowing as a strategy for restoring fertility is only possible where land is abundant.

There are always some households with insufficient cultivated land, which constantly run the risk of food shortages and lack marketable surpluses. Their lack of capital prevents them from breaking out of their poverty trap by acquiring more land, hiring extra labour, or buying new technology, unless they can earn incomes outside farming.

A crucial factor determining the supply of land at the household level is the system of inheritance. Where land is subdivided amongst male heirs, as in many dryland societies, the cultivated holding tends to become smaller with each generation, unless compensating acquisitions can be made by purchase or clearing new land. Where women inherit land, holdings may be even more fragmented. Therefore a critical question is how to gain access to additional land, or failing that, to intensification technologies which permit productivity to be sustained or increased.

Livestock: walking resources with multiple uses

The multiple uses of livestock are suggested in Table 3.2. Dryland households do not specialise in animals in the Western, commercial sense, even where no farming is undertaken. They contribute to subsistence, provide market income, transport goods and water and act as mobile savings banks. When owned by farmers, the provision of manure and farm traction are added to this list. Thus the prior question for a livestock owner is how far his or her stock holding fulfils these needs. There is usually sharp differentiation between households in the adequacy of their livestock holdings to meet economic needs (Table 3.4).

The table shows that the households that were richest in livestock were also the richest in income and in grain; yet (in this sample, though possibly not in others) they were smaller than poorer households. When the specific composition of the herds is taken into account, the diversity becomes even more marked, for wealthier households can usually afford more cattle or camels while poorer ones move into small ruminants (sheep or goats).

Herd diversification is a time-honoured strategy for coping with uncertain

Table 3.4 *Household differentiation in livestock ownership, WoDaaBe of Niger.*

Household strata	I	II	III
Number of households	2	6	6
People per household	7.5	8.8	9.5
Livestock per person (TLU)	3.6	2.3	1.3
Livestock per household (TLU)	26.9	20.2	12.2
Net income per person ('000 CFA)	32	10	1
Net cereal inflow per person (kg)	161	110	89

Notes:
TLU: livestock converted into Tropical Livestock Units (1,250 kg cow = 1 TLU)
CFA: West African franc
Source: White (1990).

feeding resources, though some pastoral communities, such as camel breeders in the arid zone, specialise (and take risks accordingly). Household livestock holdings in the drylands vary immensely on this scale of specialisation, from relatively large camel or cattle herds, through mixed holdings of small ruminants, cattle and one or two equines, to plough-bulls, and small holdings of one or two goats and a few chickens.

Diversification may also be a response to the difficulties of investing in the more valuable animals. The importance of livestock as investments charges herders and farmers alike with a need to find ways of acquiring more, by breeding (if they own breeding animals), purchase (using income generated from crops, animal products, or off-farm activities), or loan and contracting arrangements. Since fodder (as shown below) is still, to a significant extent, subject to common access, private rangeland may not constrain this goal of enlarging the herd.

Crops: multiple choices for kitchen or market

A crop inventory for a dryland village entirely dependent on rainfed farming might be expected to lack diversity. The opposite is found. For example, the farming system of Dagaceri (in northern Nigeria), which has 300–400 mm of rainfall in 12–15 weeks each year, draws on ten crops for subsistence and market, and there are forty-three varieties, seventeen of them sorghums (Table 3.5). Diversity is not merely botanical, but extends to their properties with regard to food and fodder value, other uses (medicinal, for example), marketability,

Table 3.5 *Crop inventory for sorghum, Dagaceri, northern Nigeria.*

Name of variety	Food value	Fodder value	Other uses	Market value	Drought escaping	Infertility coping	New(+) or old(−)
Dawar rini	o	−	+	−		+	
Jar tankwasa	+	++	−	−	+		
Mota	+	+	−	+	+	−	+
Husseini kunce	−	−	−	−	+		+
Malam Garba	+	+	−	+	+	.	+
Lara	+	+	−	+	−	−	−
Takanda	−	−	+	−	−	−	−
Dawar shayi	−	+	−	−	+	+	
Kuncin zomo	−	+	−	−	−	−	
Kaura	+	+	−	++	−	−	+
Makaho da wayo	−	+	+	−	−	+	−
Huhun kada	+	+	−	+	+	+	+
Farar tankwasa	+	+	−	+	−	−	
Dogon yaro	++	+	−	+	−	+	−
Binnamai	+	+	−	+	−	−	
Yar abubu	+	+	−	−	+	+	+
Wurommuya	+	+	−	+	++		+

Notes:
− not significant; + significant; ++ very significant; o not eaten

drought escaping (early maturity), and their capacity to cope with low fertility. Other variable properties are pest (insect and bird) and disease resistance. As the last column shows, the inventory of sorghum has been extended by the adoption of several varieties that are new to the village.

In addition to the sorghum varieties shown in the table, there are seven varieties of millet (which is the staple grain), from two to five varieties each of cowpea, groundnut, Bambara nut, sesame, melon and sorrel; okro and a very little maize are also grown. Such an inventory documents a 'menu' of options from which farmers can select under varying circumstances of rainfall, household food sufficiency, market opportunities, soil and other conditions.

In the field, the intercropping of millet with sorghum and cowpeas, and other mixtures, is characteristic. So is the conscientious attention to individual plants during the growing period. To an observer accustomed to the homogeneous fields of mechanised, chemical farming, the patterns may appear chaotic. But diversity fulfills two purposes. First, it maximises biomass production, through such mechanisms as:

(1)   the complementary leaf geometry of different plants for better light interception;

(2)   nitrogen fixation by legumes (such as cowpea or groundnuts);

(3)   the suppression of weeds;

and (4)   shading of low by taller plants in early phases of growth.

Second, diversity minimises risk, by ensuring that, given a drought or a pest attack, not all varieties are equally vulnerable, and plants of the same species are spaced apart. For market production, the profitability and risk of failure are not predictable, so diversified options are an advantage. Although the specific crops change, diversity in crop inventories is advantageous throughout the drylands.

Fodder: sharing out the biomass

Feeding the animals must take account of the spatial and temporal variability in fodder supply, as well as the differing requirements of the animals. Fodder comes from many sources: natural rangeland, enclosed paddocks (maybe improved by sowing or other methods), crop residues, browse from trees, fodder crops, hedge and wayside cuttings and weeds from cultivated fields. Livestock may graze open rangeland, they may be enclosed or tethered, or they may be stall-fed. They may move from one to another of these options at different times of the year. Most types of fodder may acquire a market value when scarce. Few dryland stockraisers can afford concentrates, though salt cures are purchased.

Table 3.6 shows an example of fodder procurement from Kenya, where significant differences exist between feeding strategies in the moist and in the dry semi-arid areas. In the former, farms are smaller and more intensively managed; fodder crops are grown on the steeply sloping banks of field terraces. In the moist areas, land is scarce, so that cattle (if not always other livestock) are often stall-fed ('zero-grazing') – that is, by cutting and carrying fodder crops, residues, grass and herbage to them in the *boma*. In the dry semi-arid areas, cattle graze on the farms, which include enclosed paddocks.

The management of feed supply through the year becomes a greater challenge where the dry season is long and when poor rains reduce the natural forage and residues available. In some systems (such as Machakos in Kenya, and on the Mambilla Plateau of Nigeria), most of the grazing land is privately owned. Its condition determines how many animals can be kept. However, these systems are the exception rather than the rule. In others, access to rangeland is held in

Table 3.6 *Methods of feeding livestock in Machakos, Kenya (1983).*

	Moist semi-arid	Dry semi-arid
Average farm size (ha)	4.5	5.6
Land use (ha)		
Crop production	2.0	2.9
Fodder crops	0.2	0
Grazing on farm and in paddocks	2.3	2.7
Forage production (dry matter, Kg/yr)		
Fodder crops	440	0
Grazing	2,150	3,320
Edible crop residues	3,000	4,350

Source: Ackello-Ogutu (1991).

common and the livestock owner has no control over its condition. When a drought occurs, the livestock owner has to decide whether to sell animals, move elsewhere, or watch them perish.

Trees: value added to the farm

Natural woodland is used, under common access, for fuel cutting and the collection of a range of commodities useful for construction, crafts, food, fodder and medicines. In lightly populated areas, each village may be surrounded by extensive woodland. Where densities are high, such woodland is found only in the interstices of the village field system. The extension of cultivated land gradually exhausts the supply of natural woodland, and grazing and cutting intensify the pressure. The increasing value of trees may, however, induce a change in management towards planting and protecting trees on farms. In the villages, shade and fruit trees may provide an almost continuous canopy. Hence the density of trees increases towards settlements, provided that land is held under secure title and the protector can reap the benefits.

It is in the context of these or other changes that smallholders' decisions about tree management are made. Case studies show that the stereotype of farmers 'mining' their wood stocks with little or no thought for the future are often very wide of the mark. Table 3.7 shows some aspects of tree management on farms in a part of Machakos District, Kenya.

The table shows that fruit tree densities increase as farm size decreases. This is an expression of the need for poor families to maximise income per hectare, which they do by combining trees with crops. Fruit trees in Machakos are usually

Table 3.7 *Fruit tree management on smallholdings, Mbiuni Location, Machakos, Kenya.*

Farm size class	I	II	III	IV
Average area cultivated	0.4	0.8	1.3	2.5
Fruit tree densities per ha:				
banana clumps	45.5	30.8	17.4	13.1
mangoes	6.8	3.8	3.0	1.6
pawpaws	4.5	2.6	4.5	2.0
lemons	0	6.8	5.1	3.6
guavas	2.3	0	3.0	0.4
Total	59.1	44.0	33.0	20.7

Source: Gielen (1982).

planted, managed and harvested by the women, and are an important expression of their economic autonomy, as well as a focus of potential competition with men for rights of access to land (Rocheleau *et al.* 1995). In the same district of Kenya, more than twenty species of indigenous trees were recorded growing on grazing land and on farms, where they are often planted and protected from animals; these trees are being used for fruit, browse, fencing and other construction and medicines. In addition there are exotic trees, usually grown by the men for timber or charcoal production.

The production of fuel is rarely in the forefront of smallholders' objectives. Rather the value of fruit, timber and other products is the primary consideration. Low value is given to female labour, and fuel collecting is left to the women in many societies. Trees that are planted and protected may only have subsidiary use as fuelwood trees. Both trees and their crops may be owned by women. However, tree farming also has costs. The evaluation of these – the risk of theft, damage, or the use of farm trees by grain-eating birds, for example – forms a part of smallholders' tree strategies.

Water: life for the lifting

Water, for domestic use and for livestock, is a condition of life in the drylands. Its availability is determined by a household's right of access to water sources, by distance and by the labour required to draw and carry it home (often, but not always, female). For sedentary communities, the water supply is linked to the settlement system through wells and surface collection sites. Common access to wells reflects the fact that communities had to mobilise considerable resources

Table 3.8 *Wells and farming households in Kala, Mali.*

	Households with no well	All households
Number of households	7	29
Persons per household	6.9	18.2
Workers per household	3.5	7.5
Cattle per household	1.7	20.8
Millet production per worker (kg)	1,016	1,541

Source: Toulmin (1992: 144, 158).

to dig and maintain them in the past. Mobile livestock producers, too, rely on their customary rights of access to such sources. These arrangements may be quite specific to cultures and environments, and private wells, or wells whose use was restricted to members of the community, were the norm rather than the exception in many pastoral areas before governments began to put down public wells and boreholes.

Table 3.8 shows a rather less usual arrangement in the village of Kala, in Mali, where owing to the relatively shallow depth of the water table (15–25 m), private wells are common. A private well attracts other peoples' livestock, whose manure becomes a resource for maintaining soil fertility on the family farm. Eleven were dug in the two years, 1980–81. Thus large households with more labour and livestock are in a better position to undertake the investment (equivalent to about £90–110) of digging wells, and subsequently maintain them; and well-owning households are able to reap larger yields and to grow in size by contracting marriages. This example illustrates how water, being scarce, may be embedded in the political economy of a dryland village.

Water scarcity, a problem that afflicts livestock producers seasonally, and sedentary communities in times of drought, dramatically increases the labour-time necessary for lifting and carrying it, and raises the bargaining power of water sellers. Labour scarcity often affects livestock-producing households during times of the year when they depend entirely on well water; it is usual for sharing arrangements to be made to overcome such crises. The Borana of southern Ethiopia use community chain-gangs to lift containers of water from their deep pit-wells up to the drinking troughs.

Improvements in the number and efficiency of wells, and in many places in the quality of water, have affected household welfare all over the drylands during the past half-century. When basic needs for water have been met, smallholders may be in a position to take up opportunities for irrigation (high-yielding boreholes, dams or natural surface waters). Boreholes which yield water throughout the year, where formerly only surface water was available in the wet season, have led in some areas to increases in livestock during the dry season, as transhumance became less necessary: a change of management that may lead to a shortage of forage.

Technologies for transformation

Dryland farmers are not passive recipients of technologies developed by others, but active problem-solvers in their own right. In doing so, they may make use of innovations from a variety of sources, as well as adapting indigenous technologies and carrying out their own experiments. An example is given in Table 3.9, which is drawn from a study of technical change in Machakos District, Kenya, from 1930–1990. The area saw a revolution in environmental management. Pushed at times by government and development agencies, and at other times by their own needs, the Akamba people adopted a range of land conservation practices on farmland in which field terracing is the most prominent (Tiffen et al. 1994).

The new technologies entered the district from multiple sources – geographically, in time, and in the institutional sense (Biggs 1989). They were pragmatically incorporated into the inventory of technical options through a variety of channels, including local travellers, market exchanges and on-farm experiments. The point to note is that the stimulus for adoption had to be internal to the system, a problem defined by the farmer rather than by the extension expert. For example, terrace construction did not take off on a sustainable basis until farmers perceived a need to capitalise their farms in this way. A majority raised the necessary capital themselves, or exploited co-operative labour. This took place thirty years or more after the first government programmes to promote soil conservation. Innovations were adapted to local needs. For example, composite maize (Katumani B, developed on the government research station of the same name) never had as large an impact as had been expected because farmers preferred to cross and combine it with local varieties to improve drought resistance and food security.

The Machakos study showed that smallholders were able to experiment with indigenous technical knowledge, accept the results of research, adapt new technologies to their own situations, learn from others' experience and from travel elsewhere, and work effectively with non-governmental organisations (Mortimore and Wellard 1991). Are the Akamba farmers unique in this respect? There is enough evidence to suggest that smallholders elsewhere in the drylands may not be far behind. Where land values, domestic demand for food and market opportunities are increasing, and given an enabling economic environment, technological change is inevitable.

Table 3.9 *Technological change in Machakos District, Kenya, 1930–90.*

New or extended technologies	Source	Stimulus
Crops		
Composite maize	Research station	Food security
Coffee	Government Coffee Board	European farmers
Tillage		
Ox-plough	Traders	Markets; labour shortage
Multipurpose tool bar	International Rural Development Programme (IRDP) extension	Lacking
Forked jembe hoe	Traders; local smiths	Steep slope gardening
Agronomy		
Row planting	Extension	Ploughing
Irrigation	Indigenous (gravity); sprinklers (traders)	Extended water supply
Pit planting	Experiments on-farm	Migration to drier areas
Fertilisation		
Manure	Indigenous; extension	Permanent fields; stall feeding of livestock
Fertilisers	Traders	Extension
Composting	Non-government agencies	Manure scarcity
Livestock production		
Crossbred cattle	Government, commercial breeders	Market; improvement of milk and manure output
Dipping	Veterinary Department	Tick control
Improved pastures	Extension; experiments on-farm	Privatisation of rangeland
Fodder crops	Grassland research	Intensification of livestock production
Stall feeding	Extension; experiments on-farm	Shortage of grassland
Conservation		
Terrace construction	Extension; other farmers	Private capitalisation
Run-off control (drains, waterways, bunds, gully checks, grass strips, sisal hedges, etc.)	Extension; other farmers	Need for productivity increase
Trees		
Agroforestry, informal	Experiments on-farm	Market for timber and fruit

Source: Mortimore and Wellard (1991).

Such change is driven by economic necessity (where subsistence is concerned) or by opportunity (where markets are concerned), and does not discriminate between sources. Rather than an opposition between innovative technologies, promoted by development agents, on the one hand, and conservative indigenous practice, embedded in culture, on the other (the traditional model), a new model of autonomous technical change based on 'mixing and matching' better describes what is happening in several dryland communities. Smallholders seem to be capable of effecting change, and even of enhancing productivity, to an extent unforeseen only a few years ago.

Dryland householders: more than farmers

Smallholders in the drylands try to ensure the economic sustainability of their families in an arid and risky environment. Their agenda is broader than the management of natural resources alone. Major questions include:

(1) Food sufficiency – are enough food grains (stored or incoming) assured until the next harvest?

(2) Markets – what to sell, when, where and for what prices? (Market sales may dispose of surpluses for profit or divest a household's resources in order to meet an emergency.)

(3) Capital – how to use market income: on animals, fixed or current investment, consumption, education, or food purchases?

(4) Alternative incomes – how to find alternative incomes to supplement those from farming?

(5) Migration (mobility) – whether some household members should travel away, in order to supplement incomes?

(6) Famine – in the event of a collapse in household income, how to mobilise social claims for help, exploit unfamiliar niches in the macro-economy, or ransack the ecosystem for famine foods?

For householders, however, these issues are inseparable from those that deal directly with managing natural resources. As the following chapters will show, economic rationales lie at the root of environmental management, which, while resting in the hands (for practical purposes) of millions of dryland smallholders, is ultimately dependent on the economic environment in which they make their decisions.

4   Risk in the rangelands

I turn first to the rangelands, more especially the arid rangelands (beyond the limit of rainfed farming), where an interpretation, for long conventional, of degradation caused by the misuse of natural resources (in this case, overgrazing) has been most coherently challenged. Recent research has put forward a new paradigm, in which the key driving factor is the variability of the rainfall.

The African rangelands have attracted controversy ever since colonial governments began to try to regulate what they saw as inefficient, degrading and unhealthy indigenous livestock enterprises, and European ranchers introduced radically new methods of management in some countries in eastern and southern

Plate 4 'Emaciated, diseased, overstocked'? Grazing the Badowoi parklands in northern Nigeria (September, 1993).

Africa. The controversy was not about the fact of degradation, which was not questioned, but about the means of controlling it and the level of coercion that was justified. Pressure for action escalated, until, in the 1930s, it was written:

> The broad facts are too well known . . . In Kenya, for instance, the livestock population has doubled in the last ten years . . . [the vegetation is] trampled and eaten to death, and forest cover stripped from the hills . . . There is only one answer – compulsory destocking, accompanied where necessary by reconditioning of land. Africans would certainly not welcome Government orders to destroy a large part of their apparent wealth. [But] As a DC in an eroded area said 'We should have to be prepared to call out the troops, and we might have to do it'. That, of course, is why nothing is done . . . Erosion is a problem above all others designed for shelving . . . And so Governments, from their apex in the Colonial Office to their bases in African villages, delay to act because they fear to use compulsion backed by the threat of force.(Huxley 1937)

Yielding to the settler and conservation lobbies, compulsory destocking was attempted in some areas by the government of Kenya in 1938, but the aggrieved stockowners organised themselves politically, lobbied the Westminster government, and secured its abandonment. Nevertheless, the diagnosis and prescription persisted in eastern Africa with remarkable continuity.

> The question why stocking rates in Zimbabwe's communal areas are so high has been asked for a long time. Officials have assumed that the cattle populations are 'exceeding ecological limits' and during the colonial period a series of destocking measures were imposed to bring the populations down to the 'carrying capacity' of the land. This debate still continues and current policy still advocates destocking, regulation of grazing and grazing schemes. (Scoones 1993)

For political reasons the overcrowded 'native' reserves were not extended in size. Instead, immunisation against major cattle diseases (rinderpest, East Coast fever) tended to increase livestock numbers, and strict quarantine controls on livestock movements attempted to contain the indigenous livestock sectors, in order to protect the commercial ranching interests.

In West Africa, lower ecological potential, more arduous conditions and an absence of policies to promote European settlement discouraged European ranching. One attempt to exploit the uninhabited forests of Bornu Province in Nigeria was abandoned as a failure (Dunbar 1970). Pastoral systems were not interfered with, except for veterinary controls on transit routes (which often crossed international borders) and immunisation programmes against the major cattle diseases (rinderpest and bovine pleuro-pneumonia). The weakness of the livestock policy of the Nigerian government was, indeed, fiercely criticised in an official study carried out towards the end of the colonial period (Shaw and Colville 1950).

The Sahelian ecosystem is now better understood as a result of major research programmes, particularly in Mali (Penning de Vries and Djiteye 1991), and so is its management by livestock producers (de Leeuw *et al.* 1993), but some expert judgement sticks to the view that the opportunistic grazing strategy of stockowners 'raises the stocking rate of the herds above the physical limits of the ecosystem' (Breman and de Wit 1983). These limits, of course, have to be defined in ecological terms in relation to production goals and the sustainability of the system (de Ridder and Breman 1993). Yet the economic efficiency of nomadic systems, in terms of value produced per hectare, compares favourably with those found elsewhere in the world (Western 1982).

The views exemplified above have not gone unchallenged. The controversy over the rangelands highlights certain conceptual issues about ecosystems and their management. These, it will be argued in later chapters, have implications beyond range management in the arid zone, in areas of somewhat higher rainfall where farming and livestock production are combined.

Concepts

Biomass productivity

The success of livestock production in the drylands depends on the amount of fodder resources and the efficiency with which they are managed. Pasture productivity, or the amount of edible biomass available from grass or other herbage, depends directly on the rainfall. Data from the Sahel of West Africa (Fig. 4.1) show an almost straight line function, with pasture productivity quadrupling (from 0.6 to 2.3 tonnes of dry matter per hectare) as average annual rainfall increases from 200 to 800 mm per year (Le Houérou and Hoste 1977). That range expresses the difference in space as one crosses the Sahel from north to south, a difference which dominates every aspect of primary production. It also expresses differences from year to year as the rainfall varies.

The productivity of biomass depends also on the types of plants and soils. In addition to herbage, animals browse trees, and the amount of foliage available for consumption in Sahelian conditions has been estimated at 1–2 kg per hectare per millimetre of rainfall (Gillet 1986), or about the same as the pasture productivity shown in Fig. 4.1. However, when trees are under heavy browsing and cutting, their output may be much lower. The third main component of fodder resources, crop residues, is a function of farming intensity in a particular area, and residues are not available at all in the arid zone, where rainfed farming is impossible.

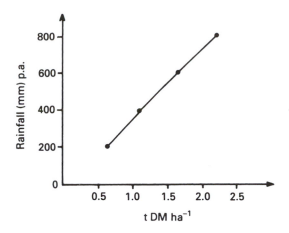

Figure 4.1 Annual rainfall and pasture productivity (constructed from data in Le Houérou and Hoste, 1977).

Biomass quality

In the West African Sahel, it used to be thought that water was the main limiting factor determining the productivity of the grasslands. The truth, however, is more complex:

> Water limits growth at the border of the Sahara. This changes over rapidly to growth limited by nitrogen (and phosphorus) with increasing rainfall to the south. Biomass increases then, but the protein content decreases. With water availability rising from 50 to 1000 mm annually the total mean production increases from nearly 0 to 4 metric tons per hectare. The protein content of the forage declines from 12 to 3 per cent. Thus low water availability produces a small amount of biomass of good quality, and higher water availability results in more biomass of increasingly inferior quality. (Breman and de Wit 1983: 1343)

This relationship is shown in Fig. 4.2. The dividing line between areas where growth is limited mainly by rainfall and areas where it is limited mainly by nutrients (phosphorus and nitrogen in particular) occurs at an annual rainfall of about 300 mm.

Another aspect of pasture quality is the nature of the dominant grasses. Not only do the dominant species vary from place to place and from year to year, but changes have occurred in the geographical distribution of annuals and perennials. Perennial grasses, which characterise the wetter savannas, grow in clumps, with root systems that survive the dry season to produce fresh growth. They do not die off totally and can be used for pasturage as long as the grass does not become too dry for animals to eat. Annual grasses, on the other hand, seed, germinate and die each year in the drier Sahel (<400 mm rainfall). On the face of it, they appear to provide less durable grazing.

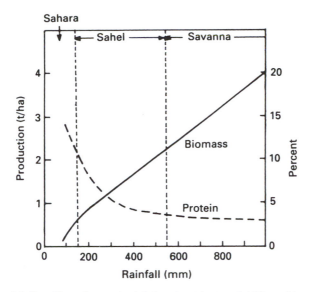

Figure 4.2 The effect of annual rainfall and nutrient availability on biomass production and its protein content in the West African Sahel. Biomass is measured in tonnes of dry matter per hectare above the ground, and protein as a percentage of the biomass at the end of September. After Breman and de Wit (1983).

The average annual rainfall in the western Sahel fell by 25–30 per cent between 1931 and 1960 and then again between 1965 and 1986. This decline corresponded with the replacement of perennial by annual species in some areas in the 1970s. For a time the change in dominant species could be understood as degradational, and was blamed by some on selective grazing by the cattle. As the perennials were overgrazed, the annuals had less competition and increased in numbers. Actually the same change took place in areas where grazing was controlled, so it was clear that rainfall decline was the more significant factor (de Wispelaere and Peyre de Fabregues 1986). The ecological zone dominated by annual grasses had, in effect, moved southwards at the expense of that previously dominated by perennials. The change made little difference to the stock carrying capacity because annuals provide good pasture, even when dead, in the judgement of local stockowners, whereas tall perennials become woody and unpalatable.

Seasonality

. The length of the growing period diminishes with intensifying aridity, and a dry season of nine months is common under unimodal rainfall regimes. During this period, biomass disappears as leaves, fruits and seeds fall, and leaves disintegrate or decompose. In the Gourma region of Mali, for example,

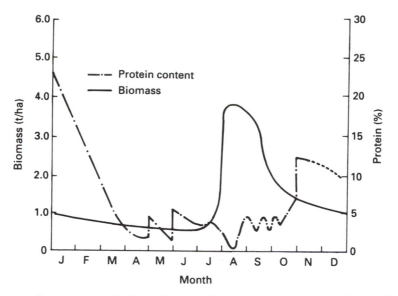

Figure 4.3 The seasonal availability of forage and its protein content, for a semi-nomadic herd in Mali in 1977. Measurements as in Figure 4.2. After Breman and de Wit (1983).

about 60 per cent of the biomass in October has been lost by the beginning of the next rains (de Leeuw *et al.* 1993). Such a seasonal pattern is shown in Fig. 4.3, which is based on the forage available to a herd of semi-nomads in Mali (Breman and de Wit 1983). The biomass fluctuates from a peak in the rainy season months of August and September to its lowest level at the end of the dry season in May and June. However, this pattern is reversed by the fluctuation in protein content, which peaks in November and is lowest in August. The step-like fluctuations in protein content (shown in the figure) are the result of periodic movements between pastures.

Trees are more complex, owing to their ability to tap underground moisture and to the phenological differences between species (Fig. 4.4). The first and most common type of tree in the Sahel is the deciduous species which produces its greatest foliage during the rainy season, and declines afterwards; a second type is the important West African tree, *Faidherbia albida*, which has an inverted leafing cycle, shedding all its foliage during the rainy season; and a third type retains some foliage throughout the year (Hiernaux *et al.* 1994). Thus *F. albida* has strategic importance for fodder in the hot, dry months before the rains when other browse and herbage are scarce. Under bimodal rainfall regimes, the relationships between foliage production and rainfall are still more complex.

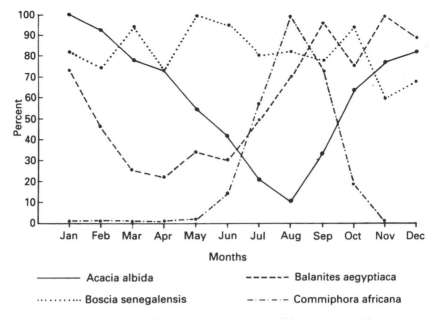

Figure 4.4 Leafing cycles of four Sahelian trees, showing leaf biomass as monthly percentages of the annual maximum. Constructed from data in Hiernaux *et al.* (1994).

Seasonality constrains pastoral specialists to move herds from place to place. For example the Zeiyadiya, who keep semi-nomadic herds of camels, cattle and small ruminants, may cover 700 km in a year between the desert, semi-desert and savannas of Darfur in the Sudan (Fig. 4.5; Ibrahim 1983).

Seasonality has implications not only for fodder supply, but for the human populations who depend on the animals. Milk provides from 40 to 70 per cent of the food supply of specialist pastoralists, and rather less (from 12 to 33 per cent) for those who combine some farming with livestock; what is not consumed is sold in order to purchase grain and other goods. Milk is most abundant during the rainy season, and becomes very scarce late in the dry season. Between February and May, which is the peak of the dry season, a cohort of Fulani men in Niger lost an average of 3.1 kg in weight, and the women lost 2.4 kg; children under five years also lost weight (Loutan and Lamotte 1984). Weight was regained in the following rainy season. In south Darfur (Sudan), pastoralists try to live on a pure milk diet in the wet season, not eating grain from six weeks to four months (Kerven 1987). Then, as grain becomes cheap after harvest, they exchange it for their increasingly scarce and valuable buttermilk.

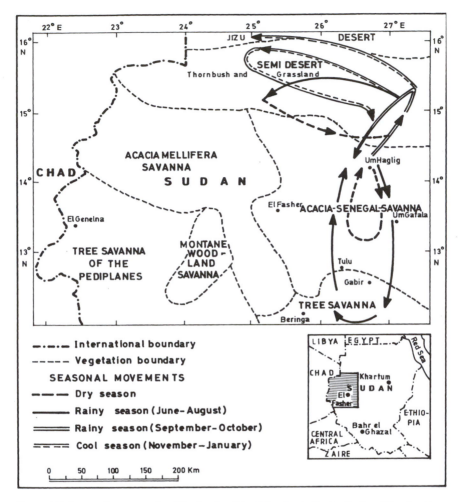

Figure 4.5 Seasonal movements of the herds of the Zeiyadiya in Darfur, Sudan. After Ibrahim (1983).

Variability

The variability of the rainfall has central significance for the new paradigm of range management in the drylands. As would be expected from the data shown in Figure 4.1, the production of herbage follows variations in annual rainfall, not only in space but also in time. But the variability of the rainfall is amplified in the production of herbage (Le Houérou 1985). Thus in the Gourma region of Mali, during the period 1984–90, the rainfall varied by a factor of less than two (between 100 and 200 mm), whereas the herbage yield varied by a factor of thirteen between the wettest and the driest years (Fig. 4.6). Another way of expressing rainfall variability is by the coefficient of variation (CV).[1] The CV for the rainfall in the same period was 37 per cent, whereas that for the mean maximum biomass was 86 per cent. The CV of annual rainfall increases with aridity, or as the annual rainfall diminishes. Thus further south in the Gourma region, the CV of the rainfall fell to 28 per cent, and that of the mean maximum biomass to 64 per cent. The level of risk facing the communities who manage dryland ecosystems is suggestively expressed in this measure.

Rainfall variability is at the root of uncertainty, or risk, in dryland ecosystems. A number of scenarios may be suggested (Fig. 4.7). In the first two of these, the rainfall (A) does not change through time, or changes little and regularly (B), so that there is zero or low variability in the amount of edible biomass for animals. Such a regime is *equilibrial* in nature, that is to say after each perturbation, it returns to the level it was at before. Such a situation does not exist in the African drylands, where seasonality is pronounced everywhere. More realistically we may postulate an equilibrial regime with high variability from season to season (C). Fluctuations in rainfall and biomass are much sharper, and in the dry season there is no growth of grass and herbs at all. Animal condition (D) reflects the pattern, but differs from it in two respects. First, it lags behind the seasonal fluctuation of biomass because time is taken to gain weight or to lose it. Second, the oscillations are less extreme because the livestock may be incapable of using all the edible biomass available in the wet season, yet can store nutrition in the dry so that their weight does not fall as much as might be expected from the condition of the pastures. If the supply of edible biomass falls far enough, the numbers of livestock fall, and there is an additional lag effect before reproduction can replace the missing animals. This scenario also shows the equilibrial pattern, in that each perturbation is followed by a return to previous conditions.

In the next scenario (E), we see a situation which more closely resembles the truth. Biomass, depending on the rainfall, fluctuates in a *disequilibrial* pattern: in other words the peaks and troughs are not equal or predictable. In some years, a peak may be followed by another peak, a trough by a second trough. Animal condition and numbers (F) fluctuate correspondingly, and danger occurs when two troughs (or two droughts) occur close together, as animals may survive in a condition of starvation across one season of shortage, but not across a period of a year or more. This pattern is disequilibrial because each perturbation is followed by a random outcome; but there is no trend, up or down, discernible in the pattern. In (G) a downward trend in the rainfall is added, shown smoothed in (H). Livestock production – average weight, or numbers – must decrease in the longer term in order to accommodate this trend. This scenario (G,H) suggests the experience of West Africa in recent decades, while (E,F) suggests that of eastern Africa.

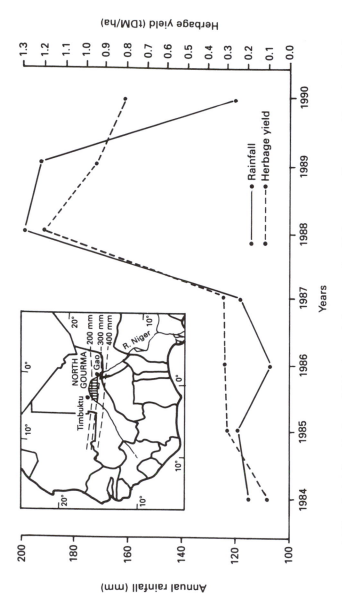

Figure 4.6 Inter-year variability of rainfall and herbage yield in the north Gourma region, Mali, 1984–90. Constructed from data in de Leeuw *et al.* (1993).

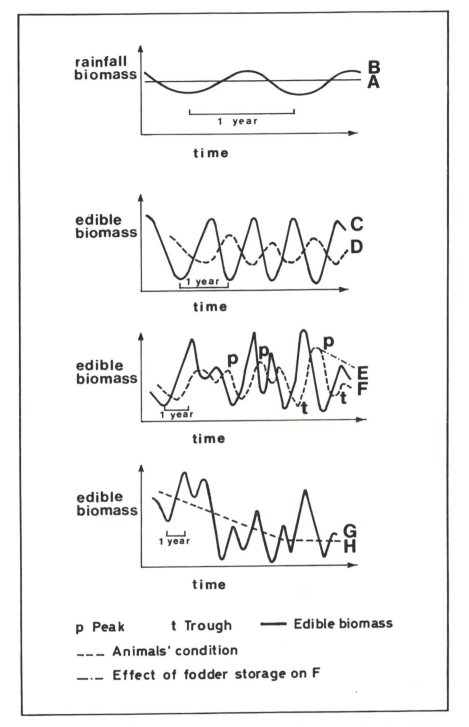

Figure 4.7 Scenarios of biomass production and animal condition under alternative rainfall regimes.

Cases

The Ngisonyoka Turkana (Ellis and Swift 1988; Ellis *et al.* 1993)

This sub-tribal group engages in the nomadic herding of cattle and small livestock in northern Kenya. In this variable and risky environment, the annual rainfall averages 180 mm, but has a CV of over 60 per cent; thus, in sixty-five years, there were nine in which the rainfall was 50 per cent or more below the mean, and twenty-three in which it was 25 per cent or more below. There are two short growing seasons, in April-June (60–90 days) and in October-December. The ecosystem is disequilibrial in nature, and is characterised by large variations in primary production from year to year, and volatile changes in livestock numbers. In Figure 4.8 two methods are used to describe this system between 1982 and 1987. One is the Normalised Difference Vegetation Index (NDVI), which is derived from earth satellite data. The other is a biomass model derived from precipitation. They are closely similar. The fluctuations are violent between years and can also be detected between seasons. In one period (1984–85) three seasonal droughts occurred in succession.

The Turkana suffered a long period of low rainfall in the 1920s and 1930s, which was followed by two decades of fluctuating rainfall. During the 1970s, rainfall was generally good, the numbers of livestock increased, and some families even became semi-sedentary. After 1980, rainfall became more erratic again, and in one drought there was a mortality rate of 50 per cent among the livestock in the region. It is clear from Figure 4.8 that the livestock owners could not be expected to fit the numbers of their animals to the biomass available (or its 'ecological carrying capacity') from one growing season to another. Neither could a minimal sustainable stocking rate be estimated, still less implemented by the Ngisonyoka. Instead, livestock numbers tend to rise during good years and crash when a prolonged shortage of biomass occurs. Taking maximum advantage of available fodder and bearing the losses when it fails is called 'opportunistic stocking' (Walker *et al.* 1981; Sandford 1983). Such a system is said to be 'event-driven' rather than 'density driven'; i.e., the controlling factor of the livestock population is fluctuating fodder supply. There is insufficient time between droughts for animal numbers to recover to a density that threatens the degradation of the range. Therefore 'overgrazing' has little meaning as an operational concept in this context.

Persistence in such a disequilibrial environment is difficult, and the Ngisonyoka make use of resources outside the region, both in good times and in

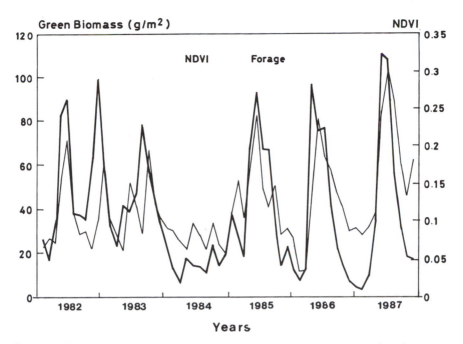

Figure 4.8 Fluctuations in biomass in Turkana, Kenya, 1982–87. After Ellis *et al.* (1993).

bad. In the past, when local pastures failed, the herds were taken to places not normally visited, invading the ranges of other pastoral groups in Uganda or the
Sudan, either by permission or by force of arms. In good years, they raided neighbours' herds in order to increase the size of their own. Trading, perhaps, offers an
alternative. Limiting the access of nomadic peoples to such external resources, by
restricting their movements, or transforming their grazing management, without
compensating strategies to cope with extreme events, threatens their very survival.
Is such a characterisation applicable to all pastoral systems?

The Borana (Coppock 1993)

On the Borana Plateau of southern Ethiopia, semi-nomadic Borana
pastoralists live in encampments and move their animals about during the year.
The plateau varies in altitude and rainfall, which ranges from 400–800 mm and
is distributed in a bimodal regime. This more favourable environment supports
perennial grasses with scattered trees. It experiences severe drought, on average,
only once in twenty years.

Assessments of the range have concluded that there is evidence of soil erosion
and of woodland encroachment on grassland communities, both of them related

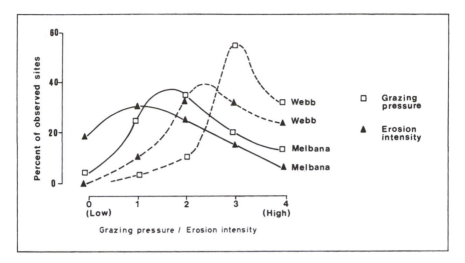

Figure 4.9 Grazing pressure and intensity of erosion in southern Ethiopia. The first location (Webb) has a high frequency of intensively grazed sites and also has a high frequency of intensively eroded sites; the second location (Melbana) has a low frequency of intensively grazed sites, and also has a low frequency of intensively eroded sites. After Coppock (1993).

to periods of intensive grazing pressure (Fig. 4.9). Erosion is linked to the removal of the grass vegetation. Woody encroachment is supposed to occur when the risk of fire is reduced by the removal of grass (and, recently, by the government's banning of bush fires), or when grazing alters the competitive advantage of grasses over woody plants.

In 1984, a severe drought reduced the cattle population by 49 per cent (30 per cent through mortality and 19 per cent through sale). However, it only took five years or so for the herds to be reconstituted. Given an interval between droughts of twenty years, there is plenty of time for the herds, after recovering, to resume an upward course in numbers, until grazing causes degradation of the range.

The Borana move their camps every five to eight years, commonly to go in search of better grazing. However, they are having increasing difficulty in locating new grazing as the numbers of people and cattle in the area increase. Their mobility is thus becoming restricted. They are becoming more sedentary as roads, markets and permanent water attract settlement. An increasing number of people in relation to livestock reduces the amount of milk available in the diet, and increases the need for grain, which is obtained through taking up farming, or through selling animal products in the markets.

There are other differences from the Turkana system besides the much higher annual rainfall. The soils of the elevated Borana plateau are fine and more prone to erosion than the sandy plains of Turkana. The perennial grasses do not die off during drought to the extent of the annuals of Turkana, thus dampening the fluctuations in fodder supply. The changes that have been observed are interpreted as 'density-dependent', not (except occasionally) as 'event-driven'.

This understanding of the system is, thus, equilibrial. Rangeland abandoned because of woody encroachment would gradually return to grassland as pressure on the grasses was moderated and fires became more numerous. Eventually its grazing value would recover and it would be used again. It is the disturbance of this equilibrium, through increasing numbers of stock (driven by a growing population), and through reduced mobility (the restriction of growing herds to smaller areas) that sets up a linear process of degradation.

The Borana case shows that not all pastoral systems display disequilibrial characteristics. It may be necessary to recognise a difference between wetter and drier pastoral systems; Coppock (1993) suggests that 400 mm of annual rainfall locates this difference in eastern African bimodal regimes. On the other hand, in a unimodal regime, the dry season is usually longer and more intense. What matters is the variability of the rainfall: where a high CV is found (more than 30 per cent), which usually means the drier areas, disequilibrial systems are found. A disequilibrial system is event-driven, or drought-driven, and the impact of grazing and of the livestock population on the environment cannot be discerned. In an equilibrial system these impacts can be discerned and the system moves along a trajectory which is driven by the density of the livestock population. Can these principles be extended from the ecology of the rangelands to the social and economic systems that depend on them?

The Tuareg (Lovejoy and Baier 1976; Baier 1980; Bonte 1986)

Deeply rooted in historical trading relations between the desert and the densely populated Sudan zone, the Tuareg economy was based on camel-raising, trans-Saharan trade, the exploitation of Saharan salt, livestock, raiding, and importing grain from the Sahel, which was indispensable for Tuareg well-being. Client farming communities in the south provided grain, and bases for trading and for grazing or fattening the camels. A system of social castes discriminated sharply between pure-bred Tuareg nobles and slaves or serfs of mixed blood, who were needed to provide labour for tending livestock and also for producing grain in the southern farming settlements, which were an essential part of the mobile system. The Tuareg of Aïr, for example, bred camels and small ruminants in their homeland, whence they departed on seasonal caravans to Bilma oasis (for salt), Katsina and Kano (for markets), Damergu (for grain) and Tripoli

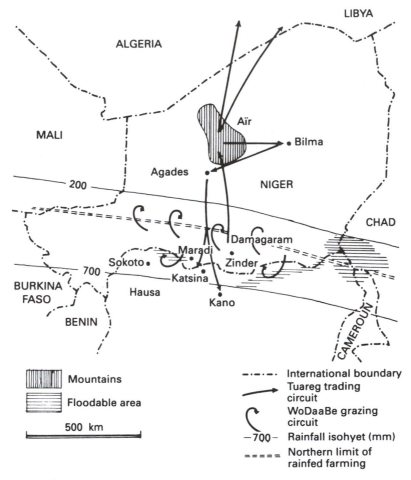

Figure 4.10 Circuits of the Aïr Tuareg and WoDaaBe of central Niger.

or Tunis (for the trans-Saharan trade), protecting their profits and trade goods in their mountain retreat (Fig. 4.10).

The abolition of slavery by the colonial governments forced a gradual substitution of market relations for those based on slavery and clientship. Some of these communities still remember their Tuareg descent, though they have since become absorbed into the settled cultures of the Sahel.

The system was adapted to the exigencies of drought:

> When drought occurred, the desert economy contracted, with nomadic Tuareg and farmers alike leaving for the extreme southern end of the trading network . . . Just as the Tuareg social structure telescoped during hard times, it expanded

again when the weather improved or political conditions returned to normal . . .
Nobles collected their personal followers and headed north . . . This spatial
mobility was the basis of the social system, which adapted to the cyclical nature
of the desert-edge climate. (Lovejoy and Baier 1976: 164–65)

However, the price of persistence in such an environment was a periodic
sloughing-off of low caste dependants, who were already marginalised by being
largely excluded from animal ownership. They remained in the south. The process
was painful.

> Droughts can be seen as a means of resolving periodic crises of pastoral over-
> production. They enforce a drastic reduction of production capacities and of the
> productivity of pastoral labour. Droughts also require the deployment of all the
> community internal and external relationships in order to reconstitute the herds
> and decimated social groups. They therefore constitute a 'cyclical' dimension to
> the functioning of these pastoral systems of production. Historically they have
> provoked restructuring, mass movement of human groups, and the establishment
> of new local hegemonies. (Bonte 1986:166–7)

The impact of the Sahel Drought of 1968–74 on a system that had already been
affected by the loss of autonomy, taxation, the ending of slave labour, the decline
of Saharan trade, market expansion and population growth, was disastrous for
many groups, who failed to recover, because their historical mode of adaptive
recovery had collapsed. The modern state is, indeed, antipathetic to the maintenance of unstable, disequilibrial systems.

The WoDaaBe (White 1987, 1990)

WoDaaBe nomads (a Fulani group) keep cattle and small stock in the
Sahel of Niger where average annual rainfall is 200–300 mm and its variability is
high (Fig. 4.10). The annual grasses of the range grow during a single short season
from June or July to October of each year. The grazing and watering of the livestock depend on movements made in response to the availability of pasture and
access to wells. However, these movements are not unconstrained. To the south
of them, sedentary farmers have occupied increasing amounts of woodland, converting it to extensively cultivated fields of groundnut, millet and cowpea, under
the influence of the growth in population and in markets. This pressure has driven
the WoDaaBe northwards into territory which they share with the nomadic
Tuareg, who occupied the area before they came. In doing so, the WoDaaBe were
themselves deprived of the possibility of taking up farming as an alternative economic strategy to livestock.

When the Sahel Drought of 1968–74 struck the WoDaaBe, they were unable
to use the strategies which had previously stood them in good stead when fodder

became scarce. The large scale movement of herds to the south was prevented, and so was diversification into farming. Neither could they protect their herds against starvation, nor were they able to subsist by crop production until they were able to reconstitute them. Unlike the Tuareg, the WoDaaBe have an egalitarian social structure, which values the sharing of animal wealth through institutionalised loans. So poverty was not concentrated in an underclass who could be 'sloughed off' but rather had the effect of reducing *all* households below the level of economic viability. Thus like the Tuareg, these WoDaaBe suffered a critical change in their adaptive capability which can be put down to the new constraints affecting their access to resources.[2]

Others were more fortunate, finding grazing opportunities in interstices among farmlands further south. Around Gouré, in eastern Niger, the WoDaaBe learnt that grazing was available in Nigeria, where farmers' encroachments on scheduled grazing areas had been forbidden. In 1984, faced with the elimination of their home rangelands around Gouré, they entered Nigeria, where they had never been before (Mortimore 1989a). This was not regular transhumance, therefore, but a dislocation of people who took an emergency step to cope with the impending loss of their entire livestock capital. Neither was it a refugee movement. It was a concerted movement intended to be temporary, to cope with a crisis of climatic origin. They relied on rights of access to the scheduled grazing areas, open to them on grounds of ethnic affinity with the resident Ful'be pastoralists. As they moved southwards, the grassland was eaten up as the tide overflows the seashore. But the resident Ful'be accepted the accelerated destruction of their own grazing resources with resignation. It meant that they, too, would have to move their animals south, their normal schedules disrupted.

Unstable, resilient systems

The arid zone provides an environment of uncertainty in which rainfall variability drives the ecosystems and determines some of the major constraints under which human communities have to live. The mobile systems of livestock production seem to provide the most efficient way of exploiting such environments. However, not all livestock production systems appear to be fundamentally disequilibrial (Behnke *et al.* 1993), as the cases reviewed above suggest.

A way of incorporating uncertainty-as-norm, as opposed to uncertainty-as-aberration, into an understanding of the drylands is suggested in the concept of the unstable, resilient ecosystem in which the relationships between faunal and floral species persist while their populations fluctuate, as proposed by Holling (1973: 17).

> Resilience determines the persistence of relationships within a system and is a
> measure of the ability of these systems to absorb changes . . . Stability, on the
> other hand, is the ability of a system to return to an equilibrium state after a tem-
> porary disturbance . . . [In] areas subjected to extreme climatic conditions the
> populations fluctuate widely but have a high capability of absorbing periodic
> extremes of fluctuation. They are, therefore, unstable using the restricted
> definition above, but highly resilient.

A more precise definition of resilience offered later by Holling and his colleagues is that 'resilience is the ability to adapt to change by exploiting instabil-
ities, rather than the ability to absorb disturbance by returning to a steady state
after being disturbed' (Walker *et al.* 1981). These authors' conclusion is that the
resilience of ecosystems decreases as their stability increases. The relevance of these
ecological concepts to the drylands and their management is clear from the cases
reviewed in this chapter.

Such a view has major implications for the idea of 'carrying capacity':

> The unpredictable nature of the environment is the central factor affecting not
> only attempts to measure productivity and population density in semi-arid
> rangelands, but also the applicability of the concept of carrying capacity that is
> used to link the two. Irregular rain falling at unpredictable places and times
> results in unpredictable primary production. Measures of grassland productivity
> may be accurate but are only valid for a particular place and time and do not
> support extrapolation to a wider area or longer term. (Holmewood and Rogers
> 1987)

The impossibility of using carrying capacity as a principle of management
under conditions of high rainfall variability, and the practice of moving animals
frequently around open access rangelands in order to accommodate spatial variability in fodder supply, show the rationality of 'opportunistic stocking' strategies pursued by African pastoralists (Sandford 1983). 'Breed, feed, and milk,
for tomorrow they die' may look like the antithesis of sustainable livestock
management – but it may approach the harsh reality for pastoralists in the arid
zone.

The cases reviewed above suggest that the concept of unstable but resilient
ecosystems, which are always under some form of human management, may have
social and economic analogues. Some parallels may be discerned between the
natural instability of arid zone ecosystems and the cultural adaptations that have
been evolved to contain it. It is reasonable to suppose that rainfall variability,
albeit less extreme in statistical terms, also poses critical challenges for farming
communities in the semi-arid zone. To these I now turn.

1 The coefficient of variation is defined as the standard deviation of the rainfall during a given period of years divided by the average rainfall and multiplied by 100.

2 The experiences of the Aïr Tuareg, and of the WoDaaBe of central Niger, are not necessarily typical of all Tuareg and Fulani people. In northeast Senegal, for example, Sutter (1987) found that resilience to drought was socially differentiated amongst the Fulani.

5 Risk for the farmer

Farming, like pastoralism, has suffered from negative stereotypes whose roots lie in colonial incomprehension of the ecological and economic constraints under which it must operate. Aubréville's caricature of agricultural land use in the savannas of West Africa (chapter 2) contains two of the main elements of the stereotype: first, shifting cultivation, with its partner in crime, bush-burning; and second overcultivation, exposing the soil to erosion by wind and water, thus depleting its nutrients. A third element was the practice of interplanting in crop mixtures, long thought to be inefficient in terms of labour use, technology and yields.

In this chapter the nature of risk in dryland farming is explored, in order to answer the question: can the concept of instability, or disequilibrium, be usefully applied to understanding semi-arid farming systems?

Rainfall variability

Rainfall variability – within seasons between seasons and over several years – plays as important a part in defining risk for the farmer as it does in managing the rangelands. The coefficient of variability of the rainfall tends to decrease as the average amount received each year increases. The regimes under which farmers operate are therefore subject to less extreme variability than those of the arid rangelands. However, it does not follow from this that the risk to their livelihoods is diminished, more especially as dryland farmers are not able to choose less risky environments in which to work.

Variability in the longer term

The best example of the implications of rainfall change for farming is provided by the millet-growing systems of the western Sahel. The northern limit of millet cultivation may be defined theoretically in terms of two criteria: its total

Plate 5 Genetic anarchy or purposive adaptation? Sorghum (above) and pearl millet (below) from villages in north-east Nigeria.

moisture requirement and the length of the growing period. According to Kowal and Kassam (1978: 109–10), the first criterion is met where the average annual rainfall reaches or exceeds 348 mm. But everywhere north of the 588 mm annual isohyet there is a risk of crop failure, through insufficient rainfall, more than once in ten years. With regard to the growing period, short-season cultivars (early millet and cowpea) require at least fifty-five days of rainfall. This requirement was met (on the basis of the long-term average rainfall until the 1960s) at Lat. 14° 40′N (Kowal and Adeoye 1973), accepting a risk of failure once in ten years. However, these theoretical limits assume a satisfactory distribution of rainfall during the season (an absence of drought) and sandy soils to which millet is adapted; they do not take account of the cropping system as a whole.

The implication of the theoretical limits is that the downward trend of the Sahelian rainfall from the 1950s to the 1980s (see Fig. 2.6) made crop production steadily more risky, as the average annual isohyets (and with them, the length of growing period isolines, Fig. 2.2) migrated slowly southwards. Successive thirty-year means trended downwards (Fig. 5.1). At Kano (Nigeria), the mean annual rainfall declined from 853 mm in 1931–60, to 714 mm in 1961–90, a fall of 16 per cent. The average annual rainfall for ten-year periods (a more sensitive indicator) declined from 910 mm in 1951–60 (a wet decade) to 632 mm in 1981–90, a fall of 30 per cent. The change in average rainfall reflected changes in the frequencies of high and low rainfall. Given the nature of the soils and the requirements of the cropping system in Kano, rainfall of less than 650 mm is critical, even if well distributed. In 1931–60, there were only three such years, but in 1961–90, there were ten, including two successive years in 1972–73 (the Sahelian Drought), and four successive years in 1981–84. After 1987, however, a recovery in the rainfall at Kano provides a reminder than even a thirty-year trend can be reversed.

In eastern Africa, annual rainfall displays no long-term negative trend (Fig. 2.6; Hulme 1994a). At a semi-arid station in Kenya (Machakos), when annual is broken down into seasonal rainfall, a century-long record (1894–1994) shows cycles instead, though the short period of records does not establish their permanence (Mutiso et al. 1991). There are two rainy seasons here, called the long rains (March–May) and the short rains (October-December), though the two are of almost the same length and produce similar amounts of rainfall. The long rains had a cycle of 9–11 years, and the short rains one of 16–22 years.

If we examine such cycles in detail (Fig. 5.2), using the records of six stations for the period 1959–88, it is clear that troughs occurred in the long rains cycle in the droughts of the early 1970s and early 1980s. The short rains also declined to a trough in 1970–74, intensifying the drought that occurred all over northern dryland Africa in those years, when there were frequent crop failures, but rose to a peak in 1984, modifying the impact of the drought in the long rains cycle (Downing *et al.* 1989). The downswing of a cycle has the same practical implications as a long-term trend in the short term. It is worth emphasising that the peaks and troughs of these measured cycles – even when inter-year fluctuations are smoothed with five-year running means – vary by as much as 100 per cent.

In southeast Africa the pattern was strongly cyclical, compared with the other two regions and, although there was a trend downwards, it was more muted than in the Sahel. In south-western Africa, some evidence for a cyclical pattern may be discerned (see Fig. 2.6).

Such trends or cycles define the technological challenge which agriculture must meet in the medium or longer term, if communities are to continue to support themselves from the land. In the Sahel, such oscillations are short wavelength reflections of the much longer wavelength movements on the southern margins of the Sahara which have been going on since the ending of the Ice Age in the northern hemisphere, and to which human responses have been necessary since prehistory (McIntosh 1992). Other drylands are analogous. The occurrence of droughts in Botswana, southern Zimbabwe, eastern Kenya and southern Ethiopia for example, is also related to longer term expansion and contraction of arid zones in the Kalahari and the Horn of Africa.

Variability between years

Of greater immediate relevance to farmers, however, is variability between successive seasons or years. In 1973, at the climax of the Sahel Drought, the minimum period of fifty-five days for millet cultivation was met at Lat. 12° 40′N in Nigeria (Kowal and Adeoye 1973). Thus, in that year, the northern boundary of arable farming with reasonable expectation of success moved southwards by a distance of over 300 km or two and half degrees of latitude (Mortimore 1989a: 43–45). In 1983 and 1984, during the next major drought cycle in the Sahel, the rainfall plunged even lower at Kano (at Lat. 12° N), which received 43 and 45 per cent less than the 1931–60 mean (Fig. 5.1). Yet notwithstanding the overall decline of Sahelian rainfall, farming takes place today further north than Kowal and Kassam's theoretical limit based on better rainfall before the 1970s. This gives some indication of the risk that some dryland farmers have to take.

Incursions and regressions, or spatial oscillations, of rainfall isohyets or LGP isolines, are most obviously evident in the Sahel, where the scale of the fluctuations from north to south and back again is large. But for practical purposes, quite small deficiencies in the rainfall may damage crops and such may occur far outside the drylands, even on the borders of the forest (Oguntoyinbo and Richards 1977).

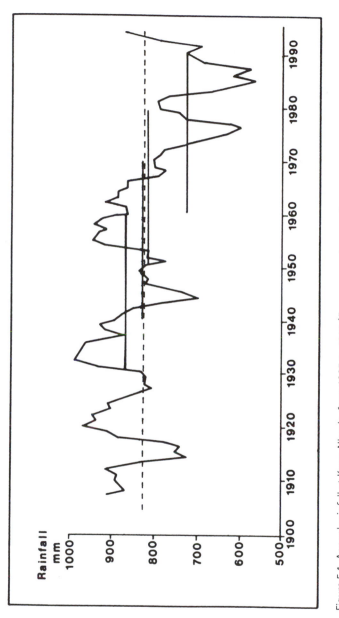

Figure 5.1 Annual rainfall at Kano, Nigeria, from 1905 to 1992 (five-year running mean).
The means are shown for 1905–92 (811 mm), 1931–60 (853 mm), 1941–70 (826 mm), 1951–80 (807 mm) and 1961–90 (714 mm).

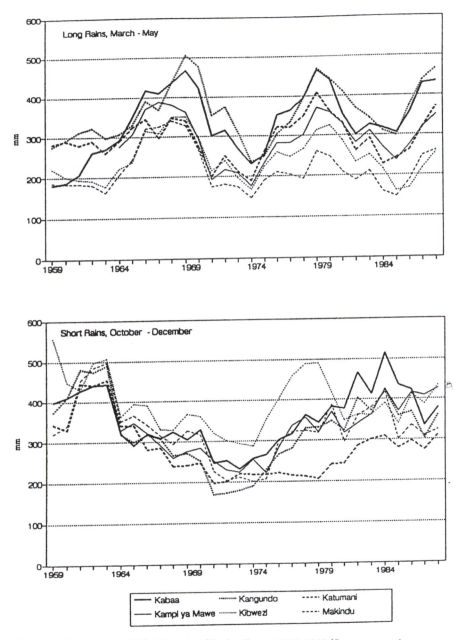

Figure 5.2 Seasonal rainfall in Machakos District, Kenya, 1957–1990 (five-year running means). After Mutiso *et al.* (1991).

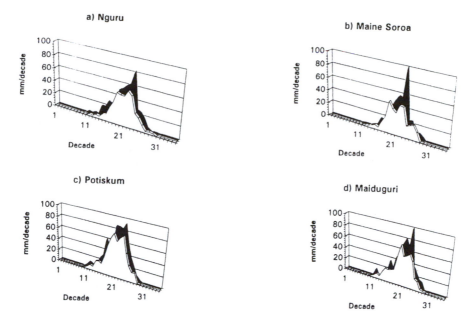

Figure 5.3 Seasonal rainfall in ten-day periods compared for 1961–70 (shown black) and 1981–90 (shown white), at four stations in Niger and Nigeria. After Hess *et al.* (1994).

Variability within seasons

Even when the total rainfall received during the growing season conforms to expectations, its distribution between months is variable and unpredictable. In West Africa, the monthly distribution of rainfall, in terms of probability, normally peaks in August. Such a peak conforms well with the growing cycle of millet. In 1984, the failure of this peak to materialise in a year of below average rainfall made an agricultural crisis. Fig. 5.3 shows how the seasonal distribution of rainfall in the north of Nigeria and south-east Niger changed between the decades of the 1960s and 1980s. Such a change, if it proved to be permanent, would have agronomic implications as important as a reduction in the annual total (Hess *et al.* 1994; Mortimore 1989a: 142–43; Sivakumar *et al.* 1993; Stern *et al.* 1981).

However, as Fig. 5.4 shows, successive years' rainfall *normally* have different configurations, to which the growing cycles of crops have to be fitted. A field cropping system is more specialised than a natural ecosystem and therefore more vulnerable to such variability. Once germinated, long intervals without rain, especially during or before flowering, may result in failure to produce any grain. Unable to predict a departure from the expected pattern, and having very few technical options with which to deal with it, they have little room for manoeu-

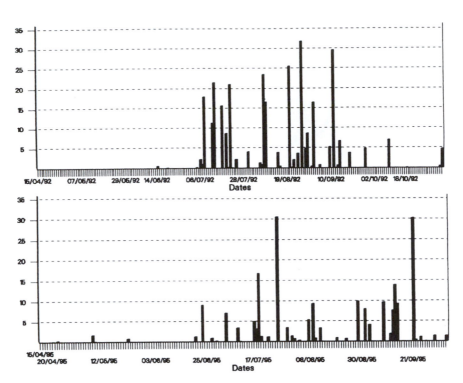

Figure 5.4 Inter-year variability in the seasonal distribution of rainfall in a Sahelian village (Futchimiram, Nigeria): daily rainfall events in 1992 (total rainfall, 310.8 mm) and in 1995 (total rainfall, 209.3 mm).

vre. This is a compelling reason for aiming at varietal and technological diversity in farming – the more proven options are available the better.

Wetlands in drylands

Rainfall variability feeds through into changes in the levels of local water-tables, in the seasonal flow of rivers and streams and in the flooding regimes of lakes and flood-plains. The natural storage of water beneath the surface dampens the oscillations between seasons and years: groundwater may be several decades old. The development of seasonally waterlogged valley bottoms and enclosed basins in the drylands took place during a long history of geophysical uplift, weathering and rainfall oscillation. They are known by such terms as *fadama* and *kwari* (in Nigeria), *dambo* (Zambia and Zimbabwe), *pan* (Botswana) and *bas-fond* (Francophone West Africa) (Turner 1986). Subsurface water and low-lying wetland have strategic significance for resource development in drylands (Adams 1992; Kolawole *et al.* 1994; Scoones 1991; Turner 1984, 1989).

Shallow sub-surface water and perennial streams have long been used for irrigated farming with hand-lifting technologies, both in West and East Africa (Adams 1993; Adams and Carter 1987; Kimmage and Adams 1990). Surface floods are used for cultivating many varieties of rice during the wet season. Flood-recession farming (using residual soil moisture) allows farming to be prolonged into the dry season, for example sorghum production on the black soils around Lake Chad and on the floor of the lake itself (Kolawole 1988). Less than a fifth of dryland populations have access to such farming resources, but wetland has a value disproportionate to its extent. In many areas its domestic value is amplified by the possibilities it offers for dry season or perennial crops (such as vegetables, sugar cane, fruit trees), rice and other products. Surface water also offers possibilities for fishing – also often aimed at the market – especially where seasonal fluctuations in water level can be exploited in trapping fish. Low-lying areas, because of their shallow water-tables, support grass and herb communities which provide grazing for livestock during dry seasons, and such resources play a pivotal role in transhumance for specialist livestock breeders (Fricke 1979).

They also provide dam sites for large-scale irrigation schemes, which have always been perceived by governments as playing a central role in the economic development of drylands, from the early colonial projects of Gezira (Sudan), Office du Niger (Mali) and the Senegal River, to latter-day schemes such as the South Chad, Bakolori and Kano River projects in northern Nigeria. Such schemes, however, are themselves at risk from variable water supply: South Chad, for example, ran into difficulties as soon as it had begun operations (Kolawole 1987).

The multiple uses of wetlands create competition between contending land uses and, in some circumstances, violent conflict between communities or individuals. There is evidence that increasing demand for wetland resources, driven by population growth, markets, or the risk of dryland farming under diminishing rainfall (Boulier and Jouve 1988), is sharpened when governments inject capital into wetland development, usually subordinating customary users' interests to what are perceived to be national priorities. They may also introduce policies discriminating in favour of irrigation farming, in pursuit of national food sufficiency targets. Inequities, expressed in the enrichment of individuals through the market for wetland products, are still less tolerable where advantage has been gained from resources under common access, at the expense of the community. Clashes develop between graziers and farmers, between upstream and downstream users, and between advantaged and disadvantaged farmers, over access to land, water or price subsidies. Such conflicts appear to be increasing in highly contested wetlands such as those of northern Nigeria (Adams 1988; Jega 1987; Kimmage and Adams 1992; Kimmage and Falola 1991; Olofin 1982).

Pests

As if rainfall variability were not enough, farmers have to contend with explosive outbreaks of insect or animal pests, or disease vectors, whose population dynamics are highly unstable. In the Manga Grasslands, on the borders of Niger and Nigeria (where the annual rainfall varied between 260 and 430 mm in 1992–95), an outbreak of a nocturnal seed-eating rodent, *Jaculus jaculus,* took place in the drought of 1983–84. It had never been seen before in some of the villages in which it appeared, not in hundreds but in tens of thousands, stealing newly planted seed for the all-important millet crop. The farmers replanted, pursuing the rats to their underground stores to try to recover the scarce seed, in a time-consuming battle of wits. Locally, this pest can destroy up to 75 per cent of grain plantings. The southward displacement of the rodents may have been explained by a shortage of natural grass seed in drier areas further north, where they were known before. However, the dramatic explosion in the population conforms with the theory of unstable ecosystems introduced in the last chapter. Subsequently the rodents stayed, permanent members of the pest community, but not in such dangerous numbers. Again this conforms with theoretical expectation (Holling 1973, Walker *et al.* 1981).

In another year, the risk may come from insect pests. The most important locusts are migrants (especially the desert locust, *Schistocerca gregaria*), whose swarming behaviour is the result of complex interactions between the amount and timing of rainfall in the desert breeding areas, wind force and direction, and conditions in the grasslands and croplands where they do the most damage (Fig. 5.5). From the farmers' perspective, the locusts arrive unannounced from outside the area and take their toll, quite beyond effective local control. International monitoring and control of the desert locust has deteriorated in many parts of northern Africa owing to the chaotic or impoverished condition of government administrations and poor international coordination. Nevertheless, an average of US $23 a year is spent on control measures (SAS 1996). Locust swarms can destroy up to 100 per cent of green crops locally, as well as fodder grasses.

Grasshoppers (the most important among many species being *Oedaleus senegalensis*) differ from migratory locusts in that they normally complete the stages of their life-cycle in the same locality. A scarcity of rainfall early in the season reduces the amount of natural grass available and concentrates their attention on the growing crops, which under careful weeding are hardier than young grass. The greatest risk of crop damage, therefore, comes early in the growing

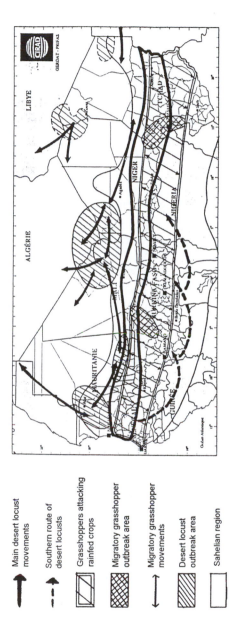

Figure 5.5 The Sahel, caught between the desert locust, *Schistocerca gregaria*, and the grasshopper, in August, 1996. After SAS (1996).

season, when the grain crops are shooting and tender. A second period of risk occurs during grain formation, when millet seed, for example, is soft and easily damaged. Whether grasshopper populations explode at these times, or at less risky times, or not at all, depends on the rainfall (heavy rain kills them), on how many eggs were deposited during the previous cycle, on predator populations (including birds such as the cattle egret) and other factors.

Grasshoppers can destroy 50 per cent or more of a millet crop. Sorghum is less vulnerable, as it ripens when the grasshopper population has begun to decrease after the rains. Technically, 'integrated pest control' can be achieved through understanding the life-cycle of the grasshopper locally, using simple and cheap methods to kill young hoppers before they can fly or lay eggs. But such measures, though less costly than chemical control, are labour-intensive, and must be organised in such a way as to prevent re-infestation from adjacent farms. Many farmers resign themselves to heavy losses. As grasshoppers infest the relatively densely populated farming zone, they cause large aggregate losses, which, though difficult to quantify, significantly exceeded those caused by locusts during the decade 1986–95 (SAS 1996).

Cowpeas may suffer damage of up to 100 per cent from other insect pests, whose dynamics are equally unpredictable for the farmer. Sharp differences in the incidence of such pests (primarily *Maruca* beetles in the Sahel) occur from year to year. Cowpeas can be grown in extremely dry conditions, where insect pressure is low: in 1995, for example, crops were produced to the north of Lat. 15° N, in Niger, with less than 200 mm of rainfall. However, the risk of drought increases as that of insect damage diminishes. Cowpea cultivation in the Sahel is thus something of a gamble and, like many forms of gambling, is extremely popular. Notwithstanding the risk involved, it is a critical component of grain–legume mixtures and potentially marketable (Mortimore *et al.* 1997).

Bird pests also fluctuate in their populations from year to year, as they too depend on variable components of the ecosystem (in particular, the supply of grass seed). Like grasshoppers, the bird hazard is intensified by an unpredictable conjunction of a scarcity of natural food with an explosion of population, leading to pressure on the grain crops during seed formation. The greatest bird pest in the Sahel is *Quelea quelea*, a small bird which breeds, migrates and roosts in enormous swarms which have been estimated to contain up to a million individuals. Localised damage to crops can be very high, 50 per cent or more. Attempts to control the Quelea bird have even resorted to dynamiting whole trees used as nesting or roosting sites.

Bulrush millet is most at risk, for its upright head provides an ideal perch for hungry birds; sorghum is somewhat better protected by its open head form, especially when inverted in a 'gooseneck', and some varieties protect their seeds by coverings or bristles. Maize, being protected by its sheath, is more or less immune to bird damage and this advantage has been a major factor promoting its popularity in eastern and southern Africa, where it has replaced millets or sorghums on a majority of family farms. The labour required for effective bird-scaring in the season of grain formation is always beyond the resources of farming households; and children of school age are needed on the farm for this task. In Yobe State of Nigeria, in 1995, an elaborate apparatus of ropes, rattles and flags could be seen suspended from trees over many farms as the precious harvest approached.

Diseases affect crops unpredictably. Those affecting indigenous grains or legumes may well be kept under control by the genetic diversity of local varieties, and their impact is absorbed by the farmer as beyond his control. But introduced market crops (for example, Allen cotton) may be much more vulnerable to disease and require chemical control at considerable cost. Insufficient technical or economic information has been collected about many diseases affecting dryland crops, especially those grown mainly for subsistence.

Managing variability: the Manga and Hausa of Dagaceri (Mohammed 1996; Mortimore 1989a)

In the remainder of this chapter, a case study is used to illustrate some of the strategies with which a dryland farming community may manage the risks of variability in rainfall and ecology. These strategies are to do with *diversity*, the classic hedge against risk of all kinds. Diversity is shown in the cropping system, in the inventory of technologies and in decision making during the agricultural year.

The village of Dagaceri is in northern Jigawa State, Nigeria. It lies on the hummocky surface of a former desert dunefield, now stable under higher rainfall, with secondary woodland, grassland and cultivation. Similar villages, ranging in size from less than 100 to more than 1,000 inhabitants, occur at intervals of five or ten kilometres across the plains. With the exception of the prominent baobab, full-grown trees are few in the heavily cut woodland or farmland alike; but the site of the village, atop its dune, is first recognisable from its wooded appearance, protected trees mingling with the perennially green shade tree, the neem. In this village live about 750 Manga and Hausa inhabitants living in 125 households.

The farming system is based on millet, sorghum and cowpea grown in mixtures, on fields which are cultivated permanently, or for several years between fallows. Farmers keep livestock, mainly small ruminants, though cattle are kept by the sedentary Ful'be nearby. The annual rainfall varied between 325 and 400 mm in the four years, 1992–95. It falls between June or July and September, or later in some years. The soils are deep, sandy and low in fertility. Left to them-

Table 5.1 *The number of cultivars in use in the farming system of Dagaceri.*

Crop	Number of varieties	Short season	Long season	Local	Introduced
Cereal grains					
Pearl (bulrush) millet	7	6	1	5	2
Sorghum	18	8	10	8	10
Benniseed (sesame)	2	1	1	2	0
Legumes					
Cowpea	6	3	3	3	3
Groundnut	2	1	1	1	1
Minor crops					
Bambara groundnut	4	3	1	4	0
Melon	2	0	2	2	0
Okro	2	2	0	2	0
Sorrel	2	0	0	2	0

Source: Mohammed 1996.

selves, they support a thorny savanna woodland. Animal manure is used to improve soil fertility whenever possible.

Diversity in the cropping system

The cropping system combines bulrush millets, which escape drought by maturing quickly, with a range of sorghums, more resistant to drought and grasshoppers, slower to reach maturity, but able to make better use of residual soil moisture after the rains have ceased. This combination aims to make the best use of whatever mix of rainfall and hazards the elements bring. It might be expected that a farming system in a high-risk Sahelian environment would have a restricted choice of cultivars. But the crop inventory of Dagaceri is remarkable for its size and diversity (Table 5.1).

The preeminence of pearl (bulrush) millet is the first pillar of the cropping system. There are seven locally identified cultivars in use; five of them, making up the majority of plantings, mature early, in ninety days, but one recent introduction matures more quickly. The ability to yield well under conditions of drought has attracted farmers in the area to new varieties, which diffused through local markets and had no contact with the formal extension system. Millet is the preferred food and its success mainly determines a family's food security in the succeeding year.

The sorghums number eighteen types, ranging from long-season varieties planted at the beginning of the rains to very fast-maturing varieties which can be planted late, take advantage of localised or residual soil moisture and produce a head of grain after the rains cease, even if not fully grown. Of these, ten varieties have been introduced to the village in recent memory, which is an indication of the dynamism in the system. Their ability to mature as fast as the millet, in years of early terminating rains, has attracted interest in such varieties, some of whose derivation is believed to have been in southern Niger. At least two, however, are known to have been promoted by extension in either Niger (nearby) or Nigeria.[1]

The second pillar of the cropping system is the mixing of nitrogen-fixing legumes with grains in alternate stands or rows. Both the cowpea and the groundnut are grown for the market. Long-season cowpeas yielded pride of place to short-season varieties, as the length of the growing period became less reliable after the 1960s. The fast-maturing variety called *dan arba 'in* arrived in the village from Niger and Chad in 1974, and achieved instant popularity in the wake of the preceding two years' catastrophic crop failures.[2] However, it did not replace the longer-season varieties, and the wisdom of this was seen when it failed in 1976. This failure was attributed to too *much* rainfall. Rainfall conditions also influence the population of insect pests, so yields are apt to vary wildly from year to year.

The groundnut, long the major export crop of northern Nigeria, virtually ceased production in Dagaceri after being hit by drought, low prices and finally rosette disease in the early 1970s. Notwithstanding several attempts to plant it in Dagaceri during the 1970s and 1980s, there was virtually no saleable crop, though seed lines were maintained. New resistant varieties made their first appearance in the area in the 1990s, but they have not restored the crop to its former popularity. The failure of groundnuts caused farmers to search their gene bank for alternatives. One option was a variety of melon called *guna (Citrullus lanatus)*. This crop had been grown, before the groundnut boom began, for its oil-bearing seeds, rich in fat and protein. After 1972, a rapid rise in its price induced a production boom, which has been sustained until the 1990s. This ground-trailing plant is sown after the harvest of the millet in September or October and only needs one good fall of rain to sustain it throughout the dry season. It has to be harvested, gutted and washed, to extract the seed, and it enters the market late in the dry season when grain prices are high and cash is scarce. However, it is vulnerable to unidentified insect pests. These, or an early end to the rains, can write off a crop at the outset.

Another alternative to the groundnut is sesame (benniseed). Varieties adapted to Sahelian conditions have long been known, but the lack of a market and the popularity of groundnuts suppressed its potential until after 1975. Tentative experiments in reviving benniseed took place in Dagaceri in the 1980s. In 1995, its promotion by agricultural extension in nearby Kano State, and a sudden improvement in its price, provided a more secure base for its recovery.

In the cropping system, therefore, the accumulated experience of the past has been united with innovative alternatives from elsewhere. Biodiversity is being managed in such a way that the uncertainties of the environment are minimised – with a range of options there is a better chance that some will do well under the conditions. The northern provenance of several new varieties of millet and cowpea invites a hypothesis of environmental change: the farming system is exchanging the characteristics of the Sudan zone for those of the Sahel in response to a corresponding shift in rainfall distribution. The need for a market crop has provoked a search for alternatives to the groundnut, subject always to the dictates of ecology.

Diversity of technologies

Diversity is also characteristic of farming technology. There are two planting times – after or before the first rain; two planting methods – in ploughed ridges or in the flat; half a dozen common intercropping patterns with the main crops alone, not to mention minor ones; and three different weeding techniques. The oldest of these is the curved hand hoe, or *fartanya,* of which there are three types – hafted or socketed into wooden handles, or smithed entirely from scrap steel, not to mention different sizes to suit women or children. This tool makes for effective but back-testing weeding and, because of its flexibility, it removes weeds thoroughly, but slowly.

Weeding, however, is the biggest operation in the farming year, because crop yields depend directly on eliminating competition from weeds; so it is done at least twice, where possible. To save labour, farmers may use the *ashasha* hoe, which is a crescent-shaped blade socketed into a long wooden handle, which permits it to be pushed through the soil from a standing position, slicing off the weeds from their roots just below the surface. It is twice as fast as the conventional hoe, but cannot easily be worked around the roots of tall, standing plants; it is most useful early in the season. It is adapted to crops planted in the flat, not those planted in prepared ridges.

A third method of weeding is with the ox-drawn ridging plough or *garma,* which can also be used for inter-row weeding, or with the cultivator, until the height of the grain crops becomes unmanageable for the bulls. This is the fastest method, but the least efficient in removing weeds (about 50 per cent effective); hand weeding is normally necessary to clean out escaping weeds from between the growing plants.

The recent history of weeding technology in Dagaceri illustrates how dryland farmers may adapt and exploit such a technological inventory under changing conditions. The profits from the groundnut boom of the 1960s permitted most farmers to expand the scale of their farming, enabling several to invest in pairs of bulls and ridging ploughs and move into the new system of pre-ridging on enlarged, cultivated fields. They hired out their plough-teams to others, so that the impact of the new technology was widespread (reaching 46 per cent of the farmers). However, in 1972 and 1973, a calamitous drought led to the loss, through death or sale, of all the bulls in the village; in 1974, only 4 per cent used ploughs, hired from another village. This created a crisis in the farming system, as cropland commitments (about a hectare per person) had become extended beyond the capabilities of many households to weed them effectively, using the *fartanya* technology.

The solution was swiftly perceived in the *ashasha*, which had already spread into the country with migrants from Niger. Its adoption was rapid, notwithstanding its unfamiliarity and, by 1980, every Manga farmer in Dagaceri was using this 'poor man's plough'. It was twice as efficient in its use of labour as the *fartanya*. Earlier studies in Niger (Raulin 1964) suggested that the choice between the *ashasha* and the *fartanya* was directly linked to the level of labour intensification.

Lower rainfall and (it is said) lower yields put a continuing premium on extending the cultivated area into fallows. But not until 1979 did plough ownership reappear in the village: in that year, two farmers had rebuilt enough wealth to buy ploughs and bulls. By 1985, thirteen years after the drought, there were once again seven ploughs and teams. This year followed the severe drought and food shortage of 1984, so the investment reflects the incomes earned outside the farm sector. (The Manga men travel as far as Lagos to earn income from trading animals and other occupations, or remain at home to manufacture fibre products for sale.) A decade later – in February, 1996 – and notwithstanding many years of poor crop performance, there were twenty-two or more ploughs, carts and pairs of bulls amongst 125 households. Now the *guna* boom is feeding agricultural profits back into farm investments. Thus some diversity in the technical options available allowed the farming system to adapt to the ecological shocks and changing economic conditions of the times.

Sequential adaptive choice

Farmers in Dagaceri do not throw down a standard technological package in the face of the elements, awaiting the unpredictable outcome with fortitude. The purpose of biological and technological diversity in farming systems in such environments is to permit choices to be made at critical points in the agricultural year (Mortimore 1982; Watts 1983). In Table 5.2 an attempt is made to portray both the options and the constraints affecting the decisions reached by households during the course of the agricultural year.

Although a majority of farmers may always appear to be following a consensual course, the briefest examination of the technical decisions reveals their number and complexity. Superimposed on this pattern of technical and economic choices and the natural and economic conditions which constrain these choices are the additional complexities of the individual households' production systems. Households differ in their resource endowments at the outset (labour, land and livestock especially). In the last column of the table, the most important economic conditions are suggested for the choices detailed in the preceding three columns.

The most far-reaching choice, which illustrates the issues facing farmers, is between the use of the ox-plough for land preparation, ridging and (with or without a cultivator) for weeding, as opposed to either of the hand hoe technologies. This allows a larger area to be cultivated and offers the possibility of enlarging profits and re-investing in additional land. If a farmer does not own a plough, waiting for one may delay the commencement of planting and miss the first rain. On the other hand, plough-ridges facilitate seedling establishment in some conditions. The use of the plough also imposes a capital requirement, not only on access to the technology itself, but for purchasing additional weeding and harvesting labour later in the season. The cost of ploughing is more easily met if inorganic fertilisers are purchased to augment yields. Although every farmer aspires to use, if not to own, a plough, because of the costs involved drought brings a correspondingly larger financial risk to plough-users. For example, the largest plough-user in Dagaceri before the drought of 1972–74 had to send his womenfolk in search of famine foods in the bush, both in 1973 and in 1974, having stripped his reserves in paying labour and buying food. Weighing up the costs, benefits and trade-offs of different options continues through the season and from year to year, always subject to an unpredictable price environment for farm inputs and output.

Instability in the farming system

The farmers' response to variability in the rainfall, in the ecology (and in the economic environment, which is explored in the next chapter) is to exploit diversity by choosing amongst cultivars, technologies and strategic options to the limit of their resource endowments. This flexibility (which is also extended into off-farm activity) is more analogous to a disequilibrial than an equilibrial model, especially when a major drought violently disturbs livelihood systems. Such an event may result in major relocations of the population, especially when famine relief agencies provide alternative survival options outside the locality. At such times, for example when Ethiopians fled into the Sudan, and western Sudanese

Table 5.2 *A framework of sequential choices available to farmers in Dagaceri.*

Operation	Natural conditions (*ital.*) and choices			Economic conditions
	no rain	**rain**		
1 LAND PREPARATION	dry flat planting	wet flat planting	ridge planting	urgency capital/labour supply
2 CULTIVAR	early millet	millet with sorghum	others	access to seed food stocks
3 FIELD PRIORITISATION	nearby fields	nearby fields	distant fields	tenure soil moisture labour time
	poor germination	**good germination**		
4 REPLANTING	replant	no replant		labour
		weeds		
5 FIRST WEEDING	ashasha	fartanya	plough/ cultivator and fartanya	capital/labour supply
		rain continues		
6 INTERPLANTING: timing and cultivars	millet-cowpea	millet-sorghum	millet-groundnut	access to seed market plans
	(a range of other mixtures of main and minor crops)			
	no rain	**rain**		
7 FERTILISATION	no fertiliser	manure	inorganics	capital/livestock
		more weeds		
8 SECOND WEEDING	ashasha (no ridges)	fartanya (ridges)	plough/ cultivator	labour/ capital supply
	poor rainfall	**good rainfall**		
9 LATE PLANTING: timing and cultivars	no planting	sorghum	minor crops	labour land
	birds		**no birds**	
10 BIRD SCARING	no protection	protection	no protection	labour equipment, trees etc.
	no yield	**poor yield**	**good yield**	
11 EARLY HARVEST (millet, cowpeas)	abandon	harvest/store	harvest/store	labour community help
12 MARKETING	none	sales/none	sales/none	need for cash
	no late rain		**late rain**	
13 GUNA	no planting		planting	access to seed labour
	no yield	**poor yield**	**good yield**	
14 LATE HARVEST	abandon or graze	harvest/store	harvest/store	labour community help
15 MARKETING	income diversification famine foods	sales/none	sales/none	need for cash size of food reserves capitalisation needs

migrated to feeding centres in Darfur in 1984, the farming system is abandoned in favour of a more hopeful alternative. But what is remarkable is that those farming populations evacuated the relief camps at the onset of the rains in 1985, returning penniless and starving to their villages (Desselegn Rahmato 1991; de Waal 1989). The systems had not collapsed; notwithstanding the divestment of household and farming capital (the loss of plough teams, even of houses in Ethiopia), they were subsequently rebuilt. At great social and economic cost, which is a measure of instability, the systems persisted, resilient. This theme is examined further in the next chapter.

1 A comparable example of cultivar diversity used against risk is that of Machakos in Kenya, where Akamba farmers were reluctant to adopt wholeheartedly the composite maize developed on the government's research station, despite its advantages of early maturity and higher yields under satisfactory rainfall, pre- ferring to maintain their local varieties, whose resistance to drought promised some yield in dry years. They deliberately mixed the old with the new varieties and allowed the composite maize to degenerate before replacing it with new seed (Mortimore and Wellard, 1991).

2 This type of cowpea, whose name means literally 'son of forty days', is named after its local reputation for giving a yield after only forty days, a matter that has not been fully researched.

6   Risk for the household

Households in the drylands face risks in three major areas. These are: the biological reproduction of the family; the attainment of food sufficiency for the household; and sustaining income for its members. In these categories, they are no different from households in other environments. However, the risks take forms which are specific to the natural and human ecology of the drylands. An assessment of risk in each of these areas leads towards the conclusion that risk management is a condition for sustaining the viability of households in the drylands. Therefore, their capability in this direction is a resource – an *internal* resource – which development interventions should seek to strengthen, not to undermine.

Plate 6 Rural capitalism or rural exploitation? A weekly market at Birniwa, Jigáwa State, Nigeria.

In this chapter, the conception of the household is broadened beyond that of a unitary group, managing a system of primary production based on farming, livestock or wild faunal and floral resources, to the idea of a more complex group, with access to other sources of income.

What is the household? Much controversy surrounds this issue. There has been a growing realisation amongst observers that residential and kinship groups do not necessarily always coincide – with each other, or with producing and consuming units. The patriarchal model of the household, in which all decisions are subject to the authority of the head, has given way to a more analytical approach to the different levels of autonomy enjoyed by individuals, in particular women and grown sons. The existence of female-headed households and of individuals living alone, once unnoticed, is now recognised. The increasing significance of monetary incomes and expenditures much complicates the pattern of transactions between members of a household and their obligations to one another. To treat the household as a 'black box' whose internal relations are beyond the scope of research investigations is increasingly unrealistic, though it may often be unavoidable.

Nor is it satisfactory to disaggregate the household into individuals, as if they were entirely autonomous: their obligations to one another are real. In many African societies, although traditional authority structures are becoming visibly weaker, household or family linkages surmount time and space (for example, the separations brought about through migration or urbanisation) to a greater degree than might be expected under conditions of such rapid social change. One way of looking at the household is as a 'network of implicit contracts' (Netting 1993). It *normally* contains a family – usually an extended one with a nuclear family and additional dependants, not necessarily related – but in some circumstances, it may contain only a small number of persons, it may lack a male head, or it may contain several families. It is a *de jure* rather than a *de facto* grouping: that is, absent members play a significant part in its economic and social life. If it is only rarely possible to draw attention to the internal differentiation of the household, the complex interactions among households and those between households and other kinds of group, it should not be forgotten that they exist.

The biological reproduction of the family

A glance back to Table 3.3 will show that, especially where families are small in size, each individual's labour contributes to the viability of the whole, and that without an adequate endowment of working adults, a family may encounter difficulties. It also shows that it cannot be taken for granted that a family will reproduce its labour force in the next generation – the fourth household illustrates this – and furthermore, only one (the first) was at that time more than replacing its male workers.

Mortality and morbidity

There are high rates of infant and child mortality in African dryland countries: 114 per thousand live births (infant mortality) and 192 per thousand (child mortality) in seventeen countries in 1991 (UNDP 1991). National statistics issued by governments, however, may be less reliable than survey data collected in smaller areas. In the Sudan zone of northern Nigeria, an infant mortality rate of 170 per thousand live births was estimated, for a population of about 40,000, in 1974–78. There was an average expectation of life of thirty-nine years (Malumfashi, Katsina State: Bradley *et al.* 1982a). In another survey, infant mortality was estimated to range between 246 and 135 per thousand in successive years, and child mortality was 154 per thousand, in 1971 (Garki, Kano State: Molineaux and Gramiccia 1980). There are low levels of preventive and curative health services. Adult mortality (which may provoke the breaking up of family units, suddenly rendered non-viable through the loss of labour), maternal mortality (which can lead to the dispersion of children), are also distressingly frequent.

Such mortality – together with much morbidity – is most common during the critical months of the growing season, when farmers most need labour. This is because disease vectors, for example the malaria parasite, are most active at these times. Malaria is a common precipitating cause of death. In Garki (northern Nigeria) there is a close correlation between seasonal mortality patterns and the incidence of biting mosquitoes, and this mortality is accounted for by infants and small children (Fig. 6.1). Malaria control reduces infant mortality, but for a large fraction, death is only delayed; other precipitating causes compete for 'high risk' children who are weakened by under-nutrition. It is not surprising that in such circumstances, families set a high value on reproduction, especially when a high incidence of infertility is also taken into account.

If the drylands are often disadvantaged *vis à vis* the more humid areas, the situation of pastoral nomadic peoples in the drylands is worse than that of the sedentary populations. Their mobility and remoteness from settlements reduces their access to health services. Mortality rates at least as high combine with *lower* fertility levels (whether biologically or culturally determined) to bring about slower rates of natural increase in these populations (Hill 1985).

Sickness threatens seasonal farm work and in years when food is scarce the labour force is more vulnerable. Given the poor provision of health services in most dryland areas, indigenous pharmacopoeias based on the natural flora play an important role. In rural Kano (Nigeria), wild or domesticated trees and shrubs

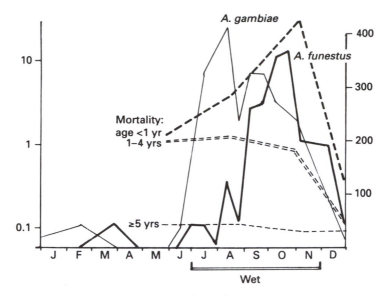

Figure 6.1 Seasonal variation in mortality rates (by age) and man-biting rates for *Anopheles gambiae* and *A. funestus*, at Garki (northern Nigeria) in 1971. The left-hand scale shows bites/man/night and the right-hand scale shows deaths/ thousand/ year; months are shown at the base, with the duration of the wet period. After Molineaux and Gramiccia (1980: 57, 235).

provide substances having prophylactic or curative properties in relation to several conditions including malaria (Etkin 1981; Etkin and Ross 1982). Some of the beneficial effects are obtained in the normal course of eating plant foods. Ethnoveterinary parallels are used by herdsmen to protect their livestock. Such systems of indigenous knowledge are an adaptive response to risk.

Fertility

In Nigeria a high gross fertility rate of 220 per thousand was found in the Malumfashi survey (Bradley *et al.* 1982b), and at Garki, one of 166 (Molineaux and Gramiccia 1980: 234). There is insufficient data to support a distinction between dryland populations and those of more humid zones in respect of fertility. The persistence of high fertility is not difficult to understand at the grassroots. On top of the risk of mortality, there is the obvious economic value of children who, in a rural system, can be soon put to work on subsistence-related activities. Children of four or five years can begin to learn agricultural tasks, help collect wild foods, or assist in food preparation for the home or for the market. In economic terms, 'the marginal utility of each additional child is strongly positive' (Gould and Brown 1996). In many societies, the social importance of the lineage sets a premium on children as the means of expanding its size and wealth (Caldwell 1982). Strongly pronatalist values are sanctioned by culture and religion.

An economic interpretation of high fertility is inadequate on its own, as the following example shows. In Kala, a Bambara village in central Mali, children make a social and religious contribution to the status of the household, as well as providing labour (Toulmin 1992). Their value to their parents as lineage descendants exceeds their economic importance, which is shown by the low status accorded to illegitimate children (of *either* sex). This example shows that fertility behaviour is culturally specific, within the context of ecological and economic risk in the drylands, and caution needs to be exercised in reaching generalisations (a caution rarely seen in the global debate). So far there is little evidence that religious *affiliation* affects fertility: both Muslim and Christian populations, for example, tend to embrace high fertility strategies in dryland Africa. The impact of *belief* is still less known. So is that of social differentiation within the village.

Dryland households are no strangers to famine, and famine highlights the dangers of inadequate risk insurance. By definition, famine-prone societies are high-risk environments in which, during crises, sons (and in some daughters) offer additional sources of income, by migrating temporarily in search of work. They also represent labour reserves, should the principal earner in the household fall ill or die. Thus a long-term response to famine can often be seen in the persistence of high fertility (Devereux 1993: 56).

In a study of a village in southern Niger ('Tudu') during the Sahelian Drought, it was found that the number of childbirths and the rate of fertility were at their highest early in 1974, at the peak of a famine which had been growing worse for two years or more (Faulkingham and Thorbahn 1975), though affected by poor health, miscarriages and weakness from hunger. In the Sahel as a whole, notwithstanding the mortality occasioned by the famine, the demographic expansion which had become established in the 1960s continued unabated in the seventies, apparently attesting to the vigour of adaptive mechanisms (Caldwell 1975). People did not see famine and a rise in mortality as a reason to change their fertility behaviour.

At the level of the household, therefore, high fertility still seems to be rational. Such a rationale runs counter to widely accepted views on 'runaway population growth'. In the words of Professor Pimentel of Harvard University (quoted in the *Guardian*, 15 July, 1994):

> To do nothing to control population numbers is to condemn future humans to a lifetime of absolute poverty, suffering, starvation, disease, and associated violent conflicts as individual pressures mount. The ultimate control of the human population will be imposed by nature.

With United Nations agencies, international pressure groups, influential scientists and writers apparently united behind such views, the seemingly irrational persistence of high fertility in high-risk environments, and the African drylands in particular, can only be understood if the different vantage point of the household is fully appreciated. However, this is not the end of the matter. Decisions affecting human fertility are taken in the context of the wider political and economic environment. The economic environment affects fertility in at least two ways.

In Kenya, including some dryland districts, the annual rate of population growth fell from a record level of 3.8 per cent in the 1970s to 3.1 per cent in the 1980s, according to census data. This change affected the dryland district of Machakos, which conformed closely to the national average (Tiffen 1991). Since permanent migration cannot explain this change, it is certain that it reflects a fall in fertility. The Akamba people of Machakos had always sent their children to school in order to enhance their chances of gaining employment, and many migrated to Nairobi and elsewhere, earning incomes to counterbalance the increasing scarcity of farmland at home. However, during the 1980s the price of coffee, an important source of income in the district, stagnated and urban employment became increasingly difficult to obtain as the economy went into recession. The costs of educating children mounted and competition intensified these costs, for example by making many parents resort to private nursery school education, even in rural areas. Effort was also put into family planning programmes, though their impact is difficult to assess. The lesson to be drawn from this experience appears to be that fertility levels are not immutable in the drylands, and that economic growth, or stagnation, can exert a major influence.

The effects of structural adjustment policies on human fertility in the drylands are therefore likely to be felt through price and income changes. The terms of trade between urban and rural sectors, the rate of growth of urban populations and their purchasing power, the deregulation of marketing systems and the ending of import protection policies are relevant. However, the effects of global economic stagnation are hidden behind those of national policies. Any tenuous link with fertility decisions in dryland communities rather defy analysis, the more so because declining government revenues may have led to a deterioration in health services (and, by implication, infant and child mortality rates).

The second way in which economic environment may affect fertility is through migration. The marginal position of the drylands in national or regional economies leads to a continual demographic bleeding through migration. In West Africa, for example, the deep-rooted regional symbiosis which exists between the Sahel and the humid zone, together with open frontiers, has meant that ever since precolonial times, households in the Sahel may exploit resources in the south by

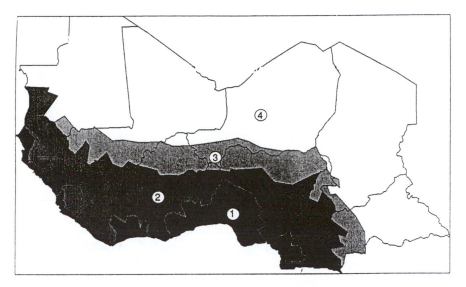

Figure 6.2 The demographic regions of West Africa, according to the West Africa Long Term Perspective Study. After Snrech *et al.* (1994).

Zone	Per cent area	Per cent of popn., 1990	Annual increase 1960–90 (%)	Per cent urban 1990	Annual urban increase (%)
1	7	41	3.2	55	5.9
2	25	28	2.6	30	6.4
3	13	25	2.4	32	7.5
4	55	6	1.7	22	6.0

means of seasonal or longer-term migration. As Fig. 6.2 shows, there is a gradient in the rate of population increase from 3.2 per cent per annum in coastal regions to 2.4 per cent in the semi-arid zone (where the bulk of the population of the drylands are concentrated) and only 1.7 per cent in the arid zone (Snrech *et al.* 1994). The maintenance of high fertility in dryland households helps to guarantee enough male (and sometimes female) children to sustain such patterns of regional interdependence. It is a mistake to assume, as protagonists of population limitation usually do, that people must expect to support themselves only from local resources.

Food sufficiency for the household

Seasonal climates impose a pattern on the production and storage of food at the household level. Market prices fluctuate seasonally, rising to a peak when food is scarce. At certain times of the year this seasonal dimension to rural poverty (Chambers *et al.* 1981) intensifies the vulnerability of low-income households. A famine crisis occurs when such vulnerability is extended, through exceptional scarcity or high prices, to a wider spectrum of the population – to the better-off households as well as the poorer ones.

Seasonality

Seasonal food producing systems must have a storage capability. In dryland climates, cereal grains (millet, sorghum, maize) store well. The losses from storage pests and deterioration, in village granaries constructed of straw or clay, may amount to as little as 4 per cent a year (e.g., Hays 1975). Few cost-effective technical improvements can be made. Cowpeas, however, are subject to insect depredations in storage, and have to be managed more carefully. Treatment with insecticides can greatly improve their keeping qualities. Do dryland households, therefore, merely need to store their production from the growing period in order to ensure a steady stream of consumption throughout the year?

Studies show that, for a majority of families, the energy needed for farming and livestock production through the year do not conform with their intake of food. Farm labour requirements peak in the wet season. For example, Gambian women, who are responsible for work on the rice farms, used four times as much energy in June–August as they did in March–May, according to an early study conducted in 1953 (Haswell 1981). Farming households near Zaria (Nigeria) also work hardest during the wet season (April–August), but their food intake has a different configuration (Fig. 6.3). Except for the month of May, it is below the average throughout the period from March to August; but it rises sharply from November to January, when the harvest is in (Simmons 1981). The implication is that when energy is most in need, food is most scarce (or costly). Nevertheless, when the labour requirements peak in May, extra food is taken out of store for consumption. This is the time for the first weeding, on which crop yields ultimately depend.

In livestock production, an incongruence occurs between the labour time spent in animal husbandry and the amount of milk available for consumption. This is illustrated in Fig. 6.4. For a herd in northern Mali, the labour requirements for watering and milking were found to be lowest when the milk production was highest, in the season of forage abundance (Swift 1981). During the long dry season, however, milk production declined steadily (with the supply of forage), while labour time doubled, as longer distances had to be travelled in search of water, and longer hours spent in lifting it from wells.

Since milk is difficult to store for long, even in butter form, specialist livestock breeders become dependent on the grain storage systems maintained by sedentary farmers with whom they are in contact. The Baggara and Fellata cattle rearers of south Darfur, in the Sudan, live on milk for several months when it is abundant, but consume more grain after the harvest, when the grain purchasing power of their increasingly scarce milk is higher (Kerven 1987). However, if the herds are dispersed from the camps during the wet season, as with the Awlad Hamid Arab camel breeders in northern Darfur, their milk is inaccessible at this time (Holter 1988, 1991). Millet must be eaten throughout the year. Thus the effects of seasonality are specific to the system in question. For growing infants and children, these seasonal changes in nutrition may be more important than for adults (Rowland *et al.* 1981).

Storage systems do not work perfectly. In Machakos, Kenya, where there are two short farming seasons (March–May and October–December), the food stored in 119 households was found to be below the average for the year during all months from September to February, falling to its lowest level from mid-November to mid-December, during the short rains (Fig. 6.5). The data were collected in 1974–75 (Onchere and Sloof 1981). After the maize was harvested, there was a sudden increase in stored food in December and food stocks improved steadily through the March–May wet season (the long rains), until beginning to fall again in August.

Production failure or market failure?

The 'hungry season', which is attested in the literature and folklore of farming communities, arises from the failure of the household economy to deliver food in a steady stream throughout every year. As far as grains are concerned, this failure cannot be attributed to storage systems, as they are (in general terms) adequate in the drylands.

A food surplus is an essential aim in an uncertain environment. In only two of thirteen years (1974–86) did *most* families in Dagaceri (Nigeria) manage to grow their year's grain requirements, still less satisfy their needs for cash, or secure a reserve for the future. This sequence included the drought cycles of 1972–73 and 1983–84. The average amount of arable land available (1.1 hectare/person), at average yields, could be expected to produce, *with satisfactory rainfall*, about 900 kg of cereal grain and 200–450 kg of cowpeas or groundnuts. Allowing for the loss of a third by weight in threshing, the grain output would feed three persons for a year at 190 kg/year.[1] According to farmers' own estimates of their requirements, it would feed only two. A smaller amount of arable land would reduce the output accordingly. Given the unavoidable fluctuations in the rainfall, and the risk from pests or disease, achieving this notional level of productive capacity is

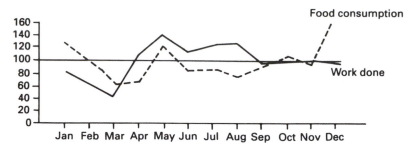

Figure 6.3 Indices of food consumption and work done in farming households in Hanwa, Zaria, Nigeria, 1970. 100 = monthly average (1970–71). The households owned no cattle. After Simmons (1981).

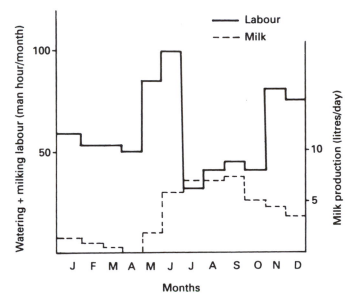

Figure 6.4 Labour inputs and the production of milk in a herd of twenty-five cattle in north Mali. After Swift (1981).

an erratic struggle. Is land shortage, then, a cause of production failure in the dry-lands?

The output of food grains (or any crop) is determined by six factors:

(1)   the amount and distribution of rainfall;
(2)   the incidence of crop pests and disease;
(3)   the soil nutrients available;
(4)   the amount of labour time invested in weeding;

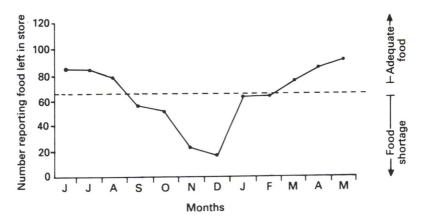

Figure 6.5 Food storage by households in Machakos District, Kenya, in 1974. After Onchere and Sloof (1981).

(5) the capital invested in technologies, particularly labour-saving cultivation; and

(6) the area cultivated, which depends in turn on (4) and (5).

The first factor (rainfall) is for practical purposes outside the farmer's control, and so usually is the second (pests and disease). Soil nutrients can be ameliorated with inputs, which cost money. Family labour can be extended with hiring, and sometimes by drawing on community help; these strategies also have a cost. New technologies, and the acquisition of cultivation rights on additional land, require capital. Thus poverty, defined as a lack of fixed and working capital, inhibits the expansion of the productive capacity of the household farm.

Even in densely populated, land-scarce systems such as those of the Kano and Sokoto close-settled zones of Nigeria (Mortimore 1967; Goddard *et al.* 1972), land scarcity is not necessarily the most important limiting factor. Among a small sample of thirteen households in Tumbau, Kano, it was found that there are both land-surplus and land-scarce holdings (Yusuf 1996). Economic differentiation amongst households sees to that.

The effect of production failure on the food sufficiency of households is amplified by the impact of the grain market. It has long been an accepted fact of life in seasonal farming systems that much food is sold immediately after harvest in order to provide cash for other needs. Later, food is bought back to feed the family during the hungry season (Fig. 6.6). The upward movement of prices from the post-harvest glut to the end-of-season scarcity (100 per cent is common) meanwhile ensures that the household can impoverish itself by these transactions.

Of the 120 households, 73 per cent *both* sold and bought, and only 3 per cent

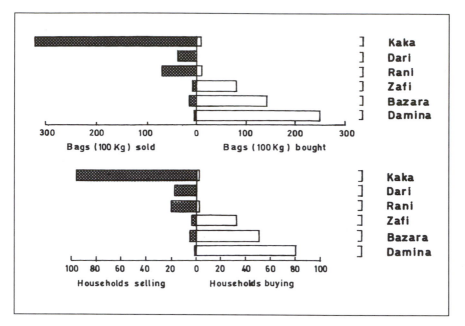

Figure 6.6 Grain selling and buying in Dagaceri, Nigeria, October 1992–September 1993 (120 households). The seasons are as follows: Kaka, October–November; Dari, December–mid-February; Rani, mid-February–March; Zafi, April–May; Bazara, June; Damina, July–September (rains).

neither sold nor bought. Thus participation in the grain market is all but universal in this village. Of those who sold, nearly all did so immediately after the harvest, but some were able to continue selling later when the price was improving. The average amount both sold and bought per household was three and a half bags, if we exclude the activities of one trader. It is thus clear, from this brief analysis, that success in playing the market may have as much effect on household food sufficiency as actual output. More grain sold early, and less bought late in the season, spells food insufficiency for poor households.

Thus poor households have difficulty in producing a grain reserve. Their poverty also prevents them from maintaining it, as their urgent need for income (not to mention gifts, religious obligations like *zakkat* (tithes), taxation, or bribes) constantly makes demands on it. A parallel argument may be applied to livestock producers.

Famine

This year [1914] the effect of shortage showed itself in all its ghastliness. The gaunt ghost of famine stalked abroad through Kano and every other part. The stricken people tore down the ant-hills in the bush to get at the small grains and chaff within these storerooms. They wandered everywhere collecting the grass burrs of the *kerangia* to split the centre pod and get the tiny seed. They made use of every poor resource their ingenuity could think of, and ravenous in their hunger, seized on anything they could steal or plunder. Mothers could not feed their babies at their breasts and cows' milk lacked, for the pasture had dried up and cattle were just skin and bone. The great city of Kano drew the starving thousands from the country in the faint hope of scouring in the streets and markets to pick up what they might, or beg the charity of the townsfolk. Not only the Nigerians but thousands from French country [Niger Colony] drifted down across our borders, passing through villages en route all bare of food to offer them. They died like flies on every road. One came across them in the town markets, emaciated to skeletons, begging feebly for sustenance, or collapsed into unconsciousness where they sat. (Hastings, 1925: 111)[2]

If the appropriate response to the seasonality and uncertainties of dryland environments is to maintain food reserves, why do poor households fail to do so? Is it because of a failure to *produce* a reserve, or a failure to *maintain* it? The discussion above has attempted to show that both of these answers help to explain why households may have insufficient food on a seasonal basis. Famines intensify these seasonal patterns of food shortage, and extend their temporal, social and spatial distribution.

A famine may be defined as a failure of primary production systems in conjunction with a failure of food procurement systems. In the literature on famines in general, there is a controversy concerning whether it is food that is scarce or whether it is the means to procure it (Devereux 1993). If it is food that is scarce, the famine is a *supply driven* event. If it is the means of procurement – normally, money with which to buy – then it is a *demand driven* event. Retrospective studies of certain famines have been used to justify the view that hunger and death were the result, not of a decline in the availability of food, but a collapse of the abilities of the poor to procure food that was available in the markets or elsewhere. In Sen's (1981) original exposition of this theme, the case rests heavily on an interpretation of the Bengal famine of 1943–44. His analyses of African famines (and of the Sahel famine of 1968–74 in particular) were more ambiguous. Using FAO statistics, he claimed that the hypothesis of 'food availability decline . . . despite its superficial plausibility in explaining the Sahelian famine . . . delivers rather little'. But every firsthand account of the famine links it directly with the drought cycle that began, in some areas, as early as 1968, and reached its climax in 1972–74. Sen's error was in opposing two apparently contradictory hypotheses, instead of analysing the links between them.

Where there is generalised poverty, it is inevitable that there is a close link between a failure of subsistence production and hunger. Poverty, or inadequate endowments of land and livestock, prevents households from maintaining an adequate level of production to ensure food reserves ('direct entitlements', according to Sen), often even for a single year, as the cases above illustrate. It stops them from creating a demand in the market for imported food ('indirect entitlements'). Poverty of resource endowments, and poverty in incomes, create vulnerability to food scarcity even in good years. But it needs a trigger to extend this effect in time and space, and such a trigger, in the drylands, has usually been a major drought. The crop failures and losses of livestock that follow such an event have intricate (and little documented) effects on storage and market systems, and repercussions throughout the economy.

Famines are embedded in the remembered history of dryland communities. For example, in Darfur in the Sudan, twenty-two famines occurred between 1885 and 1985 (Table 6.1). The names by which these famines are remembered reflect the shortage of grain, or the resort that was had to famine foods, or the hardship and suffering that resulted, sometimes causing deaths (de Waal 1989). The agency of drought is prominent in the local understanding of the causes of famine.

The contemporary description of famine in northern Nigeria in 1913–14, reproduced above, has much in common with the images produced by the television cameras at Korem in Ethiopia in 1984, even if it had less impact on the conscience of the world. The account was not exaggerated: an elderly eye witness interviewed in Danbatta District in 1973 could remember seeing starving refugees on the road southwards, the villagers having nothing to give them.

In 1972–73, famine returned to northern Nigeria (Mortimore 1973), and vast losses of crops and livestock were reported in both years of the drought, the second surpassing the first in its ferocity (Fig. 6.7). The uneven impact of the drought, owing to spatial variability in rainfall patterns, is discernible, though there was a gradient of intensity from south to north, as was expected.

A famine is not a necessary consequence of production failure. Famines do not often occur in countries with sound market infrastructures and access to international markets, alternative sources of income or insurance systems, or where effective assistance is provided by governments or foreign relief agencies. It is the lack of these provisions that can be related to major famines in dryland Africa, such as the Sahel Famine of the early 1970s (Copans 1975) and the famines in the Sudan (Shepherd 1988; de Waal 1989), Ethiopia (Desselegn Rahmato 1991) and Somalia in the 1980s; it was the availability of some of these conditions that permitted Kenya and Botswana, for example, to cope with the drought cycle of the early 1980s (Downing et al. 1989). In northern Nigeria, the drought of 1972–74 had a devastating impact, which was eventually mitigated, not so much by relief efforts (though these were significant in places), as by improved access to the urban markets created by oil revenues and derivative incomes (van Apeldoorn

Table 6.1 *Famines recalled in Darfur, 1885–1985* (de Waal 1989: 71–72).

Years	Districts	Examples of names	Cause
1888–1890	All Darfur	*Sanat Sita, Jano, Ab Jildai*	War, forced migration, locusts, cattle disease
1900	South-west Darfur	*Salim, Alabas*	War, etc.
	Mellit	*Um Mukheita*	Drought
	Kebkabiya	*Siniin*	War
1910	Dar Masalit	(no name)	War
	All Darfur	*Julu, Um Sudur, Dulendor*	Drought, war
	Southwest Darfur	*Um Sider*	War
1920	Western Darfur Dar Masalit	*Kuburu, Ab Tokolai, Bedawita*	Locusts, suppression of revolt
	Northern Darfur	*Ab Malwa*	Drought
1930	Northern Darfur	*Kadis Dakhal, Sei Kiri*	Locusts
	Eastern Darfur	*Um Rotel*	Locusts
	Northern Darfur	*Ab Habaya*	Locusts
1940	Northern Darfur	*Ab Tokolai, Um Goldi*	Drought
	North and West Darfur	*Khafaltina, Um Regeba, Um Mukheita, Abu Arobain*	Drought
1950	Dar Masalit	*Rujal Jafal*	Epidemic disease
1960	Um Kedada	*Meliss*	Drought
	Kutum-Kebkabiya	*Abu Arba*	Drought
1970	North and west Darfur	*Ab Sotir, Sanat Kruul*	Drought and Chadian refugees
1980	All Darfur	*Sanat Ju', Reagan*	Drought

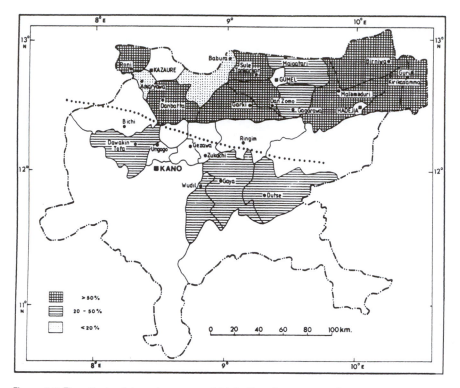

Figure 6.7 The effects of drought on crop yields in Kano State, Nigeria (old boundaries), in 1973: villages reporting 10 per cent of normal or less (n=631 villages). The seventeen districts included in the survey are shown hatched; other areas were not surveyed.

1981). When a drought of equivalent intensity occurred in 1984, these resources were exploited more successfully and its effects were mollified. At the local level, in Wollo, Ethiopia, 'in crisis circumstances a community with a more developed market system, and a greater involvement in the exchange process, has a better chance of survival than a community where the opposite holds true' (Desselegn Rahmato 1991: 143).[3]

On the other hand, arguments have been advanced that the penetration of the market, and in particular the effect of international markets in diverting agricultural resources from food to export crops (sometimes, as in French colonies in West Africa, assisted by official coercion), had malignant effects. In the 'Peanut Basin' of Senegal, for example, it has been argued that groundnut profits led households to divert the factors of production from food crops to export, thereby weakening the resistance of indigenous production systems to food shortages when rainfall failed. Meanwhile, the profits available from market production disrupted the social relations of production which had been based on the family, and undermined the traditional structures of co-operation between households and the support made available to weaker members of the community. The export of soil nutrients in the groundnuts, without replacement from fertilisers, is claimed to have caused soil degradation. Thus the system was preconditioned to failure, when the Sahel Drought struck in the 1970s (see Copans 1983; Copans 1975; Franke and Chasin 1980).

The thesis of disintegration in the peasant mode of production, first developed in Senegal, was extended by other scholars to other parts of Francophone West Africa (Raynaut 1977) – where coercion was sometimes used to obtain cotton for export – and to northern Nigeria (Shenton and Watts 1979; Watts 1983a). The new conditions also led to the disintegration of the socio-political order which had linked farmers and pastoralists (in particular, the Tuareg) in economic space, altering the balance of political power and economic advantage in favour of seden-tary farmers (Bonte 1986). Destitution overtook many once proud pastoral fam-ilies.

There is no doubt that famine must be understood in the context of the his-torical processes and the political economy of the region in question, and both colonial intervention and the 'development' process played an important part (Kates et al. 1981; Leftwich and Harvie 1986). However, the test of a predictive thesis must be in its outcome, and the West African production systems which were the focus of this discussion in the years following the Sahel Drought of the 1970s have turned out to be more resilient than expected. Food production in the Sahel as a whole, in fact, has recently followed the rate of population growth, with a time-lag of about three years (Snrech et al. 1994). Dependency on food aid, which for many years was the central activity of the Comité Inter-Etats pour la Lutte contre la Sécheresse Sahel (CILSS) countries (Somerville 1986), has been brought under control in the 1990s.[4] Such regional trends imply that a majority of households are sustaining both their production systems and their livelihoods.

Famines do not occur in cycles or trends. A link between major production fail-ures and rainfall events can usually be demonstrated. Even so, setting up Famine Early Warning Systems (FEWS) that can alert the authorities in time to take cor-rective action is often costly and may be complex (Davies et al. 1991). However, predicting the failure of food procurement systems is far more difficult, as it depends on social and economic processes, which are little monitored, or imper-fectly understood. At the household level, the link between rainfall (and pests or disease) and output is uncontroversial. But the forces that determine actual market prices – the ultimate arbiters of hardship for the household – are usually hard to understand or predict. Famine, in the drylands as anywhere else, results from a conjunction (in time and space) of food production and procurement failures. They demonstrate that instability in the economic systems of the drylands is an enemy to be feared as much as ecological disequilibrium (Davies 1996; Mortimore 1991).

Famine foods

The collapse of subsistence production leads to a vigorous search for alternative foods, illustrated in the quotation at the beginning of the last section. The women are the repositories of collective knowledge about edible substances in the ecosystem. Their normal gathering activities take on a new intensity and the range of what is eaten is extended, according to the depth of the crisis, to less and less palatable plants. Such a crisis occurred in northern Kano State, Nigeria in 1973–74. At the peak of the *yunwa* (or 'hunger') only 60 per cent of households were eating the usual evening meal with any starch content (grain or cassava), 59 per cent having bought it in the market. The remaining 40 per cent were eating vegetable foods, or nothing.

The ten most common plant species that were in use for food at the time are shown in Table 6.2. The variety of parts used is notable. Many of the trees were indigenous species preserved on farmlands for their economic value. The same survey found thirty-seven other tree, shrub and herb species which were in use for food, whose frequency could not be estimated; many of these occurred in the natural vegetation, or in regrowth on fallow land. Many of the leaves, fruits and roots that feature in such a list are used in better times to supplement the staple foods, and not only by the poor, but they are brought into different and intensive use during times of food shortage. Other famine foods are recorded in the literature, including digging up termitaria for the tiny stores of collected grain found therein, a practice observed in 1914 and photographed by a Nigerian newspaper in Borno State in 1973. The seeds of *Cenchrus biflorus* (Starburr) are still eaten in the Sahel (Bernus 1977).

Resort to famine foods intensifies pressure on trees, shrubs and herbs that grow on farmland or in the natural vegetation, but whose existence is threatened by woodland clearance and by modern methods of farming. Because the need for them is erratic and unpredictable, the conservation of this type of biodiversity is problematic. Some of the most common, such as *Cassia obtusifolia*, grow as weeds on waste ground and along roadsides. Others will be more easily suppressed. The conservation of knowledge is also important, and this is tied up with the economic position of women, who are usually responsible for harvesting famine foods.

Table 6.2 *Trees commonly used as food in northern Kano State, Nigeria, in the famine of 1972–74.*

Name	Parts used	Per cent of families (N=125)	Per cent of villages (N=631)
1 *Leptadenia hastata*	leaves	60	64
2 *Ficus* spp.	fruit, some leaves, aerial roots	35	53
3 *Cassia obtusifolia* (syn *C. tora*)	seedlings	44	19
4 *Sclerocarya birrea*	fruit, leaves (?), kernels	35	20
5 'Loranthus' spp. (parasite)	leaves	30	41
6 *Boscia senegalensis*	berries	14	–
7 *Urena lobata* (wild type)	leaves, calyces, flowers	10	–
8 *Moringa oleifera*	leaves, roots, young pods, seed oil	9	6
9 *Parkia biglobosa*	pod pulp, seeds, flowers	7	–
10 *Adansonia digitata*	leaves, seeds, pod pulp, green fruit, young root, bark	no data	

Sustaining incomes

Market production

The primary strategy for realising a monetary income from the natural resource endowment of the drylands, as everywhere, is the sale of market crops or animal products (milk or livestock). Farming systems that became dependent on the world market for sales of groundnuts, cotton, sisal or other crops during colonial times have paid for the benefits of such participation in the price fluctuations that afflict the market as unpredictably as those of the rainfall. In addition, they have shared with more humid regions the systematic taxation of farm incomes through monopsonistic state marketing boards which used a percentage of revenues to subsidise other sectors of the economy. However, the production of food for domestic markets is also susceptible to price and other uncertainties as African economies wrestle with inflation, policy changes and political instability.

The history of groundnut production in northern Nigeria illustrates both the benefits and the risks of participation in the world market (Fig. 6.8). Embraced with alacrity, as soon as the new railway provided an outlet, the export crop was brought to market in such quantities that it had to be stacked in the streets of Kano in 1911 (Hogendorn 1978). The price was so good that cotton, the government's preferred option for Kano farmers, never got off the ground, and fortunes began to be made by traders. Exports of the 'blessed groundnut' (as the *African Mail* called it) increased from 50,000 tons in 1916 (six years after the arrival of the railway) to 872,000 in 1962–63, when, reaching the height of the boom, Nigeria was Africa's leading producer.

However, stagnating prices meant that producers' income from the crop never got ahead of output after 1950. A large proportion of the value of the crop was being skimmed off by the government's marketing board and diverted to other sectors of the economy (Forrest 1993; Helleiner 1966). Price improvements were not passed on to farmers, and delays in the announcement of prices until after planting was completed, illegal profits by middlemen, and other bottlenecks gradually reduced the value of the crop to growers. Producing households were on a treadmill, having to commit increasing amounts of land and labour in order to maintain the real value of their crop: a long way from the heady days of 1911. A fall of 25 per cent in the price, after the record buying season of 1966–67, brought about a swift collapse in production for export. The downward curve of purchases was immediately followed by a decline in the rainfall, and its demise was finally sealed when rosette disease wiped out the crop in 1975.

Northern Nigerian farmers turned increasingly to producing food for the growing urban market: cowpea, sorghum (guinea corn) and millet. The history of prices between 1970 and 1986 shows some of the uncertainties in producing for the domestic market (Fig. 6.9). The rainfall departures from the mean for 1931–60 (usually *below* the mean) provide a backcloth to a pattern of erratic fluctuations underlain by a strong inflationary trend for all three crops. Such a trend might have favoured producers, were it not interrupted by frequent price collapses, notably in 1976, in 1979–81 and in 1986. The inflationary trend was fuelled by the oil boom in Nigeria and affected farm inputs and the consumables required by rural households, as well as the prices offered for their produce. Since the economy has entered recession, market incentives are reduced. Yet it is a striking fact that even in villages remote from urban markets (in distance or in cost), comparative advantage is vigorously exploited, for example in producing dry season crops in the waterlogged depressions of the northeast (Ibrahim 1996).

While the experience of Nigeria is not necessarily representative of all dryland countries, instability has tended to characterise all markets, both international and domestic. Yet households *must* sell, as their cash requirements increase, even

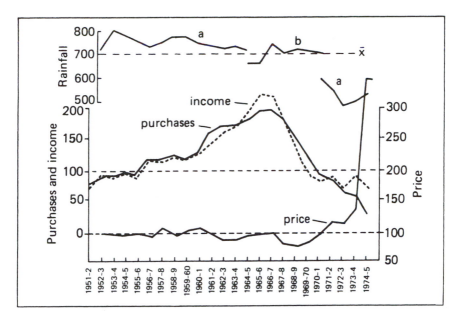

Figure 6.8 The groundnut boom in northern Nigeria,1951–75. Indices for the official groundnut price and for purchases by the Northern Nigeria Marketing Board and for 'producer income' (purchases×price) are three-year running means based on 1959–60.

if, by selling at times of low prices, they intensify their dependence on the market when prices rise (Fig. 6.5). Managing prices is as important for household viability as managing the rainfall.

Income diversification

Notwithstanding the publicity that is given, during famines, to the evidence of starvation, helplessness and relief interventions among 'famine victims', the fact is that a majority of the affected population always survives by its own effort, in what may be called the 'autonomous sector', that is, outside the relief or food aid sector (Mortimore 1991). Indeed, relief interventions may sometimes accentuate the image of distress by their own activities. Mortality rates are likely to be enhanced in relief camps, where health conditions are bad and the most distressed are concentrated (de Waal 1989). The existence of a relief operation may attract people away from alternative survival strategies. It is notable that when the rains return, the relief camps empty, as people prefer to starve on their farms, in an effort to recover self-sufficiency.

There are four levels of income diversification that may be discerned amongst

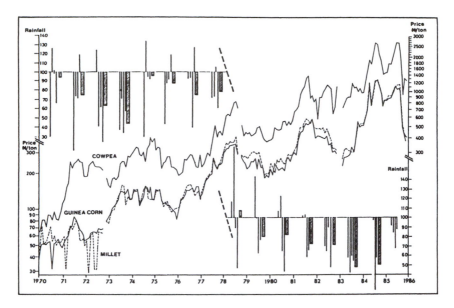

Figure 6.9 Prices of major food crops in relation to rainfall in Kano State, Nigeria, 1970–86. Rainfall is shown for the months June, July, August and September (black columns) and for the year (hatched columns) and is a composite index based on the 1931–60 mean for four stations.

the 'coping strategies' used by farmers and pastoralists in the famines that have afflicted the drylands in recent years. This ordering is based on observations in northern Nigeria, but is broadly congruent with experience elsewhere (Davies 1996; Mortimore 1989a).

The first of these is labouring for wages. Increasing monetisation in the rural economy and the differentiation of larger from smaller farmers, is generating a demand for wage labour on farms. Labour hiring acts as a mechanism for redistributing labour between seasons (workers can seek employment on irrigation schemes in the dry season), between sectors (farmers work on construction projects, for example), and between rural and urban areas (urban labourers are recruited on a temporary basis). Times of general hardship broaden recruitment, but also restrict the availability of wage money, so the labourer may have to move elsewhere. Once regarded as the preserve of farmers, this strategy is used increasingly by pastoralists in West and East Africa. During a famine, supply exceeds demand, so wages are driven down.

The second group of strategies consists in gathering, processing and selling natural resources, which may be had from the ecosystem for the cost of the labour. Wood fuel is the most common, followed in many areas by the making of mats and ropes from fibrous plants. Edible and medicinal plant products may be sold. Salt and natron may be processed from the beds of seasonal lakes. In this group of activities, like labouring, an excessive supply resulting from large scale entry of distressed people may drive down prices in a time when cash is scarce. Furthermore, these strategies depend on transport links to urban markets. Even in Nigeria – a country where roads are relatively well-developed, fuel costs low until recently and public transport unregulated – access to them is uneven.

A third strategy is liquidating assets. In every famine personal property is brought into the market and sold or pawned for sums far below the replacement value. These goods are essentially savings and their loss represents a loss of economic security which is costly to restore. This strategy is limited by the level of demand in the pawnbroker economy of remote rural areas. However, when productive assets are sold, the household's future viability is directly threatened. Livestock are the first and most common form of investments to be sold – if possible, small and less valuable animals first. The terms of trade between livestock and grain are normally unfavourable to livestock sellers during drought. So the costs of reconstituting the herd afterwards are much greater. Farmers may sell draught animals, equipment such as ploughs and eventually, the land itself (in areas where there is a land market). Such a move may prove to be irreversible where land is scarce or costly.

The fourth strategy may be loosely termed 'mobilising social networks' or claims on kin, patrons or friends. First, kinship networks are exploited in search of assistance. While this works towards redistributing wealth in normal times, in general hardship the wealthy are less able (or, perhaps, willing) to spread their own diminishing resources in this way. The same applies to the exploitation of 'patron–client' relationships, whereby a wealthier person helps an unrelated, less wealthy person in return for services of, perhaps, an intangible kind (such as loyalty). Debt may also be considered under this heading. Borrowing is likely to be within the community, as legal collateral or guarantees may not be available, and therefore depends on patterns of social relations, which define a person's entitlement to loans and creditworthiness. High rates of interest also appear to be related to the lack of legally enforceable collateral, as land is not normally used for this purpose in many African societies. Finally, public begging depends on social claims. Although Islam specifically commends almsgiving, the status of beggars is low in Muslim and in other societies and, for this reason, people may move outside the community before resorting to it.

All these are known to households as strategies to which they may resort in normal years if need be; and poor households may use them constantly. Thus a famine intensifies both the incidence of poverty in the community and the adoption of countermeasures. The first three groups of strategies are directly dependent on markets, and many can be used to accumulate wealth and improve economic security as well as to respond to an emergency. But the differentiation in wealth within rural communities, which sustains the fourth group, is historically rooted. In the past there were differences in peoples' access to resources such as farm slaves and livestock, even if, today, inequality is generated to an increasing extent by the monetisation of the rural economy.

The impact of monetisation and the privatisation of wealth on the social relations of a food crisis cannot easily be generalised. On the one hand, the rich may grow richer as they acquire, at favourable terms, enhanced resource portfolios (for example, by buying land from the starving), and shut their gates to the needy. A diminished willingness on the part of the wealthy to help the poor was a frequent complaint during the northern Nigerian drought of 1972–74 (Hill 1977; Mortimore 1989a; Watts 1983). On the other hand, relatively wealthy villagers are bound up in complex social relations with their communities and may find it difficult to resist pressures to share. There is abundant evidence that transfers to poorer households may occur, if only at the cost of consolidating their dependency. We need to discriminate between the contradictory processes of social differentiation and of 'levelling down'.

The search for alternative incomes does not consist in blind acts of desperation but is an orderly progression on the part of individuals, and the households to which they belong, through a series of options ranked on a scale of acceptability, a structure which varies from person to person according to sex, age, experience, resources and competing commitments. This conclusion, which describes the behaviour of farmers in Hausaland in 1972–74 (Mortimore 1982), seems to be generally applicable wherever studies have been carried out on 'coping strategies' in droughts (for example, Corbett 1988; Desselegn Rahmato 1991). Even when opportunities fail completely and whole families embark on painful journeys to distant sources of help, sometimes crossing frontiers on the way, this is not regarded as an irrevocable step. Claims to farmland are not relinquished, and when rain returns to their land, so do the farmers and their families – or those of them who have survived. In the same way, livestock breeders who are dispossessed by the loss of their stock attempt by all means at their disposal to save, in order to reconstitute their herds and return to customary grazing grounds.

Mobility in space

Seasonality bestows both the opportunity and, sometimes, the necessity for short-term income diversification in dryland households: opportunity because the long dry season frees time from farming (though not from livestock tending); and necessity because food shortages compel a search for alternative incomes. Income diversification opportunities within the locality are usually few, and so population mobility is called for, to centres of trade or employment. In West Africa, economic interaction between coastal and Sahelian regions has long been formalised in 'dry season migration' (Prothero 1957; Rouch 1956; Swindell 1984), as well as in the permanent transfer of population (Fig. 6.2). Young men embarked, after the harvest, on journeys southward to work on the cocoa farms of the forest belt, in the ports and cities, or in tin mines, returning when the rains called them back to their farming commitments. While away they reduced the demand on home food supplies, expressed in the ambiguous Hausa term, *cin rani*, which has been translated as 'eating away the dry season' (Prothero 1959). These movements, together with longer-term movements to both urban and rural destinations, formed a part of a complex system of regional demographic, labour, capital and information flows (Amin 1974; Cour 1993; Kuper 1965; Mabogunje 1972). Circulation (or reciprocal flows of people) in the drylands is almost certainly on a larger scale than permanent migration, especially after a regional drought occurs, and belongs to a family of movements observed extensively in the Third World (Chapman and Prothero 1984).

In southern Africa, the demand for mining labour in the gold and diamond fields of South Africa created a more formal system of labour migration from neighbouring countries, which was closely regulated by the governments concerned. Not all South Africa's neighbours were dryland countries. However, in southeast Botswana, where cultivated lands are combined with (often distant) rangeland areas in household farms, participation amongst males was very high. It has recently been replaced, to some extent, by labour in Botswana's own mines and urban areas. The effects of labour migration on agriculture seem to have been mostly negative. Crop production, already risky, has been marginalised by reliance on migrant workers' incomes, which tend to be invested in livestock rather than in farm improvements.

A case resting on negative capital flows, loss of labour, and of economic leadership has also been made for a negative impact of labour migration on the West African interior (Amin 1974). Most studies, however, are more circumspect and recognise a two-way flow in costs and benefits. Certainly Sahelians do not like to be deprived of the opportunity to move, which occurs from time to time, for example when countries close their borders. Nigeria excluded unauthorised migrants from other West African countries in 1983, including Tuareg (easily recognised by their blue-dyed turbans). They had been seeking incomes from casual employment as night guards in cities, in order to try to reconstitute their herds, which they had lost in the droughts of 1969–74. This exception proves the rule that permeable borders are essential for regional interaction at the level of the household or individual.[5]

In famine, an increased proportion of men, women and children enter the system. They make use of employment opportunities and information networks already known in their communities. The behaviour patterns are therefore highly specific to place and time. In Wollo, in Ethiopia, 22 per cent of householders had migrated out of their home areas at the peak of the famine of 1984, in search of work. However, all but an insignificant number stayed within Wollo Province, two-thirds of them staying in rural areas (Desselegn Rahmato 1991: 147). By contrast, when famine hit northern Nigeria in 1972–74, migrant workers from five villages ranged far and wide through the national 'economic space' (Fig. 6.10). In neighbouring Niger, women and children joined Tuareg migrants on the road, and farming families left their villages in their entirety.

The conclusion that population mobility in famine is an intensified version of flows and patterns that may be recognised in normal years allows it to be fitted in to general models of mobility in the Third World based on economic determinants (see Chapman and Prothero 1984; Clarke and Kosinski 1982).

Yet, notwithstanding some permanent out-migration, what is striking in many drylands is 'population immobility', or the reluctance of people to abandon home irrevocably, even under the provocation of famine. Regular circulation between home and places of seasonal or short-term employment, or trading, is a form of adaptation to new opportunities in the rapidly urbanising economies of Africa, as well as (in some societies) a continuation of an historical tradition. The risks of sacrificing claims to land and community membership are considerable in countries where political regionalism, or instability, have to be taken into account. Early observers of rural–urban migration in tropical Africa expected it to take the form familiar in European history, with the progressive transformation of rural people into urbanites and the breaking of social and cultural links. However Africa's failure to replicate an industrial revolution, to create a large working class and to provide stable employment and social security for more than a few, has produced the paradoxical result that indigenes of drought-prone, relatively unproductive and perhaps degraded drylands retain their home links with tenacity. Akamba people in Kenya invest in houses and farms at home with the income earned in Nairobi, and claims to land are jealously guarded (Tiffen *et al.* 1994). In a Hausa village near Kano, large numbers of dormant claims to farm land were found to be maintained by absent members of the community (Ross 1987).

Circulation has four advantages for the household over permanent migration (Mortimore 1982). First, it permits flexibility with regard to the commitment of time and money. Visits may be long or short, and overhead costs minimised as permanent urban residences are not required. Second, it is adaptable to the changing requirements of the life-cycle: young men, for example, are free to travel, while fulfilling their obligations on the family farm in the wet season, while their fathers

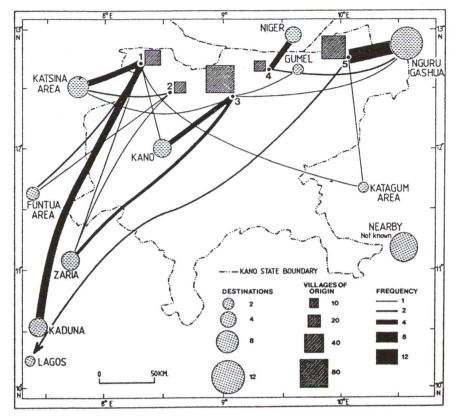

Figure 6.10 Circulation from five villages in northern Nigeria, during the famine of 1973–74.

have more responsibilities at home. Third, it is flexible with respect to destination, which may be changed as opportunity dictates between cities, rural development projects, irrigation schemes or others. Fourth, access is retained to resources and community at home. A bi-local residence pattern allows the best of both worlds to be realised for the individual or the household.

Thus population mobility is misunderstood as simply a function of the failure of primary production systems in the drylands. Rather it is a considered strategy for maintaining the household, by allocating its labour resources in response to spatially dispersed economic opportunities and temporally variable exposures to risk. The variability of the rainfall in the drylands may well be matched by the riskiness of pursuing a pot of gold. In 1976, goat-dealers from Dagaceri (in northern Nigeria), who had travelled 1,000 kilometres to Lagos, were compelled by an attempted military coup in the federal capital to rush, empty-handed, back to the safety of their village.[6]

Persisting in instability

This chapter has reviewed risk, as it affects the achievement of the bio-logical, social and economic reproduction of the household. An examination of seasonality as it affects farming and pastoral households in the drylands suggests, on the face of it, a stable equilibrium. This is because data organised in a single twelve-month series often appear to return to the point where they started (Figs. 6.3–6.5). Since data series extending beyond a single year are rare, equilibrial notions of dryland production systems tended to persist.

However, when inter-year variability is taken into account, whether in random occurrence of production failures, or in the behaviour of the markets on which households have come increasingly to depend, it becomes clear that variations in food supply and in incomes are subject to forces that are better described as un-stable.

Responses to famine show four types of behaviour:

(1)   the use of famine foods, which is a step sideways from primary pro-duction to reliance on wild foods;

(2)   divestment, which is the destruction of the capital base of production in order to divert it into consumption;

(3)   income diversification, in an attempt to extend income sources from agriculture to other sectors; and

(4)   mobility, in an attempt to find incomes in other places.

These forms of response are not those of adjustments to an equilibrial mechanism; they have the hallmarks of instability.

However, the restoration of the production systems after crisis, of farming in the first place and (where possible) pastoralism in the second place, shows their resilience, or persistence. Livestock producers are frustrated in this by their need to acquire breeding stock before they can return; farmers have their own labour, which is their chief resource. An equilibrial view of primary production systems sees the disruption caused by a major production failure as a systemic 'collapse', whereas a view which understands them as adaptively unstable directs attention instead to the sources of resilience in the system. System failure suggests that drastic interventions are necessary to transform it into something better; system resilience, on the other hand, suggests that policy should be directed towards strengthening or enabling the system to maintain those properties which facili-tate its persistence. An ability to persist is measured against economic as well as natural risk.

1 Detailed estimates using FAO formulae for energy requirements are given in Mortimore 1989a: 87.

2 It will be noticed that the city market, with its regional hinterland, commanded a better supply of food than the countryside. Groundnut exporters, using the new railway (completed in 1911), even brought back consignments from the river port of Baro in order to take advantage of the escalating prices in Kano. Although the colonial administration tried to organise some relief, it is likely that the small scale and high cost of this exercise restricted its effects to Kano city.

3 Reference to the quotation at the beginning of this section will show that the prominence of a major market in a food scarcity is not new in the history of African famines.

4 The Comité Inter-États de Lutte Contre la Sécheresse dans le Sahel (CILSS), which was set up after the Sahel Drought of the 1970s, includes the following countries: Cape Verde, Senegal, The Gambia, Mauritania, Guinea-Bissau, Mali, Burkina Faso, Niger and Chad.

5 It is alleged that many Tuareg (known in Nigeria as Buzaye) abandoned their turbans, and claimed citizenship of certain villages on the Nigerian side of the border, when asked.

6 In recent years there has been a dramatic increase in the movement of refugees in Africa (Stock 1995). Many of these movements have occurred in the drylands of Somalia, Eritrea, Ethiopia, the Sudan, Chad and Angola. But, notwithstanding the similarity suggested by the common use of the term 'drought refugee', and the unpredictability of the political crises that trigger refugee movements, they fit uneasily into an economic framework. Destinations are chosen, movements take place, and links with home are broken in an essentially disorderly way, in the drylands exactly as in more humid areas. The temporal dimensions of wars and persecution are quite different from those of the rainfall (even highly variable rainfall), and displacements often become quasi-permanent.

7 Degradation

The theory of degradation

In the preceding three chapters I have located the primary source of the instability (disequilibrium) of dryland environments in the variability of the rainfall, and followed the implications of this instability (or disequilibrium) into two areas: the management of the rangelands for grazing livestock; and the management of cropping and technological systems by farmers. I have suggested that containing and insuring against such risk must be among the primary objectives of all dryland households; furthermore, that other sources of risk originating in the economy may amplify its impact. Since most dryland households (though not all) are primarily dependent on the use of natural resources, it follows that risk management must form a necessary part of their strategy.

Much of the debate about the degradation of natural resources in dryland environments ignores this fact. This, I suggest, is because the theoretical assumptions that underlie statements about degradation are not those of *instability* but of *stability*; not those of *disequilibrium*, but of *equilibrium* as being the natural order of things.

As stated by Holling (1973: 17), the difference between stability and instability is as follows:

> Stability is a property or 'ability of a system to return to an equilibrium state after a temporary disturbance'; thus the system fluctuates around a specific state. On the other hand, unstable systems have a high capacity to absorb periodic extremes of fluctuation, often under extreme climatic conditions. They can be said to be highly resilient.

Degradation is usually portrayed, not in a context of instability (as defined by Holling), but as a *disturbance* of a stable equilibrium. This assumption was illustrated in Figure 4.7, where the first model portrayed a stable equilibrium in which perturbations either do not occur, or are always followed by a return to the *status quo ante*, like the swings of a pendulum. The amplitude of the perturbations (or

Plate 7 Which came first? Moving dunes and harvesting the nutrients, Manga Grasslands (upper) and the Kano Close-Settled Zone (lower).

the magnitude of the fluctuations) and their wavelength (whether measured in months, years, decades or centuries) are immaterial in principle, though they have considerable practical implications for living communities.

The assumption of stability is seen clearly in the 'Clementsian' theory of natural vegetational succession and the climatic climax, which dominated ecology until the 1960s. According to this tradition, each combination of climatic and soil conditions produces, in time, a vegetational community which optimises the resources of light, moisture and nutrients. In the course of establishing this equilibrium, beginning theoretically with a sterile surface, the vegetation passes through a *succession* during which species alternately establish dominance, create conditions for other species, then lose ground in competition with those species. A change of climate alters the competitive advantages of the different species and leads to a re-adjustment of the plant community to the new equilibrium. It follows that for every ecozone, and every site, there is an optimal vegetation (the climatic climax). This presumably maximises biological productivity, thereby providing a baseline against which changes induced by human management may be measured.

The concept of carrying capacity rests implicitly on such an idea. The concept claims that there is a maximum sustainable yield (whether of forage for wild animals or livestock, on the one hand, or of economic products such as crops for human communities on the other), which, if exceeded, leads in the short run to vegetational regression (Benkhe *et al.* 1993), and to degradation in the long run. Carrying capacity is reached, of course, after considerable modification of the natural vegetation (and even of the soils) has taken place. However, no degradation occurs before this point because soil physical and chemical properties, and the vegetational communities, recover fully after each cycle of exploitation. Farmers transfer land from crops to fallow and herdsmen move their animals elsewhere. However, when such cycles become shortened beyond a critical level, the recovery process is aborted.

Hence the link between degradation and the growth of population densities in Africa was expressed, in pioneering work in the 1930s, in terms of a 'Critical Population Density' (Allan 1965), beyond which land degradation is predicted. Methods were proposed for measuring such a 'CPD', under conditions of unchanging agricultural technology. Faced with evidence of land degradation in the native reserves of northern and southern Rhodesia and in Kenya, the colonial governments were ready to blame it on population increase, but reluctant to face the logic of extending the boundaries of the reserves, at the expense of privileged European settlers who had established themselves outside. The idea of the critical population density was therefore linked with the political economy of land alienation, and is less appropriate where legal restrictions to land access, such as reserve boundaries, are not in effect.

Nevertheless, a direct link between population and land degradation came to be taken as axiomatic in official statements of governments, donors and international agencies, until the 1980s. For example, a director of the United Nations Environment Programme stated:

> Each piece of land has what we call its carrying capacity . . . When that number is exceeded, the whole piece of land will quickly degenerate from overgrazing or overuse by human beings. Therefore, population pressure is definitely one of the major causes of desertification and the degradation of land. (Tolba 1986)

In such a 'classic' view, the weaknesses of an analogy between animals and humans is overlooked. Animals cannot develop technologies to increase the efficiency of land management. In fact the concept has been elaborated, under the name 'population supporting capacity', to take account of different levels of technological development in agriculture (FAO 1982). As technology becomes more intensive, the supporting capacity rises. Tolba's exposition also ignores the impact of other, non-demographic, factors on land use, especially markets. Yet it is clear that few systems of crop or livestock production anywhere in the world are now beyond such influences.

Meanwhile, the value of the concept, even for grazing management, is being questioned (Bartels *et al.* 1993). Its definition is controversial, its estimation complex, and its appropriateness in African conditions called into question on the grounds of the variability of the rainfall, the spatial mobility of herds, and the importance of crop residues, *vis à vis* natural pastures, for feeding livestock. Others suggest distinguishing between 'ecological carrying capacity' (in which the conservation of the land is the primary objective) and 'economic carrying capacity'. This is defined in terms of the animal feeding requirements for meeting particular production goals: for example, beef production has different criteria of efficiency from multiple goals such as 'milk-traction-manure' (Behnke *et al.* 1993; de Leeuw and Tothill 1993). Given this uncertainty in range management science, where the concept has its theoretical roots, great caution is needed in using it to understand the more complex relations between mixed production systems and environmental change.

The theory of human-induced degradation, therefore, states (in its traditional form) that owing to the carrying capacity, either of animals or of humans, being exceeded, not only is there a failure of food supply, with a Malthusian outcome of starvation and death (an outcome which is seen quite often in the faunal populations of natural ecosystems), but in addition, there is an unsustainable 'mining' of the bio-productivity under human management. For example, overgrazing causes the deterioration of rangeland; overcultivation causes the loss of soil nutrients and the erosion of the soil itself; overcutting causes the loss or deterioration of woodland; overdrawn wells or boreholes cause the lowering of water tables. To the negative effects of population pressure must be added the demands of markets for primary products coupled with the needs of the people for cash incomes. Thus the upward curve of exploitation (whether driven by population pressure or by market forces) diverges exponentially from the curve of

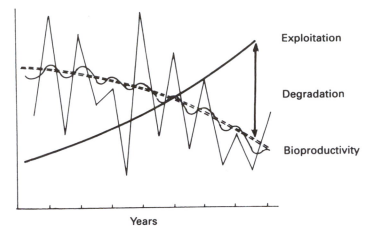

Years

Figure 7.1 Relationships between the exploitation of natural resources, bioproductivity and degradation, according to a conventional view. Three curves are shown for bioproductivity: regular and irregular fluctuations and a smoothed trend.

declining bio-productivity, leading to a situation where the land permanently loses the ability to recover its productivity, even with the passage of time (Fig. 7.1).

At this point, *reversible* degradation gives way to *irreversible*.

> In exceptionally fragile ecosystems, such as those on the desert margins, the loss of biological productivity through the degradation of plant, animal, soil and water resources can easily become irreversible, and permanently reduce their capacity to support human life. Desertification is a self-accelerating process, feeding on itself, and as it advances, rehabilitation costs rise exponentially. Action to combat desertification is required urgently before the costs of rehabilitation rise beyond practical possibility or before the opportunity to act is lost forever. (UNEP 1977a: 3)

Desertification, according to Mainguet (1994: 16), is 'the ultimate step in land degradation: irreversibly sterile land, meaning irreversible in human terms and within practicable economic limitations'. But the difficulties of defining irreversible degradation in the field – either in technical or in economic terms – have led others to retreat from this concept. Warren and Khogali (1991: 6) define degradation as a 'persistent decrease in the productivity of vegetation and soils', in which the drylands differ from other climates mainly in the relative importance of wind erosion, salinisation and seasonality. This difference shifts the emphasis from the *end-state* of desertification to the *process* of degradation.

A conception of a disturbed equilibrium on a linear trend (Fig. 7.1) implies that the objective of remedial action is to restore the land to a state of stable equilibrium: if not to pristine nature, with a climatic climax vegetation on mature soils, then at least to a sustainable level where removals from the soil or vegetation are matched by recuperation. This is the necessary conclusion of the traditional view.

The literature on degradation is too often silent on the question of system closure. If a grazing or farming system is closed – that is, there are neither exports nor imports of bio-productive resources (a situation only possible in theory) – everything may be recycled in some form. For example, some soil nutrients are returned to the land in animal dung or human waste; wood is returned in the ash from fires; crop residues are returned as dung or as green manure. On the other hand, if a system is open, export takes place: for example, in soil nutrients incorporated in the economic yield of crops, livestock or other products sold in the market; in soil eroded and carried outside the area by wind or water, to be deposited elsewhere; in timber sold to cities for fuel or for construction; or in water evaporated from irrigation plots.

Since most dryland systems are *partly* open – combining export of economic products to the market with a strong emphasis on subsistence production – the question of degradation (or its opposite – sustainability) is bound up with the efficiency of recycling of the bio-productive resources (to the extent that the system is closed) and with the replacement of exported bio-productivity by imports, for example fertilisers (to the extent that the system is open). Conventional representations of degradation emphasise the export of bio-productive resources – in crops, livestock, eroded soil – and may ignore or under-estimate recycling or imports (including those from natural processes, such as flooding). Assessing the balance between exports and imports on the one hand, and bio-productive cycling on the other, is, however, necessary for a meaningful assessment of degradation or sustainability.

Cases

'Soil mining' in southern Mali (Berckmoes *et al.* 1990; van der Pol 1992)

Southern Mali receives an average annual rainfall ranging from less than 700 to more than 1200 mm (1956–85) and has the best agricultural potential of any region of Mali. It is occupied by populations whose average density is 29 per square kilometre. They grow millet, sorghum, maize, cotton, groundnuts, cowpeas and rice and keep cattle and small ruminants. Cotton was introduced, by government policy, in the 1950s, and a company (the Compagnie Malienne de Développement du Textiles, or CMDT) is responsible for promoting the crop, providing all agricultural services in the region and also for rural development. Cotton exports are vital to the Malian economy.

By the 1980s, three trends were apparent. First, the growth of the population (at about 2.5 per cent per annum) was driving an increase in the cultivated area, which was estimated to be at the rate of 7 per cent over three years, though the trend varied from farm to farm. Second, cotton output was increasing, but four-fifths of the increase was accounted for by extensions to the cultivated area and only one-fifth by increased yields. Third, these extensions were facilitated by the increasing use of ox-ploughs, affecting 69 per cent of producing units in 1987–88.

In two of the CMDT's *régions*, Sikasso and Koutiala, 9 per cent and 21 per cent of the area (respectively) were under cultivation in 1986–87. Sikasso is in the wetter, southern part of the area (1000–1200 mm average rainfall), verging on sub-humid, while Koutiala is further north (700–900 mm). Only about half the areas in both *régions* are considered to be cultivable; in the *cercle* of Sikasso, 41 per cent of this is being used, or had been used in the past; but in Koutiala, this figure was 92 per cent. Taken at face value, these figures imply that in Koutiala (and areas like it), the reserve of unused but good quality land will soon disappear, to be incorporated into the system of cultivation with recuperative fallows. According to the FAO (1980), recuperative fallows cease to be fully effective when more than one-fifth of the cultivable area is under cultivation, in conditions comparable to these. If, as estimated, only half the land is cultivable (a low fraction by Sahelian standards), then Sikasso has already reached this level and Koutiala has doubled it.

These statistics suggest that the farming system of southern Mali cannot continue to grow indefinitely by means of extensions to the cultivated area (or extensification); and that intensification in the form of soil nutrient inputs is already necessary in some areas, especially in the northern, more densely occupied *régions*. Structural adjustment policies, however, which have been adopted by the government of Mali, have increased the cost of fertilisers, and the levels of use have declined since the 1970s. On the assumption that intensification depends on the use of imported nutrients, the sustainability of the system appears, therefore, to be in question. Programmes to reduce soil erosion and to promote the use of organic fertilisers have been implemented.

An attempt was made to estimate the nutrient balances in southern Mali using crop data for 1986–89. The balance for each nutrient (nitrogen, phosphorus, potassium, calcium, magnesium) is the difference between exports and imports. Exports take the following forms: uptake in economic crops; losses through soil leaching and erosion; and (for nitrogen) volatisation to the atmosphere. Imports take the following forms: fertilisers; manure; the weathering of soil minerals; deposition in atmospheric dust; crop residues incorporated into the soil; and (for nitrogen) fixation from the atmosphere. The estimates for these parameters were based on the best available measurements at comparable sites. The results for the two nutrients of prime importance in the Sahel are shown in Figure 7.2. They suggest that there was a deficit of 47 per cent for nitrogen, but that for phosphorus the exports and imports approximately balanced. The picture varied, however, from crop to crop, as their nutrient requirements and fertilisation varied. For potassium, there was a deficit of 43 per cent, for calcium an equilibrium and for magnesium a deficit of 38 per cent.

Translating these findings into economic terms, the study concluded that 'soil mining' – or the use without replacement of soil nutrients – amounted to 40 per cent of the value of farmers' total income from agricultural activities. The view of the farming system which is offered by this interpretation is, therefore, one of an equilibrial system disturbed by unbalanced nutrient management, and set on a trend similar to the one shown in Figure 7.1.

It is important to note that such balances for large areas rely on measurements for individual nutrients, or estimates, which may not be representative of all conditions, and that the difficult methodology offers several opportunities for error. Among these may be included the following:

(a) the recuperation of nutrient stocks under fallow is inadequately accounted for in an 'export–import' framework;

(b) the practice of mixing crops, which is widespread elsewhere in Africa, undermines the validity of using individual crop production and nutrient use data as the basis for the estimation;

(c) economic yields are not all exported but may be recycled as human wastes and in other ways; and

(d) the function of livestock in grazing, and redistributing nutrients spatially through manure, is more complex than the model recognises.

Even though nutrient budgets are difficult to construct for small areas, a budgeting approach has been taken to entire countries and regions in Africa (Smaling 1993). At such a scale, a necessary reliance on official statistical series further increases the scope for methodological disagreement, and it may be questioned whether the model affords a meaningful representation.

Rangeland degradation in Botswana (Abel 1993; Abel and Blaikie 1989; Abel et al. 1987)

The southern district of Botswana has an average annual rainfall of 515 mm (1926/27–1982/83), which falls mostly between October and April, but has a variable distribution within those months. Potential evapotranspiration is

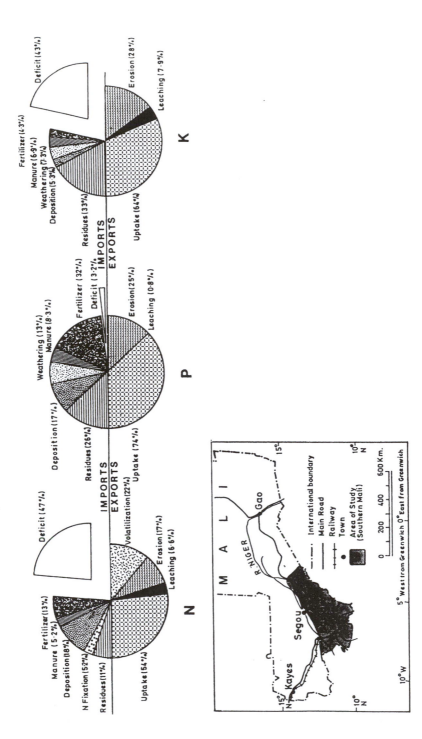

Figure 7.2 Nutrient balances under conditions of 'soil mining' in southern Mali. After van der Pol (1992).

high, owing to high temperatures, and soil moisture is frequently limiting for the growth of plants. The species composition of the grassland, and the amount of woodland, vary according to the soil parent materials, the soil profiles and topography. In this area the Batswana practise a mixed stockraising and farming system, using the ox-plough and growing sorghum, maize and beans. Cattle are customarily managed for a large part of the year from 'cattle posts' in the bush, at some distance from the villages. Off-farm incomes, earned formerly in the mining industry of South Africa, and in the last ten years increasingly within Botswana, assume a high priority among the economic strategies of households, often even coming before farming. The numbers of livestock owned by the Batswana have a strong tendency to increase owing to the social value traditionally placed on investment in cattle (Schapera 1953), favourable government policies (especially in the provision of boreholes, animal health facilities and tax incentives) and strong prices. However, major droughts (such as those of the early 1960s and 1980s) interrupt this tendency. There have been many claims that overgrazing is damaging the bio-productivity of natural ecosystems, both in communal grazing areas and in the Kalahari, where many private boreholes have been sunk.

An analysis of sequential air photography revealed that significant ecological changes occurred between 1963, 1975 and 1982 (Table 7.1). On non-arable land, woody canopy cover increased from 21 to 29 and then to 32 per cent of the total area. Arable land (ploughed and fallow) increased from 11 to 16 per cent. Kraals ('cattle posts') and the density of tracks increased, as did the frequency of relatively light-toned patches, which were interpreted as evidence of the removal of grass or surface soil. Erosion gullies also increased. The changes were not uniform over the study area, varying according to soil parent material, but the general trends were significant. They were consistent with an increase in livestock during the period, though figures were lacking.

The changes in vegetation were explained in terms of a soil moisture model (Fig. 7.3), which works as follows. An increase in the density of livestock on natural rangeland is caused either by a rise in their numbers or by a restriction of grazing land owing to the extension of arable land. The increase in grazing pressure reduces the grass cover on open grassland. This reduction in cover increases soil erosion, which removes organic material, clay and silt and causes a deterioration of soil structure. This in turn reduces infiltration from rainfall, an effect magnified by soil capping; and this means less moisture in the surface layer on which grass growth depends. Reduced infiltration also means more runoff and more erosion.

Under the woody canopy, competition with grass is reduced, so that seedlings can establish themselves when conditions are suitable; also the incidence of fires, which are damaging to seedlings, is reduced by the scarcity of grass. Once estab-

Table 7.1 *Changes in land cover, Ngwaketse area of Botswana, 1963–82.*

Land cover class	Percentage of area			Statistical significance of change
	1963 August	1975 June	1982 May	
Woody canopy	21.0	28.8	32.5	$p < 0.05$
Kraals	0.2	0.2	0.4	$p < 0.05$
Settlements	0.4	0.5	0.4	ns
Hafir or pan	0.1	0.1	0.2	$p < 0.1$
Plough-and-fallow	11.4	15.7	15.7	ns
Erosion gullies	0.3	0.3	0.7	$p < 0.01$
Light-toned patches		Increased		$p < 0.01$
Track density		Increased		$p < 0.0005$
Number of sample points	8000	8000	8000	

Source: Abel *et al.* 1987: Table 8.1

lished, the woody plants may shade out some species of grass. They act as nutrient pumps, drawing from the deeper soil profile and replenishing the surface through leaf fall, thus improving the structure of the soil and restoring infiltration. They also intercept rainfall, some of which would otherwise be lost through erosion or evaporation, and add it to the soil through stemflow. As the woody canopy increases, the grazing pressure on the remaining grassland is intensified. It is possible that the grasses eventually cease to be viable, or lose their resilience (Walker *et al.* 1981).

Losses of clay, silt and (in the short term) soil organic matter are irreversible within the time-horizon of a smallholder's planning, whereas short-term changes in the ratio of woody plants to grasses or in species composition are reversible. The study concluded that changes of the first type are degradational. The obvious solution, in order to conserve the quality of the land, is a reduction in the density of livestock. However, experimental work in Botswana shows that although destocking results in a rise in the value of output per animal, it fails to compensate for a fall in output per hectare. It is not, therefore, an economic option, especially in view of the fact that the demand for livestock, to support family livelihoods, is increased by mortality in drought and by population growth. In the eleven years, 1978–88, cattle were consistently maintained at stocking rates approximately double those officially recommended. Furthermore, it was found that even a drastic reduction in the density of livestock has only a small effect on the rate of soil loss and its determinant, vegetational cover (a reduction of 49 per

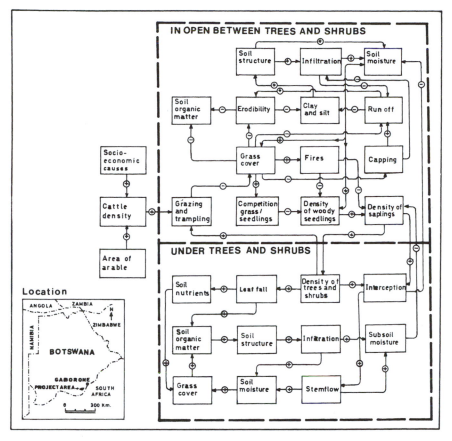

Figure 7.3 Mechanisms of change in vegetation and soils in Botswana. After Abel *et al.* (1987).

cent in the stocking rate produced an increase in vegetational cover of only 5 per cent).

The validity of such a model depends finally on demonstrating all the relationships empirically, but its general derivation from equilibrial assumptions is clear. This case study shows that dryland degradation may be subtle, if not imperceptible. Local awareness of it was found to be generally lacking: 'There is a growing perception among Batswana that land is becoming scarce. There is no general perception, however, of environmental change or degradation' (Abel *et al.* 1987: 81). In view of such ambiguities, the 'overgrazing' hypothesis, long accepted by governments in the communal grazing areas of Botswana and Zimbabwe, appears to be an oversimplification.

Soil erosion in Kondoa, Tanzania (Ostberg 1986; Mung'ong'o, 1995).

Kondoa District in central Tanzania contains the upland area of Irangi (named after the Rangi people), which is surrounded by semi-arid, almost treeless plains at an altitude of about 1,200 m. In Irangi, inselbergs rise above the sloping pediments, as high as 2,100 m above sea level. The average annual rainfall of Irangi (1970–84) is 614 mm, but in the plains it is about 550 mm. The rainy season is from December to April. Ephemeral rivers drain the area, with wide sandy beds and many gullies. Dry forest occupies 10–15 per cent of Irangi. The population of the district was estimated to be 300,000 in 1980, living at densities of less than 20 per square kilometre in the plains, but rising to over 100 per square kilometre in places in Irangi (Fig. 7.4).

The Rangi people practised an agro-pastoral system with emphasis on crop production, but gave high social value to the ownership of cattle. Erosion was already being observed in the middle of the nineteenth century, when a growing demand for grain and other provisions from trading caravans (which passed through Irangi) helped to drive an expansion of the cultivated area. Population growth added to the demand for arable land, and the Rangi expanded from their area of origin throughout the uplands and even to the surrounding plains. The clearance of woodland in order to control tsetse infestation added impetus to erosion, whose control soon became a policy priority for the colonial government. Soil wash and rills on cultivated land, the development of gullies, the loss of vegetation on grazing land and of trees on cultivated land, were the main diagnostic features. On private land, farmers built bunds and ridges along the contour, but did not attempt to stop the gullies, whose conspicuous development attracted the most attention.

The official diagnosis of the erosion crisis in Irangi was over-stocking, and a drastic decision was made to de-stock an area of 1,250 square kilometres in 1979. The entire livestock holdings of about 80,000 people – estimated at 90,000 livestock units – were removed, under compulsion, from the closed area. Employees of the regional soil conservation project policed the exclusion strictly. Soil conservation measures were stepped up on arable land (bunding, contour ridging, mulching, diversion ['cutoff'] drains), reafforestation was intensified (nurseries for tree seedlings, planting and extension advice), and gully control was introduced through check-dams and planting.

Five years later, a significant improvement in the vegetative cover in the Hills was observed. The gullies were healing and flooding had been brought under greater control. Timber for construction was less scarce. Profitable cultivation of sweet potatoes had been introduced on river-bed sites, and flood-plains, formerly reserved for grazing and liable to destructive flooding, were supporting continu-

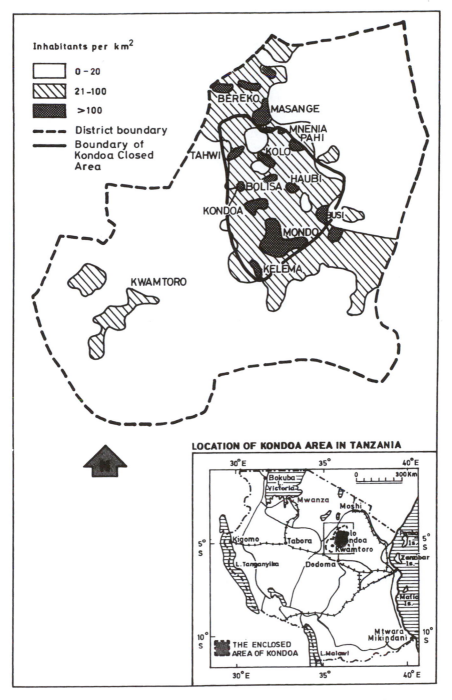

Figure 7.4 The enclosed area of Kondoa, Tanzania, with population density. After Ostberg (1986).

ous cultivation. The need for famine relief had declined. Agricultural land has since increased by 10.15 per cent, and younger men recognise that potential productivity has increased.

The price that had to be paid for these improvements was considerable. The livestock were transferred to the plains where they suffered suddenly increased mortality, representing major capital losses. Their owners made tending arrangements with friends or relatives living there, or divided their families between two locations. Manure inputs ceased on Irangi farms, provoking increased dependence on fertilisers, only partly helped by the use of mulches. Milk disappeared from the diet, unless it was purchased. Traction animals had to be brought up from the plains, with permission, for the ploughing season. Fodder could not be fully used and caused more frequent fires in the dry season. The improved vegetation gave cover for wildlife, increasing crop damage and re-infestation by the tse-tse fly. On the plains, the influx of additional stock intensified pressure on the grazings there, which are subject to variable rainfall. There was an increase in the cultivated area and an increased population became vulnerable to hunger in times of drought.

Worst of all, the need for coercion has not disappeared; disaffected persons set fire to up to 30 per cent of the regenerating vegetation and exotic tree plantations annually, and unauthorised opening of farms and illegal grazing occur in the conservation area.

> Towards equilibrium: will everything then end well in Kondoa? As the population increases, will the concern for the environment increase? Historically this turned out not to be the case. But with the support of a soil conservation programme it may be different. But . . . the soils *are* erodible. Droughts *will* strike in the future. It will always be difficult for large concentrations of people to continuously produce their own food here. (Ostberg 1986: 93)

In Kondoa, the search for a restored equilibrium through a programme of conservation was allowed to put at risk both the farming system in Irangi itself (by removing the source of manure and obstructing animal traction), and the ecology of the semi-arid plains. The coercive de-stocking of Irangi has few counterparts. In Kenya, the colonial government was forced to back down from compulsory de-stocking in Machakos in 1938 (Tiffen *et al.* 1994). In Irangi, a one-party system, the acceptance of compulsory resettlement in villages (*ujamaa*), substantial foreign aid, and a presidential visit to the area all contributed to the implementation of this drastic solution.

Conclusion

In this chapter I have attempted to show that the concept of degradation, as it is normally used, is derived from that of a stable equilibrium, and that its progression is commonly conceived in terms of departure from a baseline, which is either a stable natural equilibrium, or a modified stable equilibrium under productive management. These ideas may be implicit rather than stated. In the three case studies, an equilibrial fallowing regime in Mali (adequately replacing soil nutrients after cultivation cycles), an equilibrial stocking regime in Botswana (ensuring the stability of the natural rangeland), and a balance between cultivation and erosion in Kondoa set the baselines for the degradation agenda.

However, what is important is not how far a system or an environment has departed from a condition of stability, and what is needed to restore it, but the magnitude and direction of the trends in bio-productivity and exploitation: the curves portrayed in Figure 7.1. If the curves are diverging, under what conditions may this yawning 'degradation gap' be reduced?

Preserving or enhancing bio-productivity is *conservation*; the effect of such action is to arrest a fall in bio-productivity and eventually to reverse it. However, as many conservation projects have discovered to their cost, it is not practicable to undertake conservation in isolation from the economic environment of costs and benefits. These are reflected in the trend of exploitation, which can be modified through sustainable *intensification*, which means achieving more output from the same amount of land without incurring negative side-effects such as soil pollution. Such action slows or reverses the exploitation curve. There are both direct and indirect linkages between intensification and conservation, as will be shown in the next two chapters. *Equilibrating* the two curves means, not restoring the *status quo ante* (which is clearly an unrealistic objective), but bringing them into a dynamic balance, perhaps at a relatively low level of bio-productivity compared to that of the natural ecosystem: but one which can be improved under good management.

The cases examined in the next two chapters provide some indicators of how such an objective may be achieved – in particular, by the efforts of African smallholders themselves.

8 Intensification

The 'crisis of sustainability'

This study's findings confirm the hypothesis of strong synergies and causality chains linking rapid population growth, degradation of the environmental resource base, and poor agricultural performance.

Farmers seek to maximise production per unit of land only when land becomes scarce relative to labor. This is now occurring in many parts of Sub-Saharan Africa. The weakness of the traditional coping strategies [however] is that they are not capable of adjusting quickly enough to prevent serious negative impact of rapid population growth and increasing population pressure on soil fertility, farm size, fuelwood availability, land tenure systems.

Because agricultural technology adapted to dryland areas is so marginal, land tenure reform so exceedingly difficult to implement, and carrying capacity so low, sustainable management of dryland areas will be very problematic. (Cleaver and Schreiber 1994: 1–2, 126, 118).

In the previous chapter, it was argued that the crisis of sustainability is often represented in terms of negative feedback loops in an equilibrial system, disturbed by 'external' factors, such as the growth of the human (and livestock) populations, drought, or the market. For neo-classical economic analysts, population growth is uppermost; in socialist critiques, the market; while technical appraisals emphasise the role of rainfall and bioproductivity constraints. In this chapter, the hypotheses that population growth, rainfall variability and monetisation cause increased environmental degradation will be put to empirical test by means of a comparison of two farming systems in which these parameters vary. This exercise shows that only one of the variables, rainfall, correlates in any way with observed degradation. Increased population density and monetisation do not.

In the view of the authors quoted above, the economic impulse to maximise production per unit of land is frustrated by the unprecedented *rapidity* of population growth, the *marginal utility* of technology, *unreformed* (and, by implication, unsuitable) land tenure and *unproductive* bio-potential. The more densely populated, and monetised, of the two systems will be analysed to find the reasons for its superior sustainability.

Plate 8 Low or high inputs? Adjacent farms under contrasting management at Tumbau in the Kano Close-Settled Zone, Nigeria (September, 1994).

Table 8.1 *Comparison of two Hausa Sahelian production systems: ecology.*

	Sharken Hawsa	Tumbau
1 Average rainfall, 1969–88 (mm)	400	689
2 Decline in rainfall since 1969 (%)	20	20
3 Departure of 1973 rainfall from average (1931–60)(%)	−50	−50
4 Average length of growing period in days (FAO)	105	135
(1965–88)	<90	<120
5 Soils	aeolian sands	aeolian sands
6 Major subsistence crops	millet, early cowpea	millet, sorghum, late cowpea

Sources: FAO (1982); Sivakumar (1992); Climate Research Unit, University of East Anglia.

Two farming systems (Grégoire and Raynaut 1980; Mortimore 1993a, b; Raynaut 1980; Raynaut *et al.* 1988; Yusuf 1996)

The two systems used in this comparison are at Sharken Hawsa, in Maradi Department, Niger, and at Tumbau, in the Kano Close-Settled Zone of Nigeria (whose locations appear in Figure 8.2). Although Tumbau receives two-thirds more rainfall than Sharken Hawsa, two measures of risk (the percentage decline after 1969, and the intensity of the major drought in 1973) give similar values for the two places (Table 8.1). The difference in the length of the growing period (about a month) is responsible for the fact that sorghum (which grows to maturity in 120 days) is more important in Kano than in Maradi, where millet (90 days) is supreme.

Population density and the cultivated area

The first question is, what impact has population density on the extent of cultivation? This is explored in Figure 8.1. The profiles of the low density (Sharken Hawsa) and high density (Tumbau) systems are sharply divergent. Sharken Hawsa (with a population density of less than 50 per square kilometre) has a relatively low cultivated fraction, a high cultivated area per person and a high rate of extension. Tumbau (with a population density of 414 per square kilometre) on the contrary, has a very high cultivated fraction, a low cultivated area per person and an insignificant rate of extension.

The spatial patterns of land use are predictably different (Fig. 8.2). In Sharken

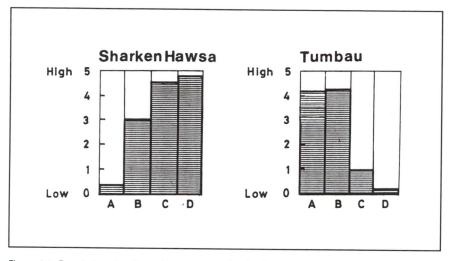

Figure 8.1 Population density and land use profiles for Sharken Hawsa and Tumbau. Constructed from data in Raynaut (1980) and Turner (1997). The vertical scale (0–5) has the following values for variables A, B, C and D.

	A Population density (persons/km²)	B Cultivated area (per cent)	C Cultivated land per person (ha)	D Annual increase in cultivated area (per cent)
5	500	100	1.5	1.5
4	400	80	1.2	1.2
3	300	60	0.9	0.9
2	200	40	0.6	0.6
1	100	20	0.3	0.3
0	0	0	0	0

Hawsa, the classic pattern of concentric land use zones shows the effect of distance costs on field cultivation, where the labour is resident in the village and must travel to the fields each day, and the supply of land is sufficient to allow some choice in locating cultivated fields. In Tumbau, on the other hand, no zonation is discernible. The population live partly dispersed, but more important is the fact that all cultivable land is claimed by someone. These spatial patterns are themselves products of the different stages reached in the process of land occupation. At Sharken Hawsa, the progression towards filling up the village *terroir* between 1957 and 1975 is apparent from the histogram. By contrast, in Tumbau, virtually all cultivable land had been in use for three decades (or more) prior to 1981.

However, the difference in population density between the two systems is not

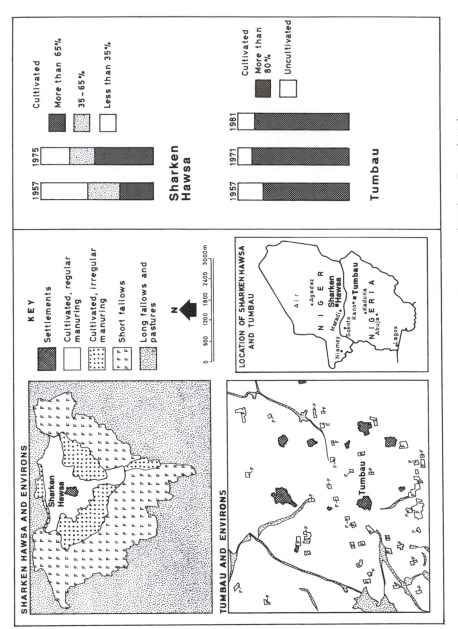

Figure 8.2 Land use in space and time, at Sharken Hawsa and Tumbau. After Raynaut (1980) and Turner (1997).

reflected proportionately in the dependent variables, indicating that other factors are at work besides population growth. Sharken Hawsa had a density approximately one-tenth that of Tumbau, yet 60 per cent of the area was under cultivation. A first hypothesis to explain this is that the demand for market crops has an effect on the cultivated area over and above the subsistence needs of the population. In Maradi Department, the falling real price for groundnuts which was paid to farmers between 1948 and 1971, forced them to extend the cultivated area in order to maintain their incomes from the crop (Raynaut 1977). An alternative hypothesis is that during the process called 'saturation', a perceptibly growing scarcity of land accelerates its acquisition and privatisation by farming households, anxious not to be left with insufficient land when the supply is finally exhausted. In Niger, this tendency has been fuelled by long-expected land tenure reform (the Rural Code) which is expected to accede land rights to those who can claim effective occupation of land that was formerly held in common, increasing rather than reducing institutional security (Lund 1993). If this is so, the land tenure reform advocated by Cleaver and Schreiber (1994) may have a *negative* effect on environmental management, in the short term. But if the extension of private ownership is followed by improved management, its long-term run effect may be beneficial.

Monetisation

Sharken Hawsa is situated eighty kilometres from Maradi, while Tumbau is only thirty-five kilometres from Kano. Kano is a major regional market and Maradi is tributary to it, acting as a bulking and distributive market for Kano. The roads infrastructure in Nigeria benefited from investments derived from oil revenues, throughout the 1970s and 1980s. In Maradi, improvements came in the late 1970s, under an integrated rural development programme (the *Programme Développement Rurale de Maradi*). Nigerian fuel subsidies kept the cost of rural transportation much lower than in Niger until after 1994, when costs rose. In terms of market access, therefore, Tumbau is advantaged relative to Sharken Hawsa.

In Sharken Hawsa, in the late 1970s, the patterns of income and expenditure varied between household heads, wives and male dependants, as they had access to different sources of income and different consumption requirements (Raynaut 1980: 47–54). The same socio-economic diversity is found in the Kano Close-Settled Zone (Hill 1977). The studies in Maradi Department showed that there were also significant differences between villages in the extent of dependence on on-farm and off-farm incomes. In Kano, too, the incidence of dry-season migration for employment was found to be greater in a more distant village than in a village close to the city of Kano; while transport and trading, not surprisingly, were more common sources of income close to the city (Amerena 1982: 155–202).

Groundnut production for the export market started in Kano with the arrival of the railway in 1911, but was much later to take off in southern Niger, where the infrastructure lagged behind, achieving major importance only after 1945. In both areas livestock, cowpeas and grain are marketed; and the Maradi area also exports tiger nuts to Nigeria. Land, labour and capital markets exist in both areas, but are much more advanced in Kano, where land sales and farm slavery were known before the colonial period, and where labour hiring and borrowing or renting of land, now involve a large proportion of households. Capital investment in agriculture (ploughs and bulls, fertilisers, other agro-chemicals, new seed) is probably further advanced per household in Maradi Department, owing to development project interventions and available credit; but on a per hectare basis, and using mostly private resources, it is higher in Kano.

The penetration of the market economy into both areas has driven change in the farming systems. However, this process began earlier in Kano (before the present century, when the city of Kano created demand for food grain, livestock and other commodities), and grew spectacularly when the new railway linked it with the coast in 1911. Indeed, Maradi is now itself tributary to the regional market of Kano, and linked with it through produce marketing and labour migration. The Kano area shows indicators of a higher general level of monetisation than Maradi: closer to its major market, it enjoys a wider range of opportunities for income diversification, and the 'commoditisation' of land, labour, capital and new technology has proceeded further. The insecurity of subsistence production in Sharken Hawsa, however, may push households towards a higher degree of dependency on monetary incomes in bad years.

Intensification and productivity

An intensity profile for each system is shown in Figure 8.3. Sharken Hawsa scores low on four out of five indicators when compared with Tumbau: the proportion of cultivated land which is regularly manured, the density of livestock per hectare; cereal yields; and density of farm trees. Data on manure applied per hectare are not available, but the level is certainly much lower than that of Tumbau. Thus the permanently cultivated system of the Kano Close-Settled Zone runs as a high input–high output system in comparison with the low input–low output system of Sharken Hawsa. The differences in the productivity of the land are greater than those of the rainfall, and show that increased population density does not necessarily lead to degradation.

A relatively high productivity on a per hectare basis does not necessarily mean

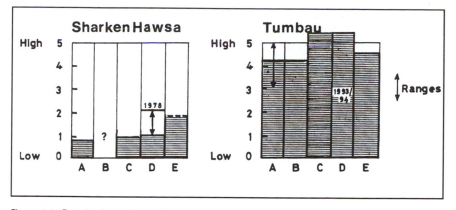

Figure 8.3 Farming intensity profiles for Sharken Hawsa and Tumbau. It should be noted that data are illustrative and, as the ranges indicate, may not be widely representative. After Bourn and Wint (1994), Cline-Cole *et al.* (1990), Harris (1995), Mortimore (1993a), Raynaut (1980). The vertical scale (0–5) has the following values for variables A, B, C, D and E:

Variables:	A	B	C	D	E
	Arable land regularly manured (per cent)	*Manure applied (tonnes/ cultivated ha)*	*Livestock density (tropical live- stock units/ha)*	*Cereal yields (kg/ha)*	*Farm trees (trees/ha)*
5	100	5.0	0.5	1000	15
4	80	4.0	0.4	800	12
3	60	3.0	0.3	600	9
2	40	2.0	0.2	400	6
1	20	1.0	0.1	200	3
0	0	0	0	0	0

food sufficiency on a per capita basis, but, at about 250 kg/person (in 1978), grain output from the Sharken Hawsa system compared unfavourably with that measured on some farms in the land-scarce Tumbau system, at 350 kg/person (in 1993–94: Harris 1996). No data are available for either system which would allow generalisation over several years and for a large number of households.

Soil fertility is maintained in Tumbau by high and increasing use of organic manure (as well as, to a limited extent, inorganic fertilisers). Organic manure is supplied primarily (though not entirely) from animals, which are more numerous in Tumbau than in Sharken Hawsa. This implies higher livestock densities per hectare as population density increases, a relationship that has been demonstrated in the Close-Settled Zone and in Nigeria as a whole (Hendy 1977; Bourn and Wint 1994). Seasonal transhumance is necessary for cattle, because of a lack of grazing areas during the wet season – with the exception, of course, of traction bulls. Other livestock depend on residues, browse and hedges. All this is in contrast with Sharken Hawsa, where manure is only put on a small proportion of cultivated land and fallows are relied on for restoring fertility on the rest. The livestock transfer nutrients from fallows and natural grazings, which cover 40 per cent of the area (though fast disappearing), to the privileged fields where they are 'night-parked' or kraaled.

A comparable transition has occurred in Kano with respect to wood fuel. Natural woodland, apart from shrubs on cattle tracks or degraded ground, is absent, yet the energy needs of the dense rural population are fully met from harvesting branches and deadwood from farm trees and field boundary hedges, and burning crop residues. (The needs of urban populations are mostly met from imports.) Tree densities are higher on the Tumbau farms, where trees of economic value are planted and protected. In Sharken Hawsa, fuel is still collected from natural woodland and farm trees are few.

The significance of these differences may be appreciated if we ask what would be the optimal use of an additional unit of labour in each system. In Sharken Hawsa (and other villages studied by Raynaut and his colleagues), a significant positive relationship was found between the area cultivated per worker and crop output per worker, which rationalises the choice of the 'extensification option'. That is to say, an extra labour unit is best spent in cultivating more land. In Tumbau, on the other hand, this option does not exist (except for those few who are able to purchase land), so the optimal use of additional labour is in soil improvement (manuring, composting), more weeding and recovering fodder from field boundaries, weeds, and residues for the animals: the 'intensification option'.

Raynaut concluded from village studies in Maradi Department, of which Sharken Hawsa was one, that:

> The intensity of the pressure of cultivation on space and the rapidity of its growth are profound and lasting factors transforming the relations between social groups and their natural environment . . . how can one explain the permanence – even progression – of a very extensive form of agriculture in the context of a rapidly increasing scarcity of available space? Does the vicious circle in which the peasants are presently entangled allow them another choice? The extension of cultivation is for them, as we have seen, the only way of safeguarding a minimum level of productivity for their labour . . . [quite contrary to] a progressive readjustment towards intensification. (Raynaut 1980: 57)

A number of factors were understood to have undermined the adaptive capability of the peasant system, effectively closing the option of intensification. These included:

(1)   the decline of collective control over natural resources;
(2)   the individualisation of land tenure;
(3)   the concentration of cultivation around nucleated villages;
(4)   monetisation (with its concomitants of market production, individualisation of economic behaviour and weakening of family cohesion); and
(5)   the rapidity of demographic growth (estimated at 2.7 per cent/year).

There is an alternative to this interpretation. This alternative proposes that the economic preconditions of intensification have not yet been met (Boserup 1965; Netting 1993). According to this hypothesis, when the supply of free land finally ceases, additional labour will be invested in the intensification option. It has been observed that in the fields close to the village, at the heart of the concentric land use system (Fig. 8.2), cereal yields may approach 1000 kg/hectare with the benefit of manuring (Raynaut 1980: 24). Such levels are comparable to those of Tumbau. However, on distant fields, with no manure and poor weeding, yields can fall below 100kg/hectare.

More recent work on agro-forestry practice in Maradi provides confirmation of the thesis. When trees were abundant, it was a rational use of labour to exploit them destructively. This destruction proceeded to the point of impairing natural regeneration around numerous villages, where there was declining soil fertility, increased erosion and a scarcity of wood. However, the scarcity impelled a spontaneous change in practice. Shrub and tree shoots were protected on land just fallowed ('défrichement amélioré': Jouet *et al.* 1996). It is a central tenet of Boserup's theory that intensification technologies are known, but await an increase in the labour to land ratio before their use can be extended.

The Kano Close-Settled Zone

Sharken Hawsa is broadly representative of many dryland production systems where population densities are low or moderate. What, therefore, is the secret of Kano's achievement in sustaining much higher densities?

Soils under annual cultivation

If dryland farming is faced with a crisis of fertility maintenance, with ever-shortening fallows unable to restore the soil, and insufficient fertilisation to compensate, it should follow that annual cultivation continued for many years causes serious degradation of its physical and chemical properties. According to conventional views of desertification, such degradation (in the drylands) eventually becomes 'irreversible'.

Table 8.2 *Soil properties under annual cultivation, Kano Close-Settled Zone, 1977 and 1990 (top 20 cm).*

Property	1977	1990	Percent change
1 Bulk density (gm/m3)	1.4	1.4	0
2 Particle size distribution (%)			
sand	90	90	0
silt	6	6	0
clay	4	4	0
3 Organic carbon (%)	0.237	0.205	−13
4 Total nitrogen (%)	0.029	0.033	12
5 Exchangeable potassium (me/100 g)	0.1	0.06	−40
6 pH, soil water	5.9	6.1	3

Note:
Exchangeable calcium, magnesium and sodium recorded changes of 0, 0 and 7 per cent respectively.

At some fifty-nine sites in the Kano Close-Settled Zone, upland soils under rainfed cultivation, which were sampled first in 1977 (LRDC 1979), were re-sampled after thirteen years in 1990. Both sets were analysed alongside each other for standard physical and chemical properties (Essiet 1990; Mortimore 1993b). These soils are sandy and situated on flat or gently sloping interfluves, whose parent material is aeolian drift which was deposited in dunes during the last trans-gression of the Sahara Desert, and under the control of wind formations which were essentially the same as those which still transport dust to the area today (McTainsh 1984).

The results were contrary to degradational expectations (Table 8.2). The phys-ical properties had not changed at all – the soils had been cultivated by hand and had not been exposed either to mechanical cultivation or to irrigation, both of which may cause physical degradation under semi-arid conditions in northern Nigeria (Essiet 1990; Mortimore 1989b; 1993b). The chemical properties were more variable but only in potassium could a large change be discerned (and given the very low values, it may not be significant).

This evidence indicates that these soils, under long-term, annual, rainfed cultivation, are stable with respect to most of the standard fertility indicators. Although the values tend to accord with low levels of fertility, they are by no means incapable of producing crops, as the yields show. If, therefore, soil fertility can be stabilised in semi-arid conditions under a high and increasing population density, then agricultural intensification can be compatible with ecological sustainability.

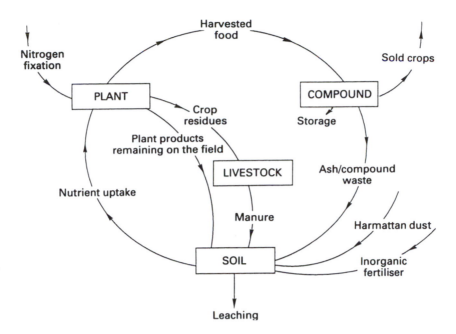

Figure 8.4 Nutrient cycling in the farming system of the Kano Close-Settled Zone, 1993–94. After Harris (1996).

The maintenance of fertility is the prime objective of soil management by the smallholders. How is this goal achieved?

Nutrient cycling (Harris 1996)

The Kano system integrates crops, livestock and trees in a nutrient cycle whose efficient management is the key to farmers' economic welfare. This cycle is shown in Figure 8.4.

Small quantities of nutrients are imported through nitrogen fixation, the use of inorganic fertiliser (nitrogen, phosphorus and potassium) and through net deposition of the Harmattan dust (cations and micronutrients) and exported when crops are sold. The key to the success of the system is the integration of crops and livestock, involving the recycling of nutrients within the system. Crop residues, especially those of legumes, are used as fodder. Small ruminants, kept in the compound at night (and throughout the day in the growing season) convert the 'free' nitrogen fixed by the legumes, and also weeds from the fields, into manure. This, together with compound waste, is returned to the fields during the following dry season. Cereal residues are grazed in the fields during the day in the

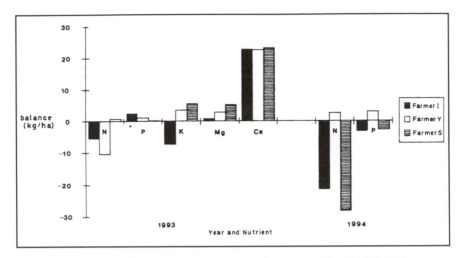

Figure 8.5 Nutrient balances on three Tumbau farms, in 1993–94. After Harris (1996).

dry season, and in the compound at other times. Trees recycle nutrients from deeper soils, depositing them in leaf fall, or providing browse which is again converted into manure.

When the nutrient flows, shown in Figure 8.4, were measured on farmers' fields, nutrient balances could be constructed for the two farming seasons, 1993 and 1994 (Fig. 8.5). The balances varied from field to field, depending on fertilisation practices and crop rotations. Manure or fertiliser may be rotated around a farmer's fields during a period of several years. Planting a legume crop ensures that some nitrogen is fixed from the atmosphere. The amount of nutrients removed depends on the economic yields, which in turn depend on rainfall. The amount of residues determines the amount of manure, unless there are insufficient livestock to use them fully. The nutrient balances show that in any one year, a farm holding (or a field) may have either a surplus or a deficit. It is the balance of nutrients over time that determines sustainability. The sustained use of farmland without complaint of land degradation or declining yields is evidence that nutrient inputs and outputs must be balanced over the long term.

Farm trees (Cline-Cole *et al.* 1990a, b)

According to popular literature on desertification, urbanisation creates an irresistible demand for fuelwood which induces rural people to cut down trees in ever-widening aureoles of deforestation surrounding cities. Such a claim has been levelled against Kano (Eckholm and Brown 1977), but the evidence refutes it.

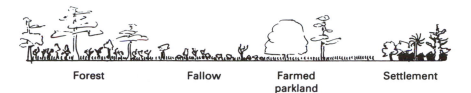

| Forest | Fallow | Farmed parkland | Settlement |

Figure 8.6. A West African model of trees, land use and settlement.

Stage:	Forest	Fallow	Farmed parkland	Settlement
Tree density (Trees/ha)	538	53	22	>22
Timber volume (m³/ha)	41	4.8	12.4	>12.4

Data from Cline-Cole *et al.* (1990b).

The disappearance of natural woodland, as cultivation was extended, increased the value of trees, not merely as fuel, but more significantly for medicines, food, fodder and timber. Trees are a major component of a complex human ecology of subsistence that did not disappear along with natural vegetation, but assumed a new, intensively managed mode. They contribute to a practice of 'ethnopharmacology' by the Hausa which uses parts of trees and other plants in the treatment of sickness and supplies valuable elements in the diet of rural people (Etkin 1981; Etkin and Ross 1982). Trees could be harvested, and their ability to grow on farmland without negative effects on crop performance increased the productive value of the land. Trees were thus first protected, when the bush was cleared, then later planted, and their presence represented a form of investment. Conservation found a place in the political economy of trees in the nineteenth and early twentieth centuries in Kano (Cline-Cole 1994). In many other parts of West Africa, farmed parkland surrounds settlements and there is an increase in the size and maturity of trees, and in their density, as one approaches towns and villages (Pullan 1974). Contrary to the myth of deforestation, dense populations are tree-friendly, provided that land and tree tenure protects their owners' rights (Fig. 8.6).

In the Kano farmlands, the last stages (farmed parkland and settlement) now extend everywhere, and densities of farm trees of up to fifteen per hectare are common. The resistance of this indigenous system of agroforestry to fuelwood pressures, both of demand (from urban markets) and of supply (meeting domestic cash needs), is testified by evidence from air photography and survey (Fig. 8.7). In two large areas, interpretation of photography showed that the density of farm trees was maintained from the early 1960s until the late 1980s. Surveys conducted on the ground, in representative quadrants, showed that when seedlings were

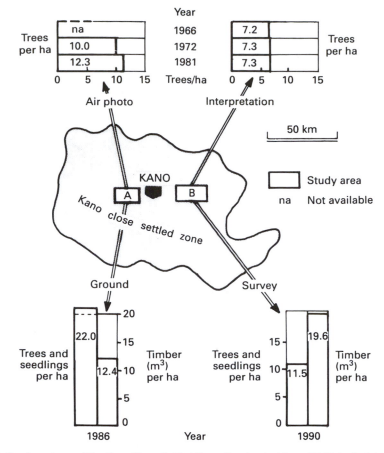

Figure 8.7 The farm trees of the Kano Close-Settled Zone. Constructed from J.E. Nichol's data in Cline-Cole *et al.* (1990a), Mortimore (1993b).

included, the densities were considerably higher, and the age-distribution of the trees (measured by girth), taking all species together, showed that regeneration was taking place through protection and planting.

The maintenance of tree stocks during that period is remarkable, as it included two major drought cycles (1972–74 and 1983–84). During these droughts, mortality increased among some tree species, notably the valuable *Faidherbia albida* (gawo), and the need for income to purchase food put pressure on farming households to cut wood for fuel. This is another illustration of how dryland farmers regard capital protection as a higher priority than meeting short term consumption needs, even in conditions of hardship (de Waal 1989).

Until the 1960s, the inner Close-Settled Zone – within a radius of 25–30 km of the city – provided nearly all of urban Kano's wood fuel. Every day, processions of thousands of farmers' donkeys carried wood into the city, returning later in the day with city manure for the farms (Mortimore and Wilson 1965; Mortimore 1972). Far from threatening environmental destruction, this traffic in wood provided an economic basis for its conservation. As the urban population grew, from 250,000 in 1962 to about 1.5 million in 1991, the escalating demand from urban residents could no longer be met by this means and, with the aid of cheap Nigerian petrol, a rapidly improving road infrastructure and private transport investments, the demand was diverted to areas of natural woodland at distances of 300 km or more (Cline-Cole *et al.* 1990a). The trees of the farmlands, protected by the value of their harvests, continued to supply rural energy requirements, but became marginal in the urban fuelwood trade. The fuelwood 'problem' is thus not one of excessive *rural* consumption, but rather a coupling of accelerating *urban* demand with a weak institutional structure for the protection of remote natural woodlands.

Long-term evidence (Mortimore 1993a)

The most compelling attribute of the system described in Kano is its longevity. It was already receiving commendations in travellers' accounts of the nineteenth century. Table 8.3 shows that for at least the last three decades, virtually all land in the Tumbau area has been under annual cultivation. Fallows were estimated to occupy not more than a third of farmland as long ago as 1913 (Gowers 1913, quoted in Mortimore 1974). Since 1962, the density of the rural population has risen by 80 per cent and the amount of cultivated land per person has fallen by 45 per cent. Yet, as the last column in the table shows, on farm holdings which are broadly representative, it is still possible to be self-sufficient in grain, at least in terms of biological requirements (the average requirement of grain per person is 190–200 kg/year, and the output achieved on these farms was 350 kg/person in 1993–94). Most agriculturalists would agree that the modest grain yields (about a tonne per hectare) could be improved given more inputs.

The highest population densities and the smallest average landholdings are found in the peri-urban Close-Settled Zone (within 10 km of the city). On the basis of small samples, studies found that as few as 20–25 per cent of households were self-sufficient in grain in the 1960s and 1970s (Mortimore and Wilson 1965; Hill 1977: 117–38). Among the remainder, grain-deficiency was a common occurrence, and had been for many years. The grain-deficient households were heavily committed to incomes earned off the farm, in a range of trading, primary processing, or labouring occupations which have deep historical roots in the area. As population density diminished away from the centre (from about 250 to 150

Table 8.3 *Trends in population density and land use, Tumbau, 1962–1991.*

	1962 (*district*)	1991 (LGA)	1993/1994 (*three holdings*)
Total population	81,500	149,200	16
Area (ha)	36,000	36,000	4.9
Rural population density (per sq km)	226	414	326
Land under annual or permanent cultivation (%)	86.9	87.1	100
Cultivated land per person (ha)	0.38	0.21	0.36
Cereal yields on three holdings (kg/ha)			1076
(kg/person)			350

Sources: Census data (1962, 1991); Harris (1994); Turner (1997).

persons per square kilometre in 1962), so the monetisation of the rural economy decreased, as measured by the level of commitment to groundnut production, the frequency of land purchases, the value of farmland, the amount of manure purchased and applied and the level of dependence on nonfarming incomes (Goddard *et al.* 1975; Amerena 1982).

These two factors – the maintenance of grain output in the rural zone despite diminishing cultivated land per person, and the persistence of grain-insufficiency, associated with high levels of income diversification, in the peri-urban zone – indicate that the Close-Settled Zone is an artifact of economic rather than natural factors. Why did the system not collapse under the pressure of increasing population? The answer lies in the fact that inflation affected the value of its components more or less equally, so that no imbalance, for example in the sectoral terms of trade between grain, livestock and trees, permanently undermined the value of investment in these sectors. Farmers went on manuring land, planting and protecting trees and keeping livestock.

Prospect

Can a low-density, extensive system such as that of Sharken Hawsa, intensify along 'low external input' lines like the Tumbau system? We can relate the two in terms of a single model of change (Fig. 8.8).

This model offers five options for a farming system, which reflect the decisions made by smallholders such as those of Tumbau or of Sharken Hawsa. The first is irreversible degradation. Few African smallholders wish to preside over the destruction of their natural resources and, while institutional safeguards (such as

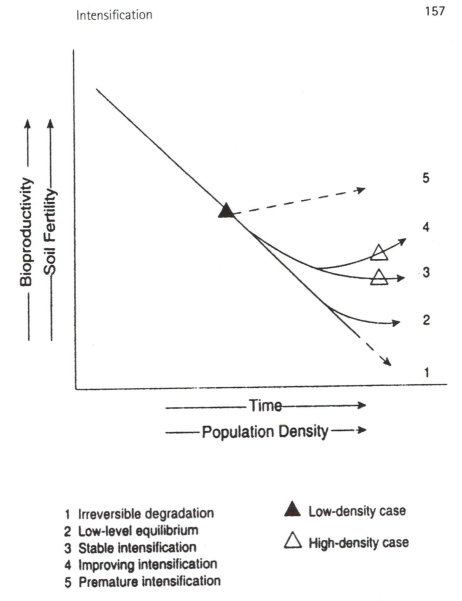

1 Irreversible degradation   ▲ Low-density case
2 Low-level equilibrium
3 Stable intensification   △ High-density case
4 Improving intensification
5 Premature intensification

Figure 8.8 The transition from degradation to intensification in a dryland farming system.

security of tenure) are sometimes lacking, poverty itself is more likely to promote careful management of private resources. The second, a low-level equilibrium, may be approached on outlying fields in Sharken Hawsa where there are no inputs and crop yields are very low. However, the model suggests that this option is but a transition to more productive management as inputs become available. Tumbau farmers, on the other hand, may either stabilise intensification (with no degradation and no yield improvement) or set it on an improving trajectory (importing inputs to support sustainable improved yields). According to this model, a low-density system proceeds on the downward curve, before the trajectories diverge. The farms of Sharken Hawsa are situated on curves 2 or 3, depending on fertility management; those of Tumbau are situated on curves 3 or 4, depending on farmers' resources of inputs. Where capital (inorganic fertilisers, ploughs, hired labour) is substituted for family labour, a farmer can promote the intensification of his holding; for this to occur, market profits, or income transferred from off-farm activities, are necessary.

The model recognises that intensification at a low population density (curve 5) is premature, because the factor ratios (principally labour to land) are not yet appropriate for intensification. In Sharken Hawsa, if the population density continues to increase, an alternative to curve 2 will soon become necessary. On the other hand, there may be constraints, either within the system itself, or in the political and economic environment, whose identification and removal is necessary. Where the possibility exists, an increase in the labour force improves the feasibility of irrigation, which although a favourite strategy against the riskiness of rainfed farming, has long been dependent on temporary or permanent movements of labour in the lightly populated Sahel (Boulier and Jouve 1988; Jouve 1996).

We conclude that population growth and monetisation are conditions of, rather than obstacles to, sustainable intensification; that the process can cope with variable rainfall; and that, in these two systems, suitable tenure institutions and technologies exist. In the next chapter, the role of technical change is examined in relation to the conservation of natural resources in Machakos.

In ending this examination of the Sharken Hawsa and Tumbau systems, however, the teasing question of the limits of intensification must be raised. As intensification almost always means increased labour inputs, and increasingly often, capital investments as well, more and more is at risk from drought or other causes of production failure; and, to the extent that the process is linked to the growth of the market, capital is at risk from price uncertainties. This is why the discovery of evidences of intensification in the drylands has provoked some surprise. Little is yet known of the levels of risk that are considered intolerable in specific systems, and of the long term trade-off between risk and effort, or between accepting risk from natural and from economic sources.

9   Conservation

Conservation has different meanings for different people. For some it implies the exclusion of humans from protected natural reserves, and for others, the protection of threatened species or habitats in ecosystems that are already occupied or exploited by human populations. The impracticability, as well as the controversial ethics, of giving human needs second place to those of 'nature', has suggested to some writers the need for a multi-purpose strategy which not merely reconciles the sometimes contradictory demands of humans and nature conservation, but goes further to integrate the economic and conservationary management of the same habitats. In urbanised and industrialised Europe, such ideas have far-reaching implications (Adams 1996).

In dryland Africa, conservation thinking has two tributary traditions. The first is the demand, emanating from conservation lobbies in northern countries and tourism ministries of African governments, for protected reserves – protected, that is, from Africans. The drylands contain most of Africa's best known tourist game parks, and tourism is a major earner of foreign exchange in several national economies. The second is the soil conservation movement, which, having its historical roots in the USA in the 1920s and 1930s, became influential in colonial governments in the 1940s and 1950s (Anderson 1984; Huxley 1937; Stocking 1996). The thrust of soil conservation propaganda, particularly in its early years, was that African smallholders were recklessly destroying their natural resources by inappropriate land use practices. This viewpoint was extended to the desertification debate in the 1970s and 1980s (see chapter 7). The seasonality and aridity of the drylands expose them to a high level of erosion risk.

Two questions arise from these preliminary considerations. First, *are* African smallholders as incapable of managing their natural resources sustainably as they have been represented to be? Second, under what conditions do the two objectives of natural resource conservation and sustainable livelihoods converge? Answers to these questions are suggested by a strategic case study of dryland management over sixty years in Machakos District of Kenya. This shows what has been achieved in *one* dryland environment.

Machakos

Machakos is inhabited by agro-pastoralists known as the Akamba, who also populate the neighbouring Kitui District. Historically, the Akamba men looked after the livestock and cleared the land, while the women cultivated small plots for food crops. In the first decade of the twentieth century, the British colonial government imposed boundaries on the indigenous peoples, to make room for white settlement in designated Scheduled Areas (the White Highlands policy). Farms and ranches of European settlers bounded the Ukambani Reserve on two sides; the other two sides abutted uninhabited Crown Lands, whose use the government controlled. Thus encircled, the Akamba, and their livestock, grew in number. It was only with independence in 1962 that the district was increased in size, from less than 7,000 to 13,600 square kilometres, by taking in Crown Land which was no longer excluded from settlement. Between 1932 and 1989, the population of the district grew from 240,000 to 1,393,000, and from the 1950s until after 1985, it grew at an annual rate of more than 3 per cent. By 1979, several locations had exceeded densities of 200 per square kilometre (Fig. 9.1).

Most of Machakos is semi-arid, with the exception of the highest hills in the central and northern area. The annual rainfall averages from 500–1000 mm and is distributed in two short rainy seasons, with a high probability of drought (see Fig. 2.3). Ninety seasonal droughts (seventy of them in runs of two or more consecutive seasons) have occurred during the past century. While the sub-humid highlands (which occupy only 10 per cent of the district) are marginally suited to coffee growing, the remainder of the district is used for growing maize, pigeon peas and beans and keeping livestock. The soils are deficient in carbon, nitrogen and phosphorus and are easily eroded.

This combination of rapid population growth, unreliable rainfall, frequent moisture stress, low soil fertility and high erodibility seems to suggest the likelihood of population-induced degradation occurring on a large scale, and this was indeed the assessment of the reserve in the 1930s and 1940s. After a series of disastrous droughts in the 1930s,

> The Machakos Reserve is an appalling example of a large area of land which has been subjected to uncoordinated and practically uncontrolled development by natives whose multiplication and the increase of whose stock has been permitted, free from the checks of war and largely from those of disease, under benevolent British rule. Every phase of misuse of land is vividly and poignantly displayed in this Reserve, the inhabitants of which are rapidly drifting to a state of hopeless

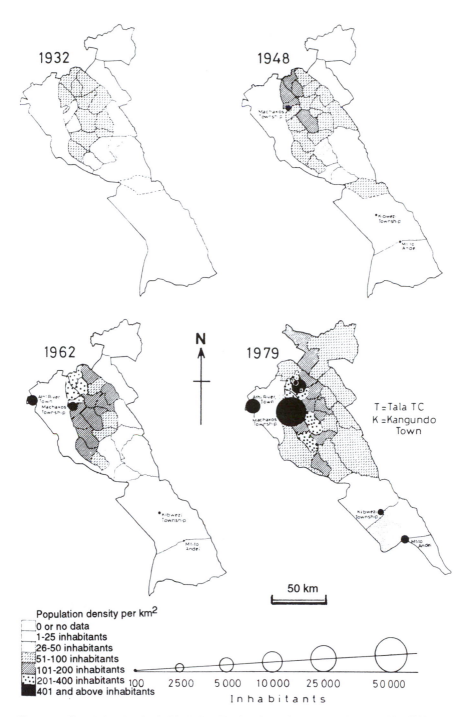

Figure 9.1 Population density in Machakos District, Kenya, in 1932 and in 1979. After Tiffen *et al.* (1994).

and miserable poverty and their land to a parching desert of rocks, stones and sand. (Maher 1937)

The government's recommendations, after commissioning eight visits and reports on Machakos between 1929 and 1939, strongly reflected an official consensus that overstocking, inappropriate cultivation, and deforestation were occurring in the reserve, which was already overpopulated in relation to its carrying capacity. Most of the permanent settlements were concentrated in the sub-humid zone.

Saving soil or water?

In 1931, an agricultural officer was posted to Machakos and he began performing soil conservation experiments with local elders. However, the slow progress of this programme of experimentation and persuasion became increasingly unacceptable, as concern over soil erosion was mounting worldwide at that time (Anderson 1984). In 1937 Maher, who was in charge of the government's soil conservation service, recommended a large-scale programme involving the compulsory removal of people from the worst affected areas. The government also made an attempt to partially destock the reserve of cattle in 1938. This was a failure, but antagonised the already suspicious Akamba.

Fear spread among the Akamba that their land rights, which by custom were established by clearing and cultivation, would be threatened if the work was done by government tractors or labour gangs. They reluctantly accepted compulsory labour on terracing and grass-planting, which was enforced by location chiefs. One person per household had to be sent; it was often a woman because many of the men were working outside the district. Initially, bench terraces constructed by throwing the soil upslope (*fanya juu*) were tried, but after 1940 the 'narrow-based' terrace (made by turning the soil downslope from a ditch) was officially promoted because it saved labour. Bench terraces did not recover official favour until around 1951, though they rapidly became popular with farmers as they were necessary for coffee growing and advantageous for horticulture, both profitable enterprises.

During the years following 1945, an aggressive 'betterment' programme was implemented by the African Land Development Board, which included soil conservation and agricultural extension. The provision of free tools to the farmers made it socially acceptable, and hostility to compulsory labour was gradually overcome. However, the real breakthrough came when compulsory work, directed by officials, was replaced in about 1956 with a variant of the traditional work party, or *mwethya*. The person responsible for calling such a group would provide neighbours with food in return for their labour. The groups were free to choose their technology, and the *fanya juu* method was usually selected. Because these groups were composed mostly of women, women came to hold leadership positions in society almost for the first time.

In the 1950s, more than 40,000 hectares of land were terraced, a situation described by one contemporary observer as a 'Machakos miracle'. However, despite this progress, a hiatus in terracing occurred as independence approached in 1962. The soil conservation programme had been corrupted, in the eyes of many Akamba, by its association with the colonial authority, which was soon to be removed. Many terraces fell into disrepair and few new ones were built. After Kenya became independent, the special funds for soil conservation were not renewed, and staff and resources were switched elsewhere. But from about 1965, a change occurred. Farmers began to terrace again on their own initiative, and to repair the works they had neglected. This was because, over the years, they had seen that crops did better on terraces. This was not the result of soil conservation *per se*. The government had earlier promoted 'narrow-based' terraces, built according to an American model by pushing earth *downslope* from the ditch, and thought to be economical with labour. But the bench or *fanya juu* terrace, which was constructed by building the bank *upslope* from the ditch, had superior moisture retention properties. This improved yields in the dry plains and, in bad years, even on the wetter hills.

Air photographs show that between 1948 and 1961 the net increase in terracing was small, owing to neglect of narrow-based terraces at the end of the period. But between 1961 and 1978, despite the lack of any large-scale government assistance, a remarkable increase occurred (Fig. 9.2). This was achieved by hiring labour (by the better-off farmers) or by participating in *mwethya*. By the 1960s, farmers were settling in large numbers in the former Crown Lands, where, after an initial phase of shifting cultivation, they began to introduce the same conservation techniques.

The drought of 1975 prompted new soil conservation programmes, which were supported by the Swedish government, the local Catholic diocese (supported by some non-governmental organisations) and the European Community (the Machakos Integrated Development Programme). Soil conservation was organised on a catchment basis, especially in the areas of new settlement in the extended district, where farmers had not been able to gather their own resources for the task. In the 1980s, more than 4,500 km of terraces were constructed annually with donor or agency support, compared with a peak of about 5,000 km in the 1950s. However, air surveys show that during the 1980s the actual total constructed was 8,500 km a year. About half, therefore, was the work of farmers unassisted by donors – even at the peak of agency activity. By 1985, 54 per cent of the district's arable land was considered to be adequately conserved and, in hilly areas, no less than 83 per cent. Almost all terraces were of the *fanya juu* or bench type. The achievement may be judged by comparing photographs taken in 1937 with the same sites as they were in 1991(Plate 9).

The Machakos story shows the importance of a substantial improvement in

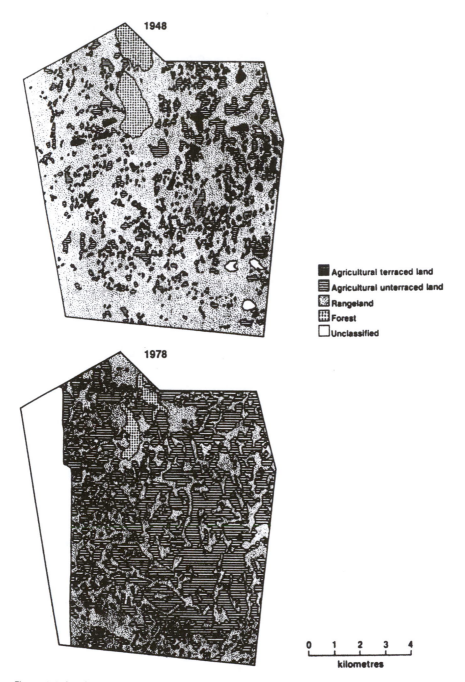

Figure 9.2 Land use and terracing in Masii in 1948 and in 1978. After Rostom and Mortimore (1991).

Plate 9 Resources – natural or human? Landscape transformation at Kiima Kimwe. Machakos, Kenya, photographed in 1937 (upper) and in 1990 (lower).

farmers' profits as an incentive to invest. The bench terrace, despite its higher labour demand, was adopted initially because its water conservation made possible the sale of profitable crops, such as vegetables and coffee. By conserving water, whose uncontrolled runoff is the main cause of soil erosion, bench terraces also conserved the soil and more of the nutrients in the manure that farmers placed on it. Farmers now also use the bench terraces for maize and beans as well. On the other hand, the narrow-based terrace was easily damaged and less effective. This shows the importance of offering farmers a choice of technologies. They are the best judges of the payoff in terms of cost (in work and money) and the benefits they seek. Even so, outside assistance can be of real value in introducing new technologies that farmers can add to their own observations and experiments. A range of other soil and water conservation methods have also been adopted in the district.

A farming revolution

The technical innovations were not restricted to soil and water conservation. Between 1930 and 1990, the production technologies that were either introduced from outside the district or whose use was greatly extended included thirty-five field and horticultural crops, five tillage technologies and six methods of soil fertility management. These technical options added flexibility to the farming system – a great advantage in a risky environment (see chapter 5).

Making money from farming

In the 1930s, most of the Akamba kept their capital in livestock, and occasional sales provided the necessary cash. Farmers who then cultivated for subsistence have since moved into producing market crops. There were three main movements. The first of these was coffee, which some men had learnt to grow while working on European farms. It was opened to African producers in 1954, after prolonged agitation against a restriction which had protected the interests of European producers. It was the most successful market crop until its price fell in the 1980s. Strict rules were enforced on its growing, processing and marketing, and its need for terraces helped drive the conservation movement when the coffee 'boom' of the 1970s greatly extended the numbers of producers. Although it is grown only in sub-humid hills (and a few drier locations), coffee helped to spread prosperity throughout the district through the demand of coffee growers for labour, food crops and livestock products, as well as for non-farm products and services which generated 41 per cent of rural incomes in 1982.

Sharply contrasted with coffee was the experience of cotton growing. This was promoted by the government as a market crop for the drier areas. Like coffee

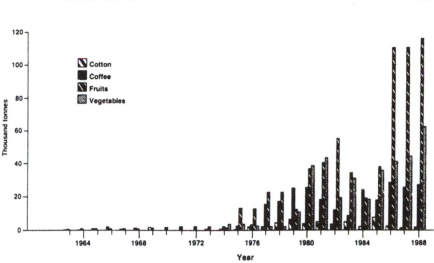

Figure 9.3 Recorded output of four market crops in Machakos District from 1963 to 1988.
After Mbogoh (1991).

growers, cotton growers received governmental assistance in the forms of extension advice, seed and fertiliser inputs, supervision, grading and pricing. But
notwithstanding public investments in roads and trucks, stores and a ginnery,
cotton production never took hold in the district, because its profitability is low;
the demands of its cultivation conflict with those of other crops; and the state
marketing system fell behind in paying the farmers. Farmers have turned their
backs on this option.

On the other hand, the third movement into market crops, fruit and horticulture, owed very little to government support. Its early promotion (starting from
the 1930s) was closely linked with the growth of Kenya's canning industry and
Nairobi's retail markets, which were often supported by itinerant Asian buyers.
The same channels now reach export markets via Nairobi airport. A generally high
value of fruit crops per hectare facilitated the skilful exploitation of wet micro-
environments even in the driest areas, as well as the development of certain technologies, such as micro-irrigation and the cultivation of bananas in pits. Women
found fruit production attractive because trees do not compete with the food
crops (for which they are often responsible) for either land or labour.

The differences between these three movements into market production (Fig.
9.3) show the diversity of the Akamba response to economic opportunities. They
also show that, given incentives, they have been innovative in both their production and marketing practices. Meanwhile, livestock sales, on which they depended
for income in the late 1930s, have declined steadily, although they remain important in drier areas and in drought years.

Experimenting with staple food options

White maize is the staple food of the Akamba. Having two short growing seasons and a high probability of drought calls for varieties that either resist drought, or escape it by maturing quickly. In 1968, the government's local research station released a drought-escaping variety known as Katumani Composite B (KCB) maize.

It was energetically promoted by the extension service. It is not known, however, how much of the maize area is planted with KCB, nor what proportion of KCB makes up total output. Of forty farmers interviewed in various locations in 1990, only a third said they grew it exclusively, and another third said they grew it along with other varieties. Thus KCB failed to usher in a 'green revolution'.

Given the unpredictable rainfall, the new maize gave farmers an additional option. The local varieties, though slower to mature, yield better in dry years. In wetter upland sites, hybrid maize (which has been outstandingly successful in other parts of Kenya) does better. In combination with other varieties, KCB strengthens rather than undermines this flexibility. Some farmers cross-pollinate KCB with the local varieties to achieve desirable traits, only buying new KCB seed every two or three years.

With and without KCB, the district managed to increase its food crop production per person in line with population growth from 1930 to 1987, and its dependence on imported food, measured per person, was less in the period 1974–85 than it had been in 1942–62. Major droughts occurred in both periods.

Introducing faster tillage

The ox-plough, introduced to the district as early as 1910, was being used by about 600, or 3 per cent, of the district's households by the 1930s. Farmers trained their cattle to plough, and ploughs were cheap. Furthermore, the technology was being developed and tested on nearby European farms where some Akamba worked. By owning ploughs, farmers could greatly increase the area they could cultivate, and this enabled them to sell maize or pulses. It also made shifting cultivation inefficient and row planting, which facilitates weeding, necessary.

After World War II, the use of ploughs increased as ex-soldiers returned from India with the money needed to buy them. Also, earnings from employment outside the district were used to buy ploughs. The government imposed a plough-based system on the newly settled area at Makueni after 1946, and provided some credit for their purchase, as did some Asian traders. Coffee, horticulture and cotton (in some years) generated investment funds for buying more ploughs. By the 1980s, 62 per cent (or more) of farmers owned a plough, with the rest being either too poor to buy one, or having fields too small and steep for ploughing with oxen.

The plough proved to be both a durable and a flexible technology. Initially, ploughs with teams of six or eight oxen were used to open new land. Lighter, two-oxen ploughs were later developed for work on small, terraced, permanent fields. The Victory mouldboard plough is now used everywhere, and for several operations – primary ploughing, seedbed preparation, and interrow weeding. It saves labour, and its use by women frees men for off-farm employment. Though much criticised on technical grounds, attempts to improve it have failed to gain wide acceptance. The 'oxenisation' of Akamba agriculture shows how capitalisation was achieved in a risk-prone dryland environment.

Fertilising the soil

Akamba farmers once relied on long fallows to replenish the soil. In the 1930s, there was very little systematic manuring and the fertility of arable land, as measured by yields, was low. The Agricultural Department favoured farmyard manure over inorganic fertilisers, and promoted composting. But it was not until the 1950s that manuring became widespread in the northern sub-humid areas, where most arable fields were by then permanent, and cultivated twice a year. The subsequent widespread adoption of manuring can be seen in the fact that by the 1980s, nine out of ten farmers were doing it, in both wetter and drier areas. Now most of the arable land in the district is cultivated twice a year – in both rainy seasons.

Manure is made in the *boma* (stall or pen) and supplemented with burned trash and waste. The amount applied is constrained by the numbers of livestock, and on how much labour, transport and cash are available when needed. A few can afford imports from neighbouring ranches. Farmers know that, under present technical and economic conditions, sustaining output depends on using *boma* manure. Few can afford large quantities of inorganic fertilisers, which are little used and then mostly on coffee.

Labour-intensive methods of soil fertility management are a part of the smallholder's logic of intensification.

Feeding the livestock

In the 1930s, the women cultivated food crops at home, while the men took the livestock to common grazing lands in the southern part of the reserve or, by permit, to Crown Lands for several months of the year. After about

1960, settlement on Crown Lands could no longer be restrained, and, as thousands of families moved into them, common access to grazing was extinguished by private enclosures. Each household must now maintain its animals on the family farm or obtain permission to use another family's land, often in return for some rent or service.

More than 60 per cent of the cattle, sheep or goats are stall-fed or tethered for part or all of the year. Cutting fodder and bringing residues to the animals when they are in the *boma* require additional labour. Fodder grass is grown on terrace banks, residues lie in cultivated fields, and feed is cut from hedges and wayside verges. The change from pasture grazing to stall feeding is most noticeable in the sub-humid hills.

The effort required to maintain livestock made grade or cross-bred cattle popular (estimated to be about 12 per cent of the total as long ago as 1983). Their milk yields and value are superior to those of the native zebu, though their increased health risks call for frequent dipping and they require more food and water. They can be kept even in the driest parts. In these ways, therefore, a reduction in access to pasture has driven a revolution in livestock keeping which extends beyond feed management to crop–livestock integration (the production of fodder on farms and manure making), adoption of more productive breeds and better health care.

Farming the trees

In the 1920s, the Forest Department believed that afforestation was necessary to arrest environmental desiccation and to fulfil the growing need for domestic fuel and construction timber. For the next several decades, the department struggled, with insufficient resources, to reserve and replant hilltop forests. In 1984, when estimates put the need for new plantations at 226,000 hectares (fifteen times the area of the government's forest reserves), the destruction of surviving natural woodland seemed imminent.

However, pictures of sites photographed in both 1937 and 1991 show little sign of woodland degradation (Plate 9). A fuel shortage on the scale predicted failed to develop, and the district does not import wood or charcoal in large quantities. The miscalculation can be explained partly by the fact that the consumption estimates on which the predictions were based ignored the use the Akamba make of dead wood, farm trash, branch wood from farm trees and hedge cuttings, for their domestic fires. A failure to appreciate a major area of innovative practice – the planting, protection and systematic harvesting of trees – also contributed to the miscalculation. Forest reservation had always been unpopular with the Akamba, who suspected the colonial government of alienating their land. Its increasing costs and difficulties forced a shift in policy from reservation to on-farm forestry promotion in the 1970s. While this shift was going on, however, a revolution was already occurring, as the following example shows.

Tree densities on farmlands in Mbiuni Location, according to a survey of 1982, averaged more than thirty-four per hectare (fourteen when bananas are excluded). Furthermore, the smaller the farm, the greater the density (Gielen 1982). The range of trees planted included both exotic and indigenous fruit and timber species. In general, the women manage fruit trees, while the men look after (and sell) timber trees. The care of trees is currently being extended from cultivated fields to grazing land, where owners manage the regeneration of woody vegetation, for timber, fuel, fodder, honey production and edible and medicinal products.

Tree farming increases the value of output per hectare, both on arable and on grazing land, without substantially increasing the labour required. Furthermore, as many trees (fruit trees in particular) are farmed by women, they add to their personal incomes.

Producing more with less

Over time, as the size of family holdings shrank owing to subdivision of the land on inheritance, the cultivated proportion of the district rose, the amount of cultivated land per person declined, and less land was left for grazing, so agricultural intensification became imperative. Figure 9.2 shows the changes in land use, and also the expansion of terracing onto all arable land, that occurred between 1948 and 1978 in one area. The progression of these changes was greater in wetter than in drier areas, and in older than in newer settled areas. Crop and livestock enterprises became more integrated within the bounds of the family farm.

Two trends – one toward intensive livestock feeding systems and the other toward permanent manured fields, often under plough cultivation – were pivotal in this transformation. The result of these trends is an increasingly efficient system of nutrient cycling through plants, animals and soil, but the changes could not have occurred without the Akamba custom that the first man to clear and cultivate the land owned it. He was then free to sell it or to pass it on to the sons of the wife who helped him to cultivate it. Older sons often established a new farm after their marriage, but, as land became scarce, they insisted on their right to share their mother's land, which earlier they might have relinquished to their youngest brother. Some of those who inherited small farms in the 1960s and 1970s sold them and moved to new land elsewhere in the district, but others stayed and invested in improving productivity. Although formal registration of

Table 9.1 *Farm sizes, investment and incomes in Mwala, Machakos, Kenya in 1980.*

Class	Farm size (hectares)	Cropped area (percent)	Cash inputs (per cultivated hectare)	Livestock (per hectare)	Net farm income (per hectare)
1	1.3	77	331	3.5	1,619
2	3.2	50	191	1.9	611
3	7.5	25	167	1.3	135
4	17.8	18	135	0.7	154

Notes:
A livestock unit is one head of cattle or five sheep or goats. Cash figures are in Kenya shillings.
Source: Rukandema *et al.* (1981).

title did not begin in Machakos until 1968, and is not yet complete, the strong customary ownership rights have ensured that the investors and their children reap the rewards of foresight.

Equally important in the transformation were the sources of investment capital. To clear and cultivate new land, build hedges or plant trees often requires hiring labour, tools or expertise. The off-farm incomes earned outside the district by Akamba men have contributed for decades to agricultural investment. Such incomes are often higher in households with smaller farms, where cash inputs and farm income per hectare, as well as cropped area and the number of livestock, may be higher (Table 9.1).

This process of intensification resulted in an overall increase in the value of output per square kilometre (at constant prices) from 1930 to 1987 (Fig. 9.4). This conclusion was reached by taking output data for the only three years for which they were available before 1974 (1930, 1957 and 1961), selecting two later years (1977 and 1987), and converting all the values into a maize equivalent at 1957 prices. Because 1957 was a good year and 1961 a drought year, the upward trend appears interrupted. A continuous series of annual data would have shown many more such irregularities, but the same trend. Although the size of the district doubled after independence in 1962, yet the upward trend continued. Output per person reflected this curve.

Facilitating change

Many social and institutional factors facilitated the agricultural changes in Machakos. Between 1930 and 1990, the often polygynous, patriarchal family, in which wives and cattle were highly valued, evolved into a smaller unit

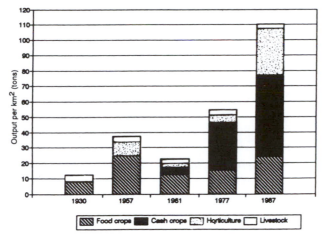

Figure 9.4 Farm output (per square km) in Machakos District, 1930–87, in constant 1957 maize prices. After Tiffen *et al.* (1994).

characterised by a greater partnership between a man and (one) wife. With the men away, the women were often left in charge of the farms. A flexible division of labour and longer working hours are called for in intensive farming, and families may pool their resources for collective effort through membership in *mwethyas*. Women's participation and leadership have been crucial to many of these groups. Although farms are smaller now than they were in the 1930s, labour is still in short supply because children and young people are at school (often to the age of twenty), and, on average, one of the adults is engaged in an off-farm activity.

Local leadership has evolved from a system of appointed chiefs, obliged to collaborate with the colonial administration and not always respected for that, into a system where there are competing organisations and interest groups, often with an elected element. These include the strong local churches as well as the political party, co-operatives and other associations. These groups enable people to articulate their needs and to obtain access to resources available at the local, district, national and even international levels. Such organisations become stronger as populations become more dense and people can interact more easily.

With more people, it also becomes cheaper per person to provide services, including education. The missions and schools, but also markets and travel, have facilitated formal education, the acquisition of technical knowledge and experimental attitudes. Education and skill training have made employment possible, for both men and women, outside the district, which in turn has brought investment funds back to house and farm.

Government attempts to influence the course of change relied too much, especially before the middle of the 1950s, on coercive or directive methods. Yet from the many techniques tried, with varying success, the Akamba seemed to gain experience that stood them in good stead when, after independence, they came to feel more in control of their resources and destiny.

Were the achievements in Machakos due to disproportionate investment of public funds? From 1947 to 1962, 32 per cent of the African Land Development Board's spending was in the district. Yet much of this was lost (for example, in subsidising terraces that were not maintained). The most lasting effects of the programme were small dams, resettlement, better farming promotion and tsetse fly control. More recently, the Machakos Integrated Development Programme did not exceed the average spending (on a per person basis) for Kenya's arid lands as a whole. The greatest proportion was on local water supplies, and its smaller soil conservation programme supplemented local efforts. Its spending on roads was often lost through inadequate maintenance, while the Akamba contributed much communal work to building feeder roads, a priority that has always been recognised and is closely linked to innovation. Particularly since independence, the government's main role in the Machakos transformation was to pursue an open market path to economic development, provide national economic infrastructure, support individual title to land and promote channels for learning and communicating new or adapted knowledge.

Contrary to the expectations expressed in the 1930s, the Akamba of Machakos have reversed land degradation, conserved and enhanced their tree stocks, invested in their farms, achieved substantial technical change, improved overall productivity and participated more fully and more profitably in the market. What happened resulted from a combination of factors: increasing population density, market growth, and a generally supportive economic environment. A positive link between productivity and improved resource management has been demonstrated.

Development planners in the past tried to transform farming systems that were seen as inefficient and technically conservative. As late as 1967, pessimism was still being expressed about the slow pace of change in Machakos (de Wilde *et al.* 1967: 84–120). In fact, the farmers have been changing their systems themselves, and, as studying them over time shows, there is room to support positive change with appropriate policies. The Machakos study showed that a high-density population in an area that is steep and dry can be sustained through a combination of exogenous practices and much local initiative.

Investing in sustainability

Over a period of sixty years, the Akamba of Machakos both put a trend of land degradation into reverse, and improved the sustainability of their livelihood system. These objectives are mutually compatible and consistent with the indigenous management of technical change – which, as we have seen, takes full advantage of new technical options when they meet recognised needs and are efficient in using the factors of production. The Machakos experience is consistent with that of the slower-evolving but more intensive system of the Kano Close-Settled Zone (see chapter 8).

For too long it was assumed that the drylands are constrained primarily by inherent productivity limitations (such as poor soil and unreliable rainfall), and that there is an inadequate economic payoff to land-improving investments (Gorse and Steeds 1987), rather than an unrealised capability for improvement through soil and water conservation and new, adapted or indigenous technologies (Reij *et al.* 1996). To a very considerable extent, these investments have, in the past, been created by labour, and are therefore within the means of capital-starved production systems. In the present, capital from outside agriculture may be employed to a greater extent than is realised, thanks to urbanisation and the growth of markets.

If the role of government and development agencies should no longer solely be understood in terms of evangelising reluctant farmers or stockbreeders with new, 'improved' technologies, it should nevertheless be clear from such case studies that there is a paramount need for an enabling policy environment, in which indigenous capital resources can be effectively mobilised, and the merits of technical options explored by farmers themselves.

This chapter is based, with the permission of Heldref Publications, on: Michael Mortimore and Mary Tiffen (1994), 'Population growth and a sustainable environment: the Machakos story', *Environment*, 36(8): 10–20, 28–32. For a critique, see: 'More on Machakos', *Environment*, 37(7): 3–5; 42–43; and for a somewhat different interpretation, Rocheleau *et al.* (1995).

10 Systems in transition

The limitations of an equilibrial view of dryland ecosystems (chapter 4) are now recognised. The concept of instability, or disequilibrium, offers an alternative basis for understanding their short-term dynamics. What of long-term changes? As soon as we extend the timeframe of our analysis, it becomes apparent that many dryland ecosystems are in transition between one state and another, or always have been in transition, driven by climate change, the progressive development of soil formations, erosion cycles, and episodic natural events like volcanic eruptions, droughts and floods. Indeed, when the timeframe is lengthened, *all* ecosystems may be vulnerable to extreme or 'surprise' events, whether they emanate from outside or from within the system, as 'accidents waiting to happen' (Holling 1987).

For policy purposes, the timescale is important. Because of their frequency, extreme events in the drylands offer a challenging laboratory for working out an appropriate interface between technology and nature. Two main management modes are available (*ibid.*). The 'technological–industrial' mode seeks to control variability and reduce diversity – as in livestock ranching systems. It thereby increases the vulnerability of both ecosystems and production systems (unless financial institutions protect the latter). On the other hand, a 'low technology' mode of management – as used by indigenous dryland peoples – seeks to adapt to variability and to exploit diversity. It thereby strengthens the resilience of both the ecosystem and the production system.

Ecosystems in transition

Short-term instability is superimposed on longer-term transitions. The historical wavelength of some of these changes (which can be measured in human generations, or even in decades) is small enough to make them relevant to natural resource management. The 'Little Ice Age', for example, had effects in Europe in the late seventeenth century, which are well-known from the historical record. This was a mere flutter in the longer term process of global warming after the last major advance of ice in the northern hemisphere. Studies of African lakes show changes in level which reflect changes in the precipitation (fluvials and inter-fluvials), which were themselves linked, through global circulation of the atmosphere, to glacial fluctuations in northern Europe (Nicholson 1978).

The Sahel shows how a progressive shortening of the timeframe (and different research methods) can link change on a geological scale with the year-by-year struggles of the smallholder. Between 18,000 and 10,000 years ago, at the time of the last major glacial advance in high latitudes, reduced rainfall extended the Sahara southwards, into what is now Nigeria, as far as Lat. 12°N (Grove and Pullan 1964; Maley 1981; McTainsh 1984, 1987; Nichol 1991). The effects of this (or an earlier) desert transgression can be seen in topographical rhythms of dunes and interdunes, land use patterns and on transformed satellite imagery (Pl. 10). Differences in soil properties between former dunes and interdunes, even when they are invisible on the ground or on air photographs, are diligently taken into account by farmers in choosing sites for the cultivation of different crops.

However, between 10,000 and 8,000 years ago, a renewal of humid conditions took place, and herding and fishing communities came into the southern Sahara. Lake Chad expanded to many times its present size, creating a beach ridge along its western shore, which still forms a prominent landmark. After 4,500 years ago, conditions became more arid, and the lake retreated to its present lower, and still fluctuating, level.

Lake-bed sediments in the Manga region to the west of Lake Chad (Lat. 13° 15' N) reveal changes which indicate that humid and relatively arid phases alternated during the last five and a half millennia (Holmes *et al.* 1997). These changes are in lithology, in the flora and fauna (pollens and ostracods) and in the amounts of carbonate, organic carbon and desert dust found in the cores. Climatic deterioration began in the Sahel, this evidence suggests, about 4,000 years ago (Fig. 10.1). Lake water became more saline, and total organic carbon decreased. The sediments became sandier and arboreal pollens declined, relative to those of grasses. Later, between about 1200 and 1000 years ago, the changing chemistry of ostracod shells indicates severe and prolonged drought, followed again by wetter conditions.

Major droughts, persisting from one to two decades, have been reconstructed from historical and other data of the last five centuries (Nicholson 1978). During the sixteenth to eighteenth centuries, droughts were less frequent and rainfall higher: this was contemporary with the Little Ice Age in Europe. Lake Chad rose. Nevertheless there were severe droughts in the 1680s and between 1710 and 1760 (Fig. 10.2). A major increase in the frequency of droughts, and a long-term fall in the level of Lake Chad, occurred after 1800. There are many historical records of

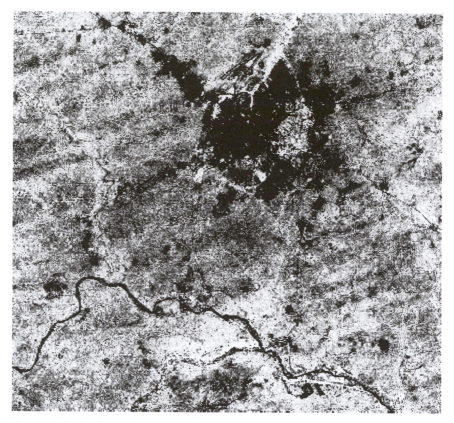

Plate 10 Urbanisation on desert dunes? The Quaternary landscape of Metropolitan Kano revealed by earth satellite imagery (Landsat TM vegetation index, Band 4/Band 2, 19 December, 1986). The darker the tone, the less the vegetation.

droughts in the nineteenth century, culminating in those of the final decade and the great drought of 1913–14 in West Africa.

Rainfall fluctuations during the period of instrumental records (of 100 years or less, in most of inland sub-Saharan Africa) show that another drier period began in the Sahel during the late 1960s (Farmer and Wigley 1985; Hess *et al.* 1994; Hulme 1992; Nicholson 1983). Such observed trends raise the question of how contemporary global warming, whether or not it is being driven by 'greenhouse gas' emissions, may affect the rainfall in dryland Africa – unfortunately, the models that are available still disagree on the direction and severity of the changes predicted for different parts of the drylands (Hulme 1994a).

The ecological significance of long-term rainfall fluctuations is suggested by short-term changes in the vegetation along the southern boundary of the Sahara,

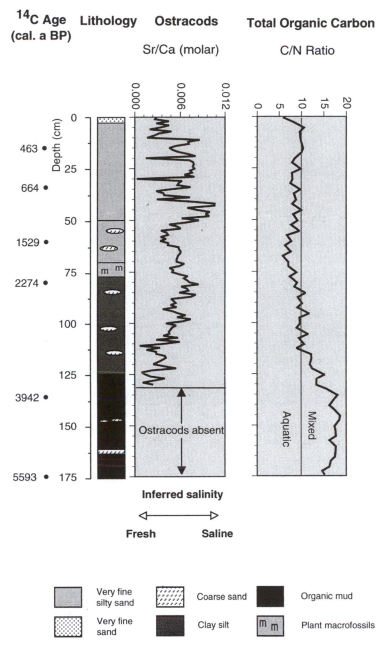

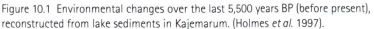

Figure 10.1 Environmental changes over the last 5,500 years BP (before present), reconstructed from lake sediments in Kajemarum. (Holmes *et al*. 1997).

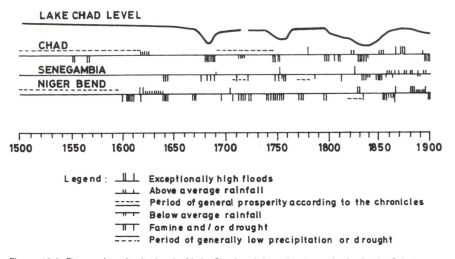

Figure 10.2 Fluctuations in the level of Lake Chad and drought chronologies in the Sahel (Nicholson 1978).

which in recent years has moved by as much as 100 km north or south between wet and dry years (Tucker *et al.* 1991) (Fig. 10.3). During the drought cycle of the early 1980s, the departure of the annual rainfall from the long-term mean increased each year, from 13 per cent in 1980 to 55 per cent in 1984; and the area of the Sahara Desert was estimated to have increased by over 15 per cent. This increase was later reversed. We must expect that these short-term changes replicate, on a smaller spatial scale and a shorter timespan, the longer-term fluctuations described above (Fig. 10.4).

The essence of the drylands is that their physical characteristics are affected by pendulum swings in time and space between relatively dry and relatively humid conditions. In both the arid and the humid zones, conditions over the long term may approach more closely the concept of a stable equilibrium, for there were 'refuge areas' where rain forests survived even during the driest climatic regressions (Thomas and Thorp 1993).

In summary, we can say that dryland ecosystems are (a) unstable and disequilibrial in the short term, and (b) transitional in the longer term. Since humans occupied the drylands, and began to use fire as a management tool, their activities have added to the complexity of ecological change. For example, deforestation in the Sahel has been linked, in theory, with changes in surface reflectance or in soil moisture, which in turn may affect the rainfall; and grazing by domestic livestock is a contributory factor in the encroachment of thorn thickets in southern and eastern Africa (chapter 7).

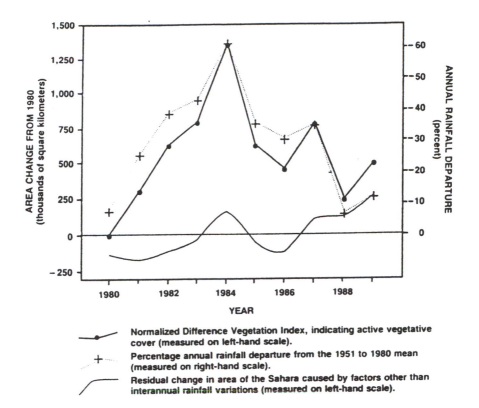

Figure 10.3 Change in the area of the Sahara from 1980 to 1989 (Hulme and Kelly, 1993 after Tucker *et al*. 1991).

Production systems in transition

How should we conceive of change in human systems? It was argued in chapters 4, 5 and 6 that they, too, show unstable or disequilibrial character-istics. Opportunistic stocking or cropping strategies, adaptive technological capa-bilities and diversification (both technical and economic) are all forms of response to the risks imposed by such instability. Human systems also change through time in response to slow changes in the ecosystem. A prehistoric example of such response was the contraction of human settlements around permanent water in the southern Sahara, as the rainfall declined, pastures diminished and hunting or collecting became more difficult 5–4,000 years ago. The origins of crop cultiva-tion in lake basins and river valleys may have been associated with climatic

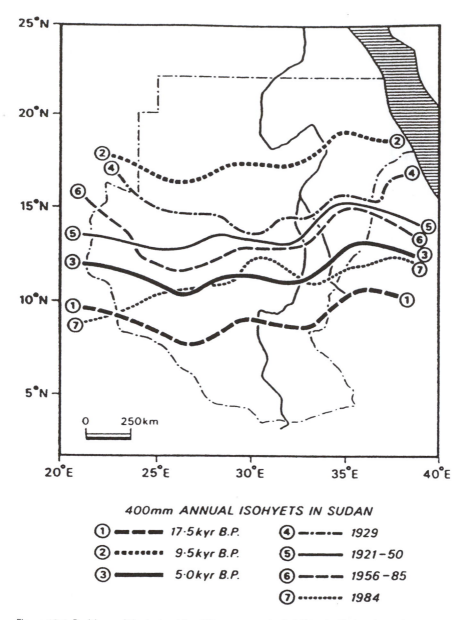

Figure 10.4 Positions of the isohyet for 400 mm annual rainfall in the Sudan, for various centuries in the Holocene and years in the twentieth century. After Hulme (1990).

desiccation in northern Africa and the Near East; certainly they were contemporaneous with it.

However, it is often difficult to say to what extent a given transition is caused by exogenous natural factors and to what extent by endogenous or internal ones. Such is the case with the degradation hypothesis: disentangling the effects of short-term climatic events (especially droughts) and long-term climate change (especially rainfall decline), on the one hand, from those of population growth, land tenure, markets, technological change, or others (each of which is the subject of a feedback hypothesis) is so difficult that some authorities have preferred to use the vague idea of a 'nexus' of interrelated factors whose interactions, though accepted, cannot yet be specified in exact terms (Cleaver and Schreiber 1994).

If degradation is a loss of bioproductivity in a system in transition, then it is more important to understand the dynamics of the system as a whole than merely measuring (or estimating) single indicators like soil or vegetational loss. Where we look for such indicators, we are quite likely to find them. For example, the *World atlas of desertification* records soil degradation and water erosion, of medium or high severity, throughout most of England (UNEP 1992: 10, 14). How relevant is such an assessment? Since the Middle Ages, English farming has evolved from low-productive, short-fallow systems to capital-intensive methods where output is dependent primarily on input levels, where over-production must be controlled by quotas and subsidies. This transformation, including technological change, the substitution of capital for labour, the transfer of rural labour to cities, and the complete monetisation of production systems, was not incremental but dynamic. That is to say, neither the direction nor the structure of change could have been accurately predicted at the outset.[1]

The degradation hypothesis (chapter 7), because it dwells on indicators, predicts negative incremental change and certain outcomes for dryland production systems. It denies – or underrates – the possibility of dynamic transition to structurally different systems. The Kano and Machakos systems (chapters 8 and 9) suggest that even under the constraints of a dryland environment, dynamic transitions are possible. In place of negative incremental change and ecological collapse, there has been dynamic transformation (of some complexity), involving changes in the relations between the components. These have included technological change, labour intensification, the beginnings of capital substitution, income diversification, monetisation, and (in Machakos) significant institutional changes. Consequently, positive incremental change has occurred, contrary to expectations, in bioproductivity and in conservation.

Four grand themes may be discerned in the dynamic transition of the production systems of Africa's drylands:

Table 10.1 *Transitions in the human systems of the drylands.*

Transition	Components	Arbiter of change
Land use intensification	Labour/capital intensification Crop–livestock integration Conservation Tree husbandry	Population density Technologies Investment resources Value of products
Economic diversification	Monetisation Income diversification Mobility	Urbanisation Markets
Institutional change	Changes in law or custom Social differentiation New division of labour Education Development interventions	Institutional reform Wealth distribution Gender and age roles Access to education Government finance
Demographic transition	Fertility behaviour	Mortality Fertility preferences

(1)   land use intensification,
(2)   economic diversification,
(3)   social institutional change, and
(4)   demographic transition (Table 10.1).

On them depends sustainability, both of natural resources and of economic livelihoods. As we examine these transitions, it is clear that they are much more than cultural responses to irresistible exogenous factors. Degradation has often been linked to a deterministic view of adaptative behaviour, as shown in the following quotations from popular publications:

> No other region [than Africa] more tragically suffers the vicious cycle of poverty leading to environmental degradation, which leads in turn to even greater poverty. (Bruntland 1987)

> The rural poor, many of whom live in environmentally fragile areas, are both the main victims and the unwilling architects of soil degradation. (OXFAM 1993)

> Increasing numbers of poor families can only stay alive by destroying their own natural resource base. (Camp 1992: 25)

On the contrary, these transitions should be understood as purposive and open-ended. They are characterised by jagged trend lines, indicating reversals as well as advances. They incorporate their own internal feedback mechanisms, that is to say, the adoption of certain strategies creates the preconditions for other

Table 10.2 *The intensification of crop production.*

Dryland constraints	Steps	Livestock interaction
	10 Labour-saving technologies introduced (plough ...)	Livestock for traction
Labour export to urban or humid zone	9 Scarcity of labour	
Few technical options?	8 Productivity improvements: higher value crops tree inter-crops new inputs agronomic changes	Browse for livestock
Moisture more limiting than soil	conservation investments	Risk of damage to works
	7 Increased effort on refertilisation	Livestock for manure Crop residues for livestock
Moisture limiting	6 Increased effort on weeding to save moisture and nutrients	
Rainfall variable	5 Crop yields per ha decrease	Limited supply of manure
Slow natural recovery of fertility	4 Fallow fraction decreases (fallow frequency decreases)	Less grazing for livestock
	3 Cultivated fraction increases (cultivation frequency increases)	
	2 Available land per person decreases	
	1 Agriculturally dependent population increases (population density increases)	

adaptive changes. Whether the outcome is degradation or sustainable resource management, whether it is greater poverty or economic growth, and whether it is increased or diminished social differentiation, must be judged from the results of empirical observations, rather than from intuitively cyclical models of change that permit only one conclusion.

The transition of intensification

Generalising from the Kano and Machakos case studies, the steps of intensification in a cropping system may be schematically represented as ten steps of a 'ladder', which must be climbed (Table 10.2). At all stages in the model, basic

Table 10.3 *The intensification of livestock production.*

Dryland constraints	Steps	Crop interactions
Seasonal variability of biomass	9 Productivity improvements: enclosure of private pastures higher value stock animal health improvements replanting	
	stall-feeding, cut-and-carry conservation investments	Animals available for traction, more manure
	8 Purchase or production of fodder	Mixtures, rotations, fodder plots
	7 Increased use of residues	Privatisation of residues Manuring fields
Surface water scarce	6 Increased effort watering animals	Restricted access to wells
	5 Splitting and diversifying herds to use biomass efficiently	
Patchy grazing	4 Increased effort moving herds	Barriers to movement
Low biomass of natural vegetation	3 Available pasture per animal unit decreases	Increased cultivation
	2 Livestock population density increases (animal units per ha increase)	
	1 Dependent population increases	

dryland constraints affect the outcomes; and the Table also suggests that the inter-action of crops with livestock is an indispensable part of the process. Towards the top (step 8), the market has a profound impact on progression, adding profitable options which in turn generate investment, as in Machakos (chapter 9).

For livestock producers, the ladder of intensification can be represented in another way (Table 10.3). Again the starting point is an increase in the human population, triggering an increase in livestock; and the market comes into play in step 9. Crop interaction is well-developed at this stage, except where aridity pre-cludes cropping.

The integration of crop and livestock production takes place at rising steps in the two 'ladders', and it is difficult to see how small producing units in rainfed areas can move to high levels of either intensity or market integration without it, as specialised production is more dependent on external inputs, which tend to be uneconomic in dryland conditions. This model of intensification is a special 'dry-lands case' of the general model first formalised by Boserup (1965). The impact of dryland constraints is felt at several steps in the crop production 'ladder', in particular on soil moisture constraints on crop growth, and in the few technical options available (though this constraint may have been exaggerated). On the livestock production 'ladder', they are felt on pasture distribution and productivity, on water availability, and in the effects of seasonality and variability on the technical options available.

Agricultural intensification driven by increasing population density was observed in the African drylands before Boserup published her thesis, for example in northern Nigeria (Grove 1952, 1961; Mortimore and Wilson 1965; Prothero 1962) and northern Ghana (Hunter 1967). Many studies and syntheses subsequently investigated its wider validity in Africa (Gleave and White 1969; Netting 1993; Prothero 1972; Turner *et al.* 1993). The relations between crop–livestock integration and the 'Boserupian' hypothesis in Africa have been explored empirically and formally by Pingali *et al.* (1987). A trend towards more integrated crop and livestock production has been observed throughout the major agro-ecological zones of Africa (McIntire *et al.* 1992), and in the semi-arid zone in particular (Mortimore and Turner 1991).

Can the transition to more intensive forms of land use continue indefinitely? Commercial systems in the north have maintained their momentum by means of imported nutrients (inorganic fertilisers). The same solution has often been promoted for African systems of crop production – though it has usually been recognised that for livestock production, fertilisation of pastures cannot be economic. Estimations of the amounts of critical nutrients exported from Africa in groundnuts or cotton suggested that, without compensating imports, the systems would eventually destroy their natural capital. For example, in the 'peanut basin' of Senegal, four-year groundnut rotations without fertiliser were estimated to lose 10–15 kg/ha of phosphorus, 42–63 kg/ha of potassium and 26–44 kg/ha of calcium (Jones and Wild 1975: 211). Groundnuts do not deplete soil nitrogen because their root nodules fix it from the atmosphere. However, in northern Nigeria, it was estimated that 25,000 tons of superphosphate were needed annually to replace the phosphate removed in the export crop of groundnuts in the sixties (*ibid.*: 143–44). Such estimates have been used to link environmental with political exploitation. 'Thus colonial profit-making in peanuts and African poverty at the producer level combined to set in motion a spreading wave of environmental degradation' (Franke and Chasin 1980: 70).

More recently, nutrient budgets have been estimated to balance nutrient losses from all sources with nutrients imported to the system and, not surprisingly, there is more evidence of losses than of gains in tropical Africa (Smaling 1993). One such estimate claims that annual nutrient losses (from exports of economic products from the farm, leaching and volatisation) are running at four times the average level of fertiliser use in sub-Saharan Africa (Stangel 1995). A modelling approach, based on simplified functions of millet and livestock production, crop–livestock interactions, the nitrogen content of the soil and population growth in a Niger farming system produced the conclusion that 'Mineral fertiliser use is an essential technology for increasing the food and feed supply from crop-land and pastures, and for raising farmers' incomes' (McIntire and Powell 1995).

On the other hand, a few intensive systems that have been studied carefully suggest that the scope for raising the productivity of 'low external input agriculture' (Reijntjes and Moolhuijzen 1995), using indigenous technology, may have been underestimated. It is a question of how efficiently nutrients are cycled, or manipulated to achieve the production goals of the farmer, and whether further gains can be made. In the Kano Close-Settled Zone (chapter 8), inorganic fertilisers became widely available only after 1981, and by 1990 they were again scarce and costly, verging on uneconomic. They cannot therefore be given credit for the productivity and sustainability of the system (Harris 1996), which has maintained itself for at least a century at high intensity.

Thus there is a policy choice between seeking improvements in the efficiency of nutrient cycling, on the one hand, and encouraging dependency on imported chemical fertilisers, on the other. The economics of the second option are marginal in the drylands (except where irrigation or high value market crops are concerned), notwithstanding its energetic promotion (for example, van der Graaf and Breman 1993). The shortage of cash at the critical time of year, and the riskiness of short-term investments under variable rainfall, argue that the most realistic approach is to provide an economic and institutional environment for farmers and livestock producers to maximise the productivity of their existing systems with minimal external inputs.

Systems of primary production can change when critical labour or input thresholds are passed, and productivity curves can be stabilised or pointed upwards (Fig. 8.8). A case has been made that tree management in Maradi (Niger), formerly exploitative in nature, has begun to exhibit conservationary practices under the driving force of scarcity (Jouve 1996; Jouet et al. 1996). A new research agenda is called for to understand systems in these dynamic terms.

The transition of economic diversification

The monetisation of dryland rural economies followed in the wake of the colonial promotion of export crops (especially in West Africa) and of labour migration (especially in southern Africa). However, the continuing importance of the subsistence sector in the household economy of smallholders is in itself a testimony to the risks attached to dependence on the market. In most parts of the drylands, it is only when the subsistence sector breaks down (owing usually to a drought or war), that the household becomes completely dependent on monetary income, and that is temporary – unless, as with livestock specialists, it may take several years to return to animal ownership.

The search for alternative incomes begins at home and ends with migration to distant places of employment; thus in food crises, the incidence of both local off-farm activities and short-term mobility increase sharply, to be followed by a drop when household food stocks recover. The growth of the urban and industrial sector is vital to the use of these strategies by more and more households. Owing to a shortage of data, informal economic activity outside agriculture is difficult to assess, but it has positive links with agriculture in Africa as a whole (Haggblade *et al.* 1989). Improved access to opportunities for diversifying incomes assisted resettled populations from areas of West Africa affected by river blindness to improve their living standards in the long term (McMillan 1995). Income diversification was found to be further developed in communities prone to frequent food shortages than in wetter areas further south (Reardon *et al.* 1988).

Risk emanating from political or economic driving factors is increasingly obvious in the drylands, where many of Africa's sudden changes of policy (e.g., the imposition of structural adjustment programmes), transgressions of human rights and wars have taken place. The drylands, however, are no different from more humid zones in their susceptibility to such risks. A case can be made that the risks emanating from the political economy have intensified since the middle of the twentieth century, with marked increases in:

(1)   the involvement of small producers in the world market;
(2)   development interventions designed to transform primary production systems;
(3)   administrative interference from centralised bureaucracies;
(4)   policy uncertainty under autocratic regimes; and
(5)   corruption, maladministration and insecurity.

Ecological risk is 'normal' in the sense of being expected, but unpredictable. Risk emanating from the political economy is sometimes so unstable that adaptive behaviour is not 'normal' in a historical sense: every crisis is new and adaptive response must be improvised. However, while the model of instability is useful, it does not describe all types of change in the economic sphere. Examples of more progressive change are the growth of the population, the extension of the cultivated area, the diminution of natural grazings, urbanisation and the growth of markets. Such changes differ not only in their time-trajectories but also in their persistence. So economic systems may also be said to be in a state of continuous transition.

The management of transition depends on three factors. First is investment. 'Booms' and 'busts' are the result of opportunistic management. In 'busts', divestment (or 'decapitalisation') occurs. The aftermath is dominated by the attempts of small producers to rebuild productive capacity (herds, plough-teams, etc.). The stabilisation or reversal of land degradation depends on investment and on the protection of investment in such crises. The terraces of Machakos, or the fertilised fields of the Kano Close-Settled Zone, are evidence of cumulative investment notwithstanding periodic crises when resources were threatened. How can cumulative investment replace cyclical 'booms' and 'busts'?

The second is the impact of development interventions and government policies. Adaptive capability, based as it is on indigenous knowledge of ecosystems, natural and cultural biodiversity, economic opportunities, and small-scale, diverse forms of response, seems *a priori* to be threatened by 'green revolution' technologies, integrated development programmes with standardised packages, intensified administrative controls and other 'top-down' and inflexible interventions. With regard to policy, the current trend away from regulation and intrusive administration in some countries is consistent with greater local autonomy and flexibility, including the capacity to select and benefit from new knowledge.

The third is the appropriation of diversity. Small farmers and stockraisers have shown themselves able to appropriate new technologies or management modes – new crops, tools, chemicals, vaccines, markets – and income earning opportunities, to extend their technical or economic options. Even as development agencies were promoting specialisation in profitable crops, multiplicity in the sources of technologies, the uses of resources (such as livestock and trees) and the choice of crop enterprises, livestock herds or income sources was becoming more, not less, characteristic. Genetic patenting by international corporations is receiving attention as a threat to such diverse resources. In Machakos, free access to technical and economic information played a role in promoting adaptive technical change (Tiffen *et al.* 1994). Such free access may not be taken for granted in future.

Social institutions in transition

The case-studies of Kano and Machakos (chapters 8 and 9) throw up very contrasting situations of social change. On the one hand, in Machakos, there have been major changes to the family, to the position of women, to leadership roles in the community, in religious affiliation, education and forms of co-operative organisation. Yet the institutional change most often called for in development literature – land tenure reform – has proved to be unnecessary. On the other hand, in Tumbau, a conservative social system, characterised by its hierarchical structure, the subservient position of women, unchanging adherence to Islam and a lack of enthusiasm for formal education has presided over change. The most important form of institutional change in Hausaland appears to be the slow erosion of the economic power of household heads *vis à vis* their male dependants (Hill 1972, 1977), a correlate of individualisation in the creation and distribution of wealth (Raynaut 1980). In Machakos, the changes were revolutionary; in Kano, they continued, in quiet continuity, processes that had been in operation for centuries.

These contrasts emphasise the importance of understanding environmental management in the drylands in its social context. This does not consist in superficially comparing 'snapshots' of present-day cultures and institutions, but rather in exposing the nature of long-term change in the social relations of agriculture, livestock keeping and other activities. These two systems have arrived at positions which are similar in important respects – high population densities, high levels of private investment and high productivity – but by very different routes. This finding suggests that the principles outlined in this book, while narrowly based on specific cases, may be applicable to a wider range of social conditions. African societies are nothing if not adaptive.

The demographic transition

Conventional interpretations of population growth in terms of demographic transition theory exemplify the use of equilibrial assumptions, both about what happened in the past and about what is expected in the future. Thus, concern is often expressed about the fact that a decisive decline in fertility rates in Africa is lagging far behind the fall in mortality rates, departing thereby from the historic experience of the urban–industrial economies. As noted in chapter 6, this lag has been explained in terms of the continuing economic and social value accorded to children (Caldwell 1976, 1982). In sub-Saharan Africa, rates of natural increase were not expected to trend downwards until after 1990, in projections prepared from data up to the 1980s (IUCN 1989). However, total fertility rates (TFRs) are now thought to be trending downwards in all but one of the dryland countries – strongly so in Zimbabwe, Kenya and Botswana, and modestly so in Nigeria, Senegal and Tanzania (Gould and Brown 1996). It is not yet clear whether this change is the beginning of an orthodox demographic transition, or a short-term adjustment to economic recession. Even so, absolute growth will continue rapidly, because in the present population, 45 per cent are under the age of fifteen, and have not yet joined the reproductive age groups.

In place of a demographic transition, many dryland societies have 'modernised' by means of a 'mobility transition'. Large families enjoy certain advantages in a context of migration, circulation and bi-local residence patterns. An influential hypothesis in the literature is that the flows of wealth between generations have an important influence on fertility behaviour. Having survived to adulthood, grown children reverse the dependency relationship which existed between them and their parents during childhood, and may be expected to support their parents with labour, or income, even if they have migrated out of the village.

However, inter-generational support can flow both ways. Financial transfers do, indeed, occur between young adult migrants and their rural parents, though this responsibility is honoured in the breach as much as in observance. However, urban migrants may receive (or collect) cheap food when visiting their villages. In eastern and southern Africa, where out-migration is extensive, and education is considered essential for obtaining urban or migrant employment, absent sons or daughters may send their children home for primary education with the grandparents. Single women with children, lacking the economic support of a husband, may see reproduction as a form of insurance against old age, even more than married people. The more members a household has, the more income streams can be generated through migratory strategies.

A study of population growth and distribution in West Africa concluded that notwithstanding rapid urbanisation, which is estimated to have reached 30 per cent of the population in 1990, the rural populations of the drylands will continue to increase in absolute terms until the year 2020 (Snrech *et al.* 1994). In eastern and southern Africa, some rural dryland populations have been more adversely affected by out-migration. But in the African drylands as a whole, it may safely be stated that most of the population is not going to go away; that evidence for falling fertility is only now beginning to appear; that increase in the productivity of land needs therefore to continue; and that dryland populations must be given access to the employment resources of the more humid zones, in order to diversify their economic base.

Better policies for dryland development

In brief, this study suggests the following conclusions that are relevant to planning and policy for the future of the drylands.

Dryland environments must continue to be managed by dryland households

Primary responsibility for making decisions about the management of natural resources in the drylands will continue to lie where it does now – with dryland households – and for three reasons. First, the intervention capabilities of African governments, increasingly debt-strapped, under-resourced, and depen-

dent on external development aid, are declining in many countries. Grand socialist experiments in centrally planned and directed economic systems (such as those
of Tanzania and Ethiopia) are being dismantled. Subsidies to encourage conservation (Mainguet 1994) are likely to remain beyond the reach of many dryland
governments. Second, development objectives for the rural sector have shifted
dramatically from overt transformation into new, more 'efficient' systems, to providing enabling structures and services, allowing farmers and livestock producers
greater autonomy. Third, confidence in the applicability of scientific prescriptions
to dryland management has been badly dented by many project failures, and
meanwhile there has been a growing recognition of indigenous knowledge
(though its adaptive capacity, especially when enhanced by education, is probably still under-estimated).

To support the conservation and improvement of dryland resources, secure rights to the benefits must be guaranteed

This does not mean that land tenure reform is necessary everywhere.
Customary tenure in many dryland countries is adequately secure, provided that
governments themselves refrain from arbitrary alienation of land. Group tenure
may provide a satisfactory alternative to individual tenure in some cultures.
However, resource access (including not only land, but trees and water) is fluid in
many communities – with, for example, livestock producers losing access to
grazing areas on account of farm expansion, or women losing access to trees or
crops taken over by men on account of their market potential. The benefits of
improvements must be enjoyed by those who invest in them.

The small scale and diversity of production units calls for locationally and culturally appropriate technical and economic options

The use of 'blue-print' development strategies (for example by early
integrated development projects), based on conceptions of the average production unit, tends to predispose project benefits in favour of better-resourced
smallholders who can fulfil the requirements and gain access to the resources on
offer, accentuating economic differentiation in the community. It is much more
difficult to create a 'menu' of options suitable for a variety of individual circumstances. However, the existence of such a 'menu' played an important part in
enabling some systems to evolve to higher productivity.

The adaptive capabilities of dryland households are their major resource

Centuries of experience in managing difficult and risky environments (something which is lacking in the formal training of the professionals who advise them) enables dryland producers to identify their production constraints and both select from and experiment with new options as they become available to them. This argues in favour of on-farm (or on-range) rather than on-station research, driven by participatory rather than by scientific priorities. New technologies are most successful where they extend the options available, rather than supplanting them, and where they permit 'mixing and matching' rather than calling for a green revolution.

Protecting investment against unpredictable crises, particularly in food availability, should become a developmental objective

A view of dryland ecosystems as inherently unstable, and of production systems as adaptive to instability, emphasises that the gains of development interventions may swiftly be lost unless they can be insured against divestment in times of famine, or (even more difficult) against changes in the economic environment that undermine their profitability. To take such an objective on board, development planning must escape from the myopia imposed by the two-, three- or five-year financial plans dictated by donors and government agencies, and also (to be fair) the short-termism demanded by local political constituencies, and address the realities of long-term change.

Enabling policies should target the improvement of productivity through the development of efficient markets

A view of dryland ecosystems as in continuous transition, and of production systems as in parallel transition, driven by economic as well as ecological forces, distracts attention from an unhealthy obsession with doomsday scenarios (and their correlates, impossibly expensive rehabilitation interventions). Instead, attention should be focused on learning the dynamics of change in the production systems and identifying policy options for supporting positive and discouraging negative change. In the cases studied in detail, the role of the market, unimpeded by price controls and restrictions on the movement of goods (especially food), has been to free up dynamic transition in production systems. While it cannot be disputed that markets create millionaires, improved access to markets can benefit the poor as well as the rich. Only an increase in the profitability of primary production can justify the investments that are necessary to improve productivity and arrest degradation.

Lasting investments in improving land productivity involve all sectors of the household economy

Sectorally specialised interventions in rural production systems resulted in the past from tunnel vision on the part of the professional departments set up to look after rural affairs. Unfortunately, 'integrated rural development' programmes may lack integration and merely reproduce those specialisms at the local level, but the smallholders who manage the drylands have no speciality, and must operate in technical, economic and social spheres simultaneously. The complexity of their decisions, and scope of their knowledge, are easily underestimated. Sectoral integration at the household level takes place at the point where scarce resources – most especially of labour – are allocated to competing activities (weeding, marketing, schooling, animal tending, etc.) and the trade-offs (both economic and social) must be evaluated. Development planning can facilitate the process of rural capital formation through understanding and supporting the economic linkages among sectors.

Drylands depend on access to national markets, cities and humid zones – including those of other countries

Notwithstanding the slow progress of most formal regional groupings in Africa, the regional interdependence of the drylands is an historical fact, which has only intensified since independence. This poses a considerable challenge to the structures of international economic co-operation that exist in Africa. Migration – especially mass movements in emergencies – is politically sensitive. There is a contradiction between a government based on a national constituency and the interests of displaced or voluntary migrants from neighbouring states. This transnational dimension of dryland management may be taken even further in the context of global environmental change. If desertification is now a global responsibility (as admitted in the International Convention to Combat Desertification), and yet the solution depends on the actions of millions of small-scale producers living in twenty or more different countries, then dryland production systems are also a global responsibility.

Population limitation will not solve the problems of the drylands

The positive outcomes of an increasing rural population density included, in Machakos (with a population of 1.3 million), the stabilisation and reversal of land degradation, increasing investment in land-improvement, technological change, higher output per hectare and per person, agricultural and income diversification and diminished vulnerability to food crises (Tiffen and Mortimore 1994). The Kano system (with more than 2.5 million inhabitants) has achieved sustained productivity for a longer period. Malthusian scenarios rest, to a large extent, on evidence of degradation in low-density systems. There, labour is scarce and none is available for intensification. Markets, infrastructure and economic diversification are constrained by the low densities (Boserup 1965). The appropriate policy priority in such circumstances is to minimise the costs of a sparse population distribution, with improvements to roads, transport, market institutions and additions to technical options for market production.

Doomsday scenarios based on present trends cannot be acceptable for the peoples of the drylands, whose adaptability is their chief resource (OECD 1988). Pathways of adaptation cannot, however, be predicted, nor is it necessary to do so. The effective mobilisation of the human, technical and management potential of drylands communities in the short and medium term is a more appropriate developmental objective.

1 Incremental change is either positive or negative and takes place through progressive additions or subtractions of the same variable; dynamic change is understood here to consist in transformation of the relations between the components of the system.

Bibliography

Abel, N.O.J., 1993 'Reducing cattle numbers on southern African communal range: is it worth it?' In: Behnke, R., Scoones, I. and Kerven, C. (eds.): 173–95.

Abel, N.O.J. and Blaikie, P.M., 1989 'Land degradation, stocking rates and conservation policies in the communal rangelands of Botswana and Zimbabwe.' *Land Degradation and Rehabilitation*, I, 2: 101–23.

Abel, N.O.J., Flint, M.E., Hunter, N.D., Chandler, D. and Maka, G., 1987 *Cattle-keeping, ecological change and communal management in Ngwaketse. Vol. II, Main report.* Norwich: Overseas Development Group, University of East Anglia.

Ackello-Ogutu, C., 1991 'Livestock production.' In: Tiffen, Mary (ed.), 'Environmental change and dryland management in Machakos District, Kenya, 1930–1990. Production profile': 45–89. *ODI Working Paper 55.* London: Overseas Development Institute.

Adams, W.M., 1988 'Rural protest, land policy and the planning process on the Bakolori Project, Nigeria.' *Africa*, 58: 315–36.

1992 *Wasting the rain: rivers, people and planning in Africa.* London: Earthscan.

1993 'Indigenous use of wetlands and sustainable development in West Africa.' *The Geographical Journal*, 159: 209–18.

1996 *Future nature: a vision for conservation.* London: Earthscan.

Adams, W.M. and Carter, R.C., 1987 'Small-scale irrigation in sub-Saharan Africa.' *Progress in Physical Geography*, 11: 1–27.

Agnew, C.T., 1989 'Sahel drought: meteorological or agricultural?' *Journal of Climatology*, 9: 371–82.

Ahlcrona, E., 1988 'The impact of climate and man on land transformation in central Sudan. Applications of remote sensing.' *Meddelanden fran Lunds Universitetets Geografiska Institutioner*, avhandlingar 103. Lund: Lund University Press.

Allan, W., 1965 *The African husbandman.* Edinburgh: Oliver and Boyd (reprinted in 1977 at Westport, Connecticut: Greenwood Press).

Amerena, P.M.J., 1982 *Farmers' participation in the cash economy: a case study of two settlements in the Kano Close-Settled Zone of Nigeria.* Ph.D thesis, University of London.

Amin, S. (ed.), 1974 *Modern migrations in West Africa.* Oxford: Oxford University Press, for the International African Institute.

Anderson, D.M., 1984 'Depression, dustbowl, demography and drought: the colonial state and soil conservation in East Africa during the 1930s.' *African Affairs*, 83(332): 321–43.

Anglo-French Forestry Commission, 1937 *Report of the Anglo-French Forestry Commission, December 1936 – February 1937.* Nigeria Sessional Paper 37 of 1937. Lagos: Government Printer.

van Apeldoorn, G.J., 1981 *Perspectives on drought and famine in Northern Nigeria.* London: Allen and Unwin.

Aubréville, A., 1949 *Climats, forêts et désertification de l'Afrique tropicale.* Paris: Societé d'Editions Géographiques, Maritimes et Coloniales.

Baier, S., 1980 *An economic history of central Niger.* Oxford: The Clarendon Press.

Bartels, G.B., Norton, B.E. and Perrier, G.K., 1993 'An examination of the carrying capacity concept.' In: Behnke, R.H., Scoones, I. and Kerven, C. (eds.): 89–103.

Behnke, R.H., Scoones, I. and Kerven, C. (eds.), 1993 *Range ecology at disequilibrium. New models of natural variability and pastoral adaptation in African savannas.* London: Overseas Development Institute.

Beinart, W., 1996 'Environmental destruction in southern Africa.' In: Leach, M. and Mearns, R. (eds.): 54–72.

Bennett, H.H., 1939 *Soil conservation.* New York: McGraw-Hill.

Berckmoes, W., Jager, E. and Kone, Y., 1990 'L'intensification agricole au Mali-sud.' *Bulletin.* Amsterdam: Royal Tropical Institute.

Bernus, E., 1977 *Case study on desertification. The Eghazer and Azawak region, Niger.* United Nations Conference on Desertification. Nairobi: United Nations Environment Programme.

   1979 'Exploitation de l'espace et désertification en zone Sahélienne.' *Travaux de l'Institut de Géographie de Reims,* 39/40: 49–59.

Biggs, S.D., 1989 'A multiple source of innovation model of agricultural research and technology promotion', *Agricultural Administration (Research and Extension) Network Paper* 6. London: Overseas Development Institute.

Biswas, M.R. and A.K. (eds.), 1980 *Desertification. Associated case studies prepared for the United Nations Conference on Desertification.* 2 vols. Oxford: Pergamon.

Bohle, H.G., Cannon, T., Hugo, G. and Ibrahim, F.N. (eds.), 1991 *Famine and food security in Africa and Asia.* Bayreuth: Bayreuther Geowissenschaftliche Arbeiten, 15.

Bonfiglioni, A.M., 1985 'Evolution de la propriété animale chez les Wodaabe du Niger.' *Journal des Africanistes,* 55: 25–37.

Bonte, P., 1986 'The Sahel: transformation and drought.' In: Garcia, R.V. and Spitz, P. (eds.), *Drought and man. The 1972 case history. Vol. 1, Nature pleads not guilty.* 150–81. Oxford: Pergamon.

Boserup, E., 1965 *The conditions of agricultural growth.* London: Allen and Unwin (reprinted, 1995, London: Earthscan).

Boulier, F. and Jouve, P., 1988 *Etude comparée de l'évolution des systèmes de production Sahéliens et leur adaptation a la sécheresse.* Montpellier: Département des Systèmes Agraires.

Bourn, David and Wint, William, 1994 'Livestock, land use and agricultural intensification in sub-Saharan Africa.' *Pastoral Development Network Paper* 37a. London: Overseas Development Institute.

Bovill, E.W., 1921 'The encroachment of the Sahara on the Sudan.' *Journal of the African Society,* 20: 174–85, 259–69.

Bradley, A.K., Macfarlane, S.B.J., Moody, J.B., Gilles, H.M., Blacker, J.G.C. and Musa, B.D., 1982a 'Malumfashi Endemic Diseases Research Project, XX. Demographic findings: mortality.' *Annals of Tropical Medicine and Parasitology,* 76: 393–404.

   1982b 'Malumfashi Endemic Diseases Research Project, XIX. Demographic findings: population structure and fertility.' *Annals of Tropical Medicine and Parasitology,* 76: 381–91.

Breman, H. and de Wit, C.T., 1983 'Rangeland productivity and exploitation in the Sahel.' *Science,* 221: 1341–47.

Bruntland, G.H. (ed.), 1987 *Our common future. Report of the World Commission on Environment and Development.* London: Penguin Books, for United Nations.

Buchanan, K.M. and Pugh, J.C., 1955 *Land and people in Nigeria.* London: London University Press.

Buonajuti, A., 1991 'External evaluation of the Plan of Action to Combat Desertification.' *Desertification Control Bulletin,* 20: 30–33.

Caldwell, J.C., 1975 *The African drought and its demographic implications.* New York: The Population Council.

1976 'Towards a restatement of demographic transition theory.' *Population and Development Review,* 2 (3/4): 321–66.

1982 *Theory of fertility decline.* London: Academic Press.

Camp, S.L., 1992 'Population pressure, poverty and the environment.' *Integration* (Japan), 32: 24–27.

Cardy, F., 1993 'Desertification – a fresh approach.' *Desertification Control Bulletin,* 22: 4–8.

Chambers, R., Longhurst, R. and Pacey, A. (eds.), 1981 *Seasonal dimensions to rural poverty.* London: Frances Pinter.

Chapman, M. and Prothero, R.M. (eds.), 1984 *Circulation in Third World countries.* London: Routledge and Kegan Paul.

Charney, J.G. and Stone, P.H., 1975 'Drought in the Sahara: a bio-geophysical feedback mechanism.' *Science,* 187: 434–45.

Chevalier, A., 1952 'La décadence des sols et de la végétation en Afrique Occidentale française et la protection de la nature.' *Bois et Forêts des Tropiques,* 16: 335–53.

Clarke, J.I. and Kosinski, L.A. (eds.), 1982 *Population redistribution in Africa.* London: Heinemann.

Cleaver, Kevin M. and Schreiber, Gotz A., 1994 *Reversing the spiral. The population, agriculture and environment nexus in sub-Saharan Africa.* Washington, DC: The World Bank.

Cline-Cole, R.A., 1994 'Political economy, fuelwood relations, and vegetation conservation. Kasar Kano, Northern Nigeria, 1850–1973.' *Forest and Conservation History,* 38: 67–78.

Cline-Cole, R.A., Falola, J.A., Main, H.A.C., Mortimore, M.J., Nichol, J.E. and O'Reilly, F.D., 1990a *Wood fuel in Kano.* Tokyo: United Nations Press.

Cline-Cole, R.A., Main, H.A.C. and Nichol, J.E., 1990b 'On fuelwood consumption, population dynamics and deforestation in Africa.' *World Development,* 18(4): 513–27.

Cloudsley-Thompson, J.L., 1984 'Human activities and desert expansion.' *The Geographical Journal,* 144: 416–23.

Collier, F.S. and Dundas, J., 1937 'The arid regions of Northern Nigeria and the French Niger Colony.' *Empire Forestry Journal,* 16: 184–94.

Cooke, H.J., 1985 'The Kalahari today: a case of conflict over resource use.' *The Geographical Journal,* 151: 75–85.

Copans, J. (ed.), 1975 *Sécheresses et famines du Sahel. 1, Ecologie, dénutrition, assistance. 2, Paysans et nomades.* Paris: Maspero.

1979 'Droughts, famines and the evolution of Senegal (1966–1978).' *Mass Emergencies,* 4: 87–93.

1983 'The Sahelian drought: social sciences and the political economy of underdevelopment.' In: Hewitt, K. (ed.): 83–97.

Coppock, D.L., 1993 'Vegetation and pastoral dynamics in the southern Ethiopian rangelands: implications for theory and management.' In: Behnke, R.H., Scoones, I. and Kerven, C. (eds.): 42–61.

Corbett, J.-M., 1988 'Famine and household coping strategies.' *World Development,* 16: 1099–1112.

Cour, J., 1993 'Retrospective demo-economic analysis and suggested long-term demo-economic picture of West Africa.' *West Africa Long Term Perspectives Study Working Paper* 2. Paris: Club du Sahel/OECD.

Dalby, D. and Harrison Church, R.J. (eds.), 1974 *Drought in Africa. Proceedings of the 1973 Symposium:* 114–26. Centre for African Studies, School of Oriental and African Studies, University of London.

Darkoh, M.K., 1995 'The deterioration of the environment in Africa's drylands and river basins.' *Desertification Control Bulletin,* 24: 35–41.

Davies, S., Buchanan-Smith, M. and Lambert, R., 1991 *Early warning in the Sahel and Horn of Africa: the state of the art. A review of the literature.* 3 vols. IDS Research Reports 20. Brighton: Institute of Development Studies at the University of Sussex.

Dessalegn Rahmato, 1991 *Famine survival strategies.* Uppsala: Scandinavian Institute of African Studies.

Devereux, S., 1993 *Theories of famine.* New York: Harvester Wheatsheaf.

Dougill, A. and Cox, J., 1995 'Land degradation and grazing in the Kalahari: new analysis and alternative perspectives.' *Pastoral Development Network Paper* 38c. London: Overseas Development Institute.

Downing, T.E., 1992 'Climate change and vulnerable places: global food security and country studies in Zimbabwe, Kenya, Senegal and Chile.' *Research Report* 1, Environmental Change Unit, University of Oxford.

Downing, T.E., Akong'a, J., Mungai, D.N., Muturi, H.R. and Potter, H.L., 1987 'Introduction to the Kenya case study.' In: Parry, M.L., Carter, T.R. and Konjin, N.T. (eds.), *The impact of climatic variations on agriculture. Vol. 2, Assessments in semi-arid regions:* 129–48. Dordrecht: Kluwer Academic Publishers.

Downing, T.E., Gitu, K.W. and Kamau, C. (eds.), 1989 *Coping with drought in Kenya: national and local strategies.* Boulder, CO: Lynne Reiner.

Dregne, H.E., 1970 *Arid lands in transition. Publication 90.* Washington, DC: American Association for the Advancement of Science.

1983 *Desertification of arid lands.* Advances in Desert and Arid Land Technology and Development No 3. Hardwood Academic Publishers.

Dregne, H.E., Kassas, M. and Rosanov, B., 1991 'A new assessment of the world status of desertification.' *Desertification Control Bulletin,* 20: 6–18.

Dunbar, G.S., 1970 'African Ranches Ltd., 1914–1931: an ill-fated stock raising enterprise in Northern Nigeria.' *Annals of the Association of American Geographers,* 60: 102–23.

Eckholm, E., 1976 *Losing ground. Environmental stress and world food prospects.* New York: Pergamon.

Eckholm, E. and Brown, L., 1977 *Spreading deserts: the hand of man.* Worldwatch Paper 13. Washington, DC: Worldwatch Institute.

Ellis, J.E. and Swift, D.M., 1988 'Stability of African pastoral ecosystems: alternate paradigms and implications for development.' *Journal of Range Management,* 41: 450–59.

Ellis, J.E., Coughenour, M.B. and Swift, D.M., 1993 'Climate variability, ecosystem stability, and the implications for range and livestock development.' In: Behnke, R.H., Scoones, I. and Kerven, C. (eds.): 31–41.

Essiet, E.U., 1990 'A comparison of soil degradation under smallholder farming and large scale irrigation land use in Kano State, northern Nigeria.' *Land Degradation and Rehabilitation,* 2: 209–14.

Etkin, N., 1981 'A Hausa herbal pharmacopoeia: biomedical evaluation of commonly used plant medicines.' *Journal of Ethnopharmacology,* 4: 75–98.

Etkin, N. and Ross, P., 1982 'Food as medicine and medicine as food. An adaptive framework for the interpretation of plant utilization among the Hausa of northern Nigeria.' *Social Science Medicine,* 16: 1559–73.

Fairhead, J. and Leach, M., 1996 *Misreading the African landscape: society and ecology in a forest-savanna mosaic.* Cambridge: Cambridge University Press.

Falloux, F. and Mukendi, A. (eds.), 1988 *Desertification control and renewable resource management in the Sahelian and Sudanian zones of West Africa.* World Bank Technical Paper 70. Washington, DC: The World Bank.

FAO, 1980 *Report on the second FAO/UNFPA Expert Consultation on Land Resources for Populations of the Future.* Rome: Food and Agriculture Organisation of the United Nations.

FAO, 1984 *Land, food and people.* FAO Economic and Social Development Series 30. Rome: Food and Agriculture Organisation of the United Nations.

FAO/UNEP, n.d. (?1983) *Provisional methodology for assessment and mapping of desertification.* Rome: Food and Agriculture Organisation of the United Nations.

FAO/UNESCO, 1977 *Soil map of the world 1:5M. Vol. VI: Africa, Sheets VI – 1, 2, 3.* Paris: United Nations Educational, Scientific and Cultural Organisation.

Farmer, G. and Wigley, T.M.L., 1985 *Climate trends for tropical Africa. A research report for the Overseas Development Administration.* Norwich: Climate Research Unit, University of East Anglia.

Faulkingham, R.H. and Thorbahn, P.F., 1975 'Population dynamics and drought: a village in Niger.' *Population Studies,* 29: 463–77.

Forrest, T., 1993 *Politics and economic development in Nigeria.* Boulder, CO: Westview Press.

Franke, R.W. and Chasin, B.H., 1980 *Seeds of famine: ecological destruction and the development dilemma in the West African Sahel.* Montclair, NJ: Allanheld, Osmun.

Fricke, W., 1979 *Cattle husbandry in Nigeria. A study of its ecological conditions and social-geographical differentiations.* Heidelberger Geographischen Arbeiten, Heft 52. Heidelberg: Universität Heidelberg.

Gielen, H., 1982 *Report on an agroforestry survey in three villages of northern Machakos, Kenya.* Nairobi: Wageningen Agricultural University and International Council for Research in Agroforestry.

Gillet, H., 1986 'Desert and Sahel.' In: Lawson, G.W., *Plant ecology in West Africa:* 174–81. Chichester: John Wiley.

Giri, J. (ed.), 1988 *The Sahel facing the future: increasing dependence or structural transformation.* Paris: OECD.

Glantz, M.H. (ed.), 1976 *The politics of natural disaster: the case of the Sahel drought.* New York: Praeger.

Glantz, M.H. and Orlovsky, N., 1983 'Desertification: a review of the concept.' *Desertification Control Bulletin,* 9: 15–22.

Gleave, M.B. and White, H.P., 1969 'Population density and agricultural systems in West Africa.' In: Thomas, M.F. and Whittington, G.W. (eds.), *Environment and land use in Africa*: 273–300. London: Methuen.

Goddard, A.D., Fine, J.L. and Norman, D.W., 1972 'A socio-economic study of three villages in the Sokoto close-settled zone. I, Land and people.' *Samaru Miscellaneous Paper 33*. Zaria: Institute for Agricultural Research, Ahmadu Bello University.

Goddard, A.D., Mortimore, M.J. and Norman, D.W., 1975 'Some social and economic implications of population growth in rural Hausaland.' In: Caldwell, J.C., Addo, N.O., Gaisie, S.K., Igun, A. and Olusanya, P.O. (eds.), *Population growth and socio-economic change in West Africa*: 321–36. New York: Columbia University Press, for the Population Council.

Gorse, J.E. and Steeds, D.R., 1987 *Desertification in the Sahelian and Sudanian zones of West Africa*. World Bank Technical Paper 61. Washington, D.C.: The World Bank.

Gould, W.T.S. and Brown, M.S., 1996 'A fertility transition in Sub-Saharan Africa?' *International Journal of Population Geography*, 2: 1–22.

Gowers, W.F., 1913 Kano Province Annual Report for 1913. Nigerian National Archives, Kaduna.

van der Graaf, S. and Breman, H., 1993 'Agricultural production: ecological limits and possibilities.' *Rapports PSS* 3. Wageningen: Production Soudano-Sahelienne, CABO-DLO, for the Club du Sahel.

Grégoire, E., 1980 *Etude socio-économique du village de Gourjae (Département de Maradi, Niger)*. Programme de Recherches sur la Région de Maradi, Université de Bordeaux II.

Grégoire, E. and Raynaut, C., 1980 *Présentation générale du Département du Maradi*. Programme de Recherches sur la Région de Maradi, Université de Bordeaux II.

Grove, A.T., 1952 *Land and population in Katsina Province*. Kaduna: Government Printer.

1961 'Population densities and agriculture in Northern Nigeria.' In: Barbour, K.M. and Prothero, R. Mansell (eds.), *Essays on African population*: 115–36. London: Routledge and Kegan Paul.

Grove, A.T. and Pullan, R.A., 1964 'Some aspects of the Pleistocene paleogeography of the Chad basin.' In: Howell, F. Clark and Bourlière, François (eds.), *African ecology and human evolution*: 230–45. London: Methuen.

Haggblade, S., Hazell, P. and Brown, J., 1989 'Farm-nonfarm linkages in rural sub-Saharan Africa.' *World Development*, 17(8): 1173–1202.

Hailey, L., 1938 *An African survey: a study of problems arising in Africa south of the Sahara*: 1056–1114. Oxford: Oxford University Press.

Harris, F., 1994 *Nutrient dynamics of the farming system of the Kano Close-Settled Zone, Nigeria*. Ph.D thesis, University of Cambridge.

1996 'Intensification of agriculture in semi-arid areas: lessons from the Kano Close-Settled Zone, Nigeria.' *Gatekeeper Series*, 59. London: Sustainable Agriculture programme, International Institute for Environment and Development.

Hastings, A.G.C., 1925 *Nigerian days*. London: The Bodley Head.

Haswell, M., 1981 'Food consumption in relation to labour output.' In: Chambers, R., Longhurst, R. and Pacey, A. (eds.): 38–40.

Hays, H.M., 1975 'The storage of cereal grains in three villages of Zaria Province, northern Nigeria.' *Savanna*, 4(2): 117–24.

Hellden, U., 1988 'Desertification monitoring.' *Desertification Control Bulletin*, 17: 8–12.

Helleiner, G.K., 1966 *Peasant agriculture, government and economic growth in Nigeria.* Yale: Yale University Press.

Hendy, C.R.C., 1977 'Animal production in Kano State and the requirements for further study in the Kano close-settled zone.' *Land Resource Report* 21. Tolworth: Land Resources Division, Overseas Development Administration.

Hess, T.M., Stephens, W. and Maryah, U.M., 1994 'Rainfall trends in the North East Arid Zone of Nigeria 1961–1990.' *Agricultural and Forest Meteorology*, 74: 87–97.

Hewitt, K. (ed.), 1983 *Interpretations of calamity.* London: Allen and Unwin.

Hiernaux, P., 1994 *The crisis of Sahelian pastoralism: ecological or economic?* Addis Ababa: International Livestock Centre for Africa.

Hiernaux, P., Cissé, M.I., Diarra, L. and de Leeuw, P.N., 1994 'Fluctuations saisonnières de la feuillaison des arbres et des buissons sahéliens. Conséquences pour la quantification des ressources fourragères.' *Revue d'Elevage Médicine vétérinaire des Pays tropiques*, 47: 117–25.

Higgins, G.M., Kassam, A.H., Naiken, L., Fisher, G. and Shah, M.M., 1982 *Potential population-supporting capacities of lands in the developing world. FPA/INT/513.* Rome: Food and Agriculture Organisation of the United Nations.

Hill, A.G. (ed.), 1985 *Population, health and nutrition in the Sahel. Issues in the welfare of selected West African communities.* London: Routledge and Kegan Paul.

Hill, P., 1972 *Rural Hausa. A village and a setting.* Cambridge: Cambridge University Press.

  1977 *Population, prosperity and poverty. Rural Kano, 1900 and 1970.* Cambridge: Cambridge University Press.

Hogendorn, J.S., 1978 *Nigerian groundnut exports: origins and early development.* Zaria: Ahmadu Bello University Press.

Holling, C.S., 1973 'Resilience and stability of ecological systems.' *Annual Review of Ecology and Systematics*, 4: 1–23.

  1987 'The resilience of terrestrial ecosystems: local surprise and global change.' In: Clark, W.C. and Munn, R.E. (eds.), *Sustainable development of the biosphere.* 292–320. Laxenburg, Austria: International Institute for Applied Systems Analysis.

Hollis, G.E., Adams, W.M., and Aminu-Kano, M., 1994 *The Hadejia-Nguru Wetlands. Environment, economy and sustainable development of a Sahelian floodplain wetland.* Gland, Switzerland: International Union for the Conservation of Nature.

Holmes, J.A., Street-Perrott, F.A., Allen, M.J., Fothergill, P.A., Harkness, D.D., Kroon, D. and Perrot, R.A., 1997 'Holocene paleolimnology of Kajemarum Oasis, Northern Nigeria: an isotopic study of ostracodes, bulk carbonate and organic carbon.' *Journal of the Geological Society, London*, 154: 311–19.

Holmewood, K. and Rogers, W.A., 1987 'Pastoralism, conservation and the overgrazing controversy.' In: Anderson, D. and Grove, R. (eds.), *Conservation in Africa. People, policies and practice.* Cambridge: Cambridge University Press.

  1991 *Masaailand ecology. Pastoral development and wildlife conservation in Ngorongoro, Tanzania.* Cambridge: Cambridge University Press.

Holter, U., 1988 'Food habits of camel nomads in the north west Sudan.' *Ecology of Food and Nutrition*, 21: 1–15; 95–115.

  1991 'Food and survival strategies in relation to drought: Arab camel-nomads and sedentary millet-farmers in northern Darfur (Sudan).' In: Bohle, H.G., Cannon, T., Hugo, G. and Ibrahim, F.N. (eds.): 101–114.

le Houérou, H.N., 1985 'Pastoralism.' In: Kates, R.W., Asubel, J.H. and Berberian, M. (eds.), *Climate impact assessment* 155–85. Chichester: John Wiley.

le Houérou, H.N. and Hoste, 1977 'Rangeland production and annual rainfall relations in the Mediterranean Basin and in the African Sahelian and Sudanian Zones.' *Journal of Range Management*, 30: 181–9.

Hubert, H., 1920 'Le dessèchement progressif en Afrique Occidentale.' *Bulletin du Comité d'Etudes Historiques et Scientifiques d'AOF* 401–67.

Hulme, M., 1990 'The changing rainfall resources of Sudan.' *Transactions of the Institute of British Geographers*, N.S. 15: 21–34.

1992 'Rainfall changes in Africa: 1931–1960 to 1961–1990.' *International Journal of Climatology*, 12: 685–99.

1994a *Climate change, desertification and desiccation, and the case of the African Sahel*. Norwich: Climate Research Unit, University of East Anglia.

1994b 'Regional climate change scenarios based on IPCC emissions projections with some illustrations from Africa.' *Area*, 26(1): 33–44.

Hulme, M. and Kelly, M., 1993 'Exploring the links between desertification and climate change.' *Environment*, 35(6): 4–11; 39–45.

Hunter, J.M., 1967 'Population pressure in a part of the West African savanna: a study of Nangodi, north-east Ghana.' *Annals, Association of American Geographers*, 57: 101–14.

Huntingdon, E., 1915 *Climate and civilization*. Yale: Yale University Press.

Huxley, E., 1937 'The menace of soil erosion.' *Journal of the Royal African Society*, 36: 357–70.

Ibrahim, A.M., 1996 'The farming system of Kaska, Yobe State, Nigeria.' *Soils, Cultivars and Livelihoods in North-east Nigeria*. *Working Paper* No 3. Kano: Department of Geography, Bayero University.

Ibrahim, F.N., 1978 'Anthropogenic causes of desertification in western Sudan.' *Geojournal*, 2–3: 243–54.

1983 'The role of nomadism in the process of desertification in Western Sudan.' *Applied Geography and Development* (German Institute for Scientific Co-operation), 22: 46–57.

1984 *Ecological imbalance in the Republic of the Sudan – with reference to desertification in Darfur*. Bayreuth: Bayreuther Geowissenschaftliche Arbeiten.

IPCC, 1994 *Radiative forcing of climate change. The 1994 Report of the Scientific Assessment Working Group of IPCC. Summary for policymakers*. World Meteorological Organisation/United Nations Environment Programme.

IUCN, 1989 *IUCN Sahel studies, 1989*. Gland, Switzerland: International Union for the Conservation of Nature.

Jaetzold, R. and Schmidt, H., 1983 *Farm management handbook of Kenya*. Vol. 2: *Natural conditions and farm management information*. Part C: *East Kenya (Eastern and Coast Provinces)*. Nairobi: Ministry of Agriculture.

Jahnke, H.E., 1982 *Livestock production systems and livestock development in tropical Africa*. Kiel: Wissenschaftsverlag Vauk.

Jega, A., 1987 'The state, agrarian reformism, and land administration in the Bakolori Irrigation Project.' In: Mortimore, M., Olofin, E.A., Cline-Cole, R.A. and Abdulkadir, A. (eds.), *Perspectives on land administration and development in northern Nigeria* 141–52. Kano: Department of Geography, Bayero University.

Johnson, D.L.(ed.), 1977 'The human dimensions of desertification.' *Economic Geography*, 53 (special issue).

Jones, B., 1938 'Desiccation and the West African colonies.' *The Geographical Journal,* 91: 401–23.

Jones, M.J. and Wild, A., 1975 *Soils of the West African savanna. The maintenance and improvement of their fertility.* Harpenden: Commonwealth Agricultural Bureau.

Jouet, Astrid, Jouve, Philippe and Banoin, Maxime, 1996 'Le défrichement amélioré: une pratique paysanne d'agroforesterie au Sahel.' 14th International Symposium on Sustainable Farming Systems, November, 1996, Colombo. Montpellier: Centre National d'Etudes des Régions Chaudes.

Jouve, Philippe, 1996 *La lutte contre l'aridité au Maghrib et au Sahel par l'adaptation des systèmes de production agricole.* Montpellier: Centre National d'Etudes des Régions Chaudes.

Kassas, M., A., Y. and Rosanov, B., 1991 'Desertification and drought: an ecological and economic analysis.' *Desertification Control Bulletin,* 20: 19–29.

Kates, R.W. *et al.* 1981 *Drought impact in the sahelian-Sudanic zone of West Africa: a comparative analysis of 1910–15 and 1968–74.* Background paper 2, Centre for Technology, Environment and Development. Worcester, MA: Clark University.

Kerven, C., 1987 'The role of milk in a pastoral diet and economy: the case of south Darfur, Sudan.' *ILCA* [International Livestock Centre for Africa] *Bulletin,* 27: 18–27.

Kimmage, K. and Adams, W.M., 1990 'Small-scale farmer-managed irrigation in northern Nigeria.' *Geoforum,* 20: 435–43.

1992 'Wetland agricultural production and river basin management in the Hadejia-Jama'are valley, Nigeria.' *The Geographical Journal,* 158: 1–12.

Kimmage, K. and Falola, J.A., 1991 'Technical change, equity and sustainability in small-scale irrigation in Hadejia-Nguru floodplain.' In: Olofin, E.A., Patrick, S. and Falola, J.A. (eds.), *Land administration and development in northern Nigeria: case studies.* 113–26. Kano: Department of Geography, Bayero University.

Kolawole, A., 1987 'Environmental change and the South Chad Irrigation Project (Nigeria).' *Journal of Arid Environments,* 13: 169–76.

1988 'Cultivation of the floor of Lake Chad as a response to environmental hazards in eastern Borno, Nigeria.' *The Geographical Journal,* 154: 243–50.

Kolawole, A., Scoones, I., Awogbade, M.O. and Vok, J.P. (eds.), 1994 *Strategies for the sustainable use of fadama lands in northern Nigeria.* Zaria: Centre for Social and Economic Research, Ahmadu Bello University/International Institute for Environment and Development.

Kowal, J.M. and Adeoye, K.B., 1973 'An assessment of aridity and the severity of the 1972 drought in northern Nigeria and neighbouring countries.' *Savanna* 2(2): 145–58.

Kowal, J.M. and Kassam, A.H., 1978 *Agricultural ecology of savanna. A study of West Africa.* Oxford: The Clarendon Press.

Kuper, H. (ed.), 1965 *Urbanization and migration in West Africa.* University of California Press.

Lambin, E.F., 1993 'Spatial scales and desertification.' *Desertification Control Bulletin,* 23: 20–23.

Lamprey, H.F., 1988 'Report on the desert encroachment reconnaissance in northern Sudan: 21 October to 10 November, 1975.' *Desertification Control Bulletin,* 17: 1–7.

Leach, M. and Mearns, R. (eds.), 1996 *The lie of the land. Challenging received wisdom in African environmental change and policy.* London/ Oxford: International African Institute/ James Currey.

de Leeuw, P.N. and Tothill, J., 1993 'The concept of rangeland carrying capacity in sub-Saharan Africa: myth or reality.' In: Behnke, B.H., Scoones, I. and Kerven, C. (eds.): 77–88.

de Leeuw, P.N., Diarra, L. and Hiernaux, P., 1993 'An analysis of feed demand and supply for pastoral livestock: the Gourma region of Mali.' In: Behnke, R.H., Scoones, I. and Kerven, C. (eds.): 136–52.

Leftwich, A. and Harvie, D., n.d. (?1986) 'The political economy of famine. A preliminary report on the literature, bibliographical resources, research activities and needs in the U.K.' *Discussion Paper* 116, Institute for Research in the Social Sciences, Institute of Social and Economic Research, Department of Politics, University of York.

Leroux, M., 1983 *The climate of tropical Africa – Atlas.* Paris: Editions Champion.

Loutan, L. and Lamotte, J.M., 1984 'Seasonal variations in nutrition among a group of nomadic pastoralists in Niger.' *The Lancet,* April 28: 945–47.

Lovejoy, P.E. and Baier, S., 1976 'The desert-side economy of the central Sudan.' In: Glantz, M.H. (ed.): 145–75.

LRDC, 1979 'The land resources of central Nigeria.' *Land Resource Study* 29. Tolworth: Land Resources Development Centre, Overseas Development Administration.

Lund, C., 1993 'Waiting for the Rural Code: perspectives on a land tenure reform in Niger.' *Dryland Network Paper* 44. London: International Institute for Environment and Development.

Mabbutt, J.A., 1985 'Desertification of the world's rangelands.' *Desertification Control Bulletin,* 12: 1–11.

Mabogunje, A.L., 1972 *Regional mobility and resource development in West Africa.* Montreal: McGill-Queens University Press.

Macleod, N.H., 1976 'Dust in the Sahel: cause of drought?' In: Glantz, M.H. (ed.): 214–31.

Maher, C., 1937 *Soil erosion and land utilisation in the Ukamba Reserve (Machakos).* Report to the Department of Agriculture (ms). Rhodes House Library, Oxford, Mss. Afr. S.755.

Mainguet, M., 1980 'L'interdépendence des mécanismes éoliens dans les zones arides du Sahara et dans leur marges sahéliennes: ses effets sur la propagation de la désertification.' In: Meckelein, W. (ed.), *Desertification in extremely arid environments:* 107–23. Stuttgarter Geographische Studien 95, Geographisches Institut der Universität Stuttgart.

    1994 *Desertification. Natural background and human mismanagement.* 2nd edn. Berlin: Springer-Verlag.

Maley, J., 1981 *Etudes palynologiques dans le bassin du Tchad et paleoclimatologie de l'Afrique nord-tropicale de 30,000 ans a l'époque actuelle.* Travaux et Documents 129. Paris: Office de la Recherche Scientifique et Technique Outre-mer.

Mbogoh, S., 1991 'Crop production.' In: Tiffen, M. (ed.), 'Environmental change and dryland management in Machakos District, Kenya, 1930–1990. Production profile.' *ODI Working Paper* 55. London: Overseas Development Institute.

Mbuvi, J.P., 1991 'Soil fertility.' In: Mortimore, M. (ed.), 'Environmental change and dryland management in Machakos District, Kenya, 1930–1990. Environmental profile.' *ODI Working Paper* 53. London: Overseas Development Institute.

McIntire, J., Bourzat, D. and Pingali, P., 1992 *Crop-livestock interactions in sub-Saharan Africa.* Washington, DC: The World Bank.

McIntire, J. and Powell, J.M., 1995 'African semi-arid tropical agriculture cannot grow without external inputs.' In: Powell, J.M., Fernandez-Rivera, S., Williams, T.O. and Renard, C. (eds.): 539–51.

McIntosh, R.J., 1992 'Historical view of the semi-arid tropics.' Carter Lecture Series, University of Florida.

McMillan, D.E., 1995 *Sahel visions. Planned settlement and river blindness control in Burkina Faso.* Tucson: University of Arizona Press.

McTainsh, G.H., 1984 'The nature and origin of the aeolian mantles of central northern Nigeria.' *Geoderma,* 33: 13–37.

1987 'Desert loess in northern Nigeria.' *Geoderma,* 33: 13–37.

Meyer, W.B. and Turner, B.L.II (eds.), 1994 *Changes in land use and land cover.* Cambridge: Cambridge University Press.

Millington, A.C., Critchley, R.W., Douglas, T.D. and Ryan, P., 1994 *Estimating woody biomass in Sub-Saharan Africa.* Washington, DC: The World Bank.

Mohammed, S., 1996 'The farming system of Dagaceri, Jigawa State, Nigeria.' *Soils, Cultivars and Livelihoods in North-east Nigeria,* Working paper 2. Kano: Department of Geography, Bayero University.

Molineaux, L. and Gramiccia, G., 1980 *The Garki Project. Research on the epidemiology and control of malaria in the Sudan Savanna of West Africa.* Geneva: World Health Organisation.

Morel, E.D., 1911 *Nigeria: its peoples and its problems.* London: Murray (reprinted 1968, London: Frank Cass).

Morgan, W.B. and Moss, R.P., 1965 'Savanna and forest in Western Nigeria.' *Africa,* 35: 286–94.

Mortimore, M., 1967 'Land and population pressure in the Kano Close-Settled Zone, Northern Nigeria.' *The Advancement of Science,* 23: 677–88.

1972 'Some aspects of urban relations in Kano (Nigeria).' In: Vennetier, P. (ed.), *La Croissance Urbaine en Afrique Noire et à Madagascar.* (2 vols.). Paris: Centre National de la Recherche Scientifique.

1973 'Famine in Hausaland.' *Savanna,* 2(2): 103–8.

1974 'The demographic variable in regional planning in Kano State, Nigeria.' In: Hoyle, B.S. (ed.), *Spatial aspects of development:* 129–46. Chichester: John Wiley.

1982 'Framework for population mobility: the perception of opportunities in Nigeria.' In: Clarke, J.I. and Kosinski, L.A. (eds.), *Population redistribution in Africa:* 50–7. London: Heinemann.

1989a *Adapting to drought. Farmers, famines and desertification in West Africa.* Cambridge: Cambridge University Press.

1989b 'The causes, nature and rate of soil degradation in the northernmost states of Nigeria and an assessment of the role of fertiliser in counteracting the process of degradation.' *Environment Department Working Paper* 17. Washington, DC: The World Bank.

1991 'Five faces of famine. The autonomous sector in the famine process.' In: Bohle, H.G., Cannon, T., Hugo, G. and Ibrahim, F.N. (eds.): 11–36.

1993a 'The intensification of peri-urban agriculture: the Kano Close-Settled Zone, 1964–1986.' In: Turner, B.L. Jnr., Kates, R.W. and Hyden, G. (eds.): 358–400.

1993b 'Northern Nigeria: land transformation under agricultural intensification.' In: Jolly, C.L. and Torrey, B.B. (eds.), *Population and land use in developing countries. Report of a Workshop:* 42–69. Washington, DC: National Academy Press.

Mortimore, M. and Tiffen, M., 1994 'Population growth and a sustainable environment: the Machakos story.' *Environment,* 36(8): 10–20; 28–32.

Mortimore, M. and Turner, B., 1991 'Crop-livestock farming systems in the semi-arid zone of sub-Saharan Africa. Ordering diversity and understanding change.' *Agricultural*

Administration (Research and Extension) Network Paper 46. London: Overseas Development Institute.

Mortimore, M. and Wellard, K., 1991 'Environmental change and dryland management in Machakos District, Kenya, 1930–1990. Profile of technological change.' *ODI Working Paper* 57. London: Overseas Development Institute.

Mortimore, M. and Wilson, J., 1965 'Land and people in the Kano Close-Settled Zone.' *Occasional Paper* 1. Zaria: Department of Geography, Ahmadu Bello University.

Mortimore, M., Singh, B.B., Harris, F. and Blade, S., 1997 'Cowpea in traditional cropping systems.' In: Singh, B.B., Mohan Raj, D.R., Dashiell, K.E. and Jackson, L.E.N. (eds.), *Advances in cowpea research.* Copublication of the International Institute of Tropical Agriculture and the Japan International Research Centre for Agricultural Sciences. Ibadan: Nigeria.

Mutiso, S.K., Mortimore, M. and Tiffen, M., 1991 'Rainfall.' In: Mortimore, Michael (ed.), 'Environmental change and dryland management in Machakos District, Kenya, 1930–1990. Environmental Profile.' *ODI Working Paper* 53. London: Overseas Development Institute.

Mung'ong'o, C.G., 1995 'Social processes and ecology in the Kondoa Hills, Central Tanzania.' *Meddellanden Series* B 93. Stockholm: Department of Human Geography, Stockholm University.

Nelson, R., 1988 'Dryland management – the desertification problem.' *Environment Department Working Paper* 8. Washington, DC: The World Bank.

Ness, G.D., 1994 'Population and the environment: frameworks for analysis.' *Environmental and Natural Resources Policy and Training Project Working Paper* No. 10. Ann Arbor: University of Michigan.

Netting, R. McC., 1993 *Smallholders, householders. Farm families and the ecology of intensive, sustainable agriculture.* Stanford: Stanford University Press.

Nichol, J.E., 1991 'The extent of desert dunes in northern Nigeria as shown by image enhancement.' *The Geographical Journal,* 157: 13–24.

Nicholson, S.E., 1978 'Climatic variations in the Sahel and other African regions during the past five centuries.' *Journal of Arid Environments,* 1: 3–24.

  1983 'Sub-Saharan rainfall in the years 1976–80: evidence of continued drought.' *Monthly Weather Review,* 111: 1646–54.

Norman, D.W., Fine, J.C., Goddard, A.D., Pryor, D.H. and Kroeker, W.J., 1976 'A socio-economic survey of three villages in the Sokoto close-settled zone', 3, Input-output study. Vol. ii Basic data. *Samaru Miscellaneous Paper* 65. Zaria: Institute for Agricultural Research.

Odingo, R.S., 1992 'Implementation of the Plan of Action to Combat Desertification (PACD) 1978–1991.' *Desertification Control Bulletin,* 21: 6–14.

OECD, 1988 *The Sahel facing the future: increasing dependence or structural transformation. Futures study of the Sahel countries.* Paris: Organisation for Economic Co-operation and Development.

Oguntoyinbo, J.S. and Richards, P., 1977 'The extent and intensity of the 1969–73 drought in Nigeria: a provisional analysis.' In: Dalby, David and Harrison Church, R.J. (eds.): 114–26.

Olofin, E.A., 1982 'Some effects of the Tiga Dam and reservoir on the downstream environment in the Kano River basin, Kano state/Nigeria.' *Beiträge zur Hydrologie,* 3: 11–28.

  1992 'Soil erosion in the drylands of Nigeria and the issue of soil life.' Report to

Cambridge–Bayero University Agropastoral Change Research Project. Kano, Nigeria: Department of Geography, Bayero University.

Olsson, L., 1985 'An integrated study of desertification. Applications of remote sensing, GIS and spatial models in semi-arid Sudan.' *Lund Studies in Geography Ser. C, General and Mathematical Geography* no 13. Lund: Lund University.

1993 'Desertification in Africa – a critique and an alternative approach.' *Geojournal,* 33: 23–31.

Onchere, S.R. and Sloof, R., 1981 'Nutrition and disease in Machakos District, Kenya.' In: Chambers, R., Longhurst, R. and Pacey, A. (eds.): 41–44.

Ostberg, W., 1986 *The Kondoa transformation. Coming to terms with soil erosion in Central Tanzania.* Research Report 76. Uppsala: Scandinavian Institute of African Studies.

OXFAM, 1993 *Africa make or break: action for recovery.* Oxford: Oxfam.

Penning de Vries, F.W.T. and Djiteye, M.A. (eds.), 1991 *La productivité des pâturages sahéliens. Une étude des sols, des végétations et de l'exploitation de cette ressource naturelle.* Wageningen: Pudoc.

Pieri, C., 1989 *Fertilité des terres de savanes. Bilan de trente ans de recherche et de développement agricoles au sud du Sahara.* Paris: Ministère de la Coopération, Centre de Coopération Internationale en Recherche Agronomique pour le Développement.

Pingali, P., Bigot, Y. and Binswanger, H.P., 1987 *Agricultural mechanisation and the evolution of farming systems in sub-Saharan Africa.* Baltimore: The Johns Hopkins University Press.

van der Pol, F., 1992 'Soil mining. An unseen contributor to farm income in southern Mali.' *Bulletin* 325. Amsterdam: Royal Tropical Institute.

Powell, J.M., Fernandez-Rivera, S., Williams, T.O. and Renard, C. (eds.), *Livestock and sustainable nutrient cycling in mixed farming systems of sub-Saharan Africa. Proceedings of an international conference, 22–26 November, 1993. Vol. II: technical papers.* Addis Ababa: International Livestock Centre for Africa.

Prothero, R.M., 1959 *Migrant labour from Sokoto Province, Northern Nigeria.* Kaduna: Government Printer.

1962 'Some observations on desiccation in North-Western Nigeria.' *Erdkunde,* 16: 11–19.

(ed.), 1972 *People and land in Africa south of the Sahara.* Oxford: Oxford University Press.

Pullan, R.A., 1974 'Farmed parkland in West Africa.' *Savanna,* 3(2): 119–52.

van Raay, J.G.T. and de Leeuw, P.N., 1976 'The importance of crop residues as fodder: a resource analysis in Katsina Province, Nigeria.' *Samaru Research Bulletin* 139. Zaria: Institute for Agricultural Research.

Raeburn, C., 1928 'The Nigerian Sudan. Some notes on water supply and cognate subjects.' Pamphlet 1. Kaduna: Geological Survey of Nigeria.

Rattray, J.M., 1960 *The grass cover of Africa 1: 10 M.* Rome: Food and Agriculture Organisation of the United Nations.

Raulin, H., 1964 'Techniques et bases socio-économiques des sociétés rurales Nigeriennes.' *Etudes Nigeriennes* 12. Niamey: Centre National de Recherche en Sciences Humaines.

Raynaut, C., 1977 'Lessons of a crisis.' In: Dalby, David and Harrison Church, R.J. (eds.): 17–32.

1980 *Recherches multidisciplinaires sur la région de Maradi: rapport de synthèse.* Programme de Recherches sur la Région de Maradi, Université de Bordeaux II.

Raynaut, C., Koechlin, J., Brasset, P., Cheung, Ch. and Stigliano, M., 1988 *Projet de Développement Rural de Maradi. Le développement rural de la région au village.* Bordeaux: GRID.

Reardon, T.A., Matlon, P. and Delgado, C., 1988 'Coping with household level food insecurity in drought-affected areas of Burkina Faso.' *World Development*, 16(9): 1065–74.

Reij, C., Scoones, I. and Toulmin, C. (eds.), 1996 *Sustaining the soil: indigenous soil and water conservation in Africa*. London: Earthscan.

Reijntjes, C. and Moolhuijzen, M., 1995 'Searching for new methods.' *ILEIA Newsletter for Low External Input and Sustainable Agriculture*, 11(2): 4–5.

Reining, P. (comp.), 1978 *Handbook on desertification indicators*. Washington, DC: American Association for the Advancement of Science.

Renner, G.T., 1926 'A famine zone in Africa: the Sudan.' *The Geographical Review*, 16: 583–96.

Richards, P., 1983 *Indigenous agricultural revolution. Ecology and food production in West Africa*. London: Hutchinson.

de Ridder, N. and Breman, H., 1993 'A new approach to evaluating rangeland productivity in Sahelian countries.' In: Behnke, R.H., Scoones, I. and Kerven, C. (eds.): 104–17.

Ringrose, S. and Matheson, W., 1991 'A Landsat analysis of range conditions in the Botswana Kalahari.' *International Journal of Remote Sensing*, 12: 1023–51.

Rocheleau, D., Benjamin, P. and Diang'a, A., 1995 'The Ukambani region of Kenya.' In: Kasperson, J.X., Kasperson, R.E. and Turner, B.L. II (eds.), *Regions at risk: comparisons of threatened environments*. Tokyo: United Nations University Press.

Rosenzweig, C., Parry, M. L., Fischer, G. and Frohberg, K., 1993 'Climate change and world food supply.' *Research Report* 3. Environmental Change Unit, University of Oxford.

Rosenzweig, Cynthia and Parry, Martin L., 1994 'Potential impact of climate change on world food supply.' *Nature*, 367: 133–38.

Ross, P.J., 1987 'Land as a right to membership: land tenure dynamics in a peripheral area of the Kano Close-Settled Zone.' In: Watts, Michael (ed.), *State, oil and agriculture in Nigeria*: 223–47. Institute of International Studies, University of California.

Rostom, R.S. and Mortimore, M., 1991 'Environmental change and dryland management in Machakos District, Kenya, 1930–1990. Land use profile.' *ODI Working Paper* 58. London: Overseas Development Institute.

Rouch, Jean, 1956 'Migrations au Ghana.' *Journal de la Société des Africanistes*, 26: 33–196.

Rowland, M.G.M., Paul, A., Prentice, A.M., Müller, E., Hutton, M., Barrell, R.A.E. and Whitehead, R.G., 1981 'Seasonality and growth of infants in a Gambian village.' In: Chambers *et al.*: 164–74.

Rukandema, M., Mavua, J.K. and Audi, P.O., 1981 'The farming system of lowland Machakos, Kenya. Farm survey results from Mwala.' *Farming Systems Economic Research Programme Technical Report* no 1. Nairobi: Ministry of Agriculture.

Sandford, S., 1983 *Management of pastoral development in the Third World*. Chichester: John Wiley.

SAS, 1996 *Lettre d'Information* 03 (13 August). Montpellier: Surveillance des Acridiens au Sahel.

Schapera, L., 1953 *The Tswana*. London: International African Institute.

Scoones, I. (ed.), 1991 *Wetlands in drylands: the agro-ecology of savanna systems in Africa*. 3 Parts. London: International Institute for Environment and Development.

——— 1993 'Why are there so many? Cattle population dynamics in the communal areas of Zimbabwe.' In: Behnke, R.H., Scoones, I. and Kerven, C. (eds.): 62–76.

Sen, A., 1981 *Poverty and famines: an essay on entitlement*. Oxford: The Clarendon Press.

Shaw, T. and Colville, G., 1950 *Report of Nigerian Livestock Mission*. London: His Majesty's Stationery Office.

Shenton, B. and Watts, M., 1979 'Capitalism and hunger in Northern Nigeria.' *Review of African Political Economy*, 15/16: 53–62.

Shepherd, A., 1988 'Case studies of famine: Sudan.' In: Curtis, D., Hubbard, M. and Shepherd, A., *Preventing famine. Policies and prospects for Africa.* 28–72. London: Routledge.

Simmons, E. B., 1981 'A case study in food production, sale and distribution.' In: Chambers, R., Longhurst, R. and Pacey, A. (eds.): 73–79.

Sivakumar, M.V.K., 1992 'Climate change and implications for agriculture in Niger.' *Climatic Change*, 20: 297–312.

Sivakumar, M.V.K., Maidoukia, A. and Stern, R.D., 1993 'Agroclimatology of West Africa: Niger.' *Information Bulletin*, 5. Niamey/Patancheru: International Crops Research Institute for the Semi-arid Tropics.

Smaling, E., 1993 *An agro-ecological framework for integrated nutrient management with special reference to Kenya.* Ph.D thesis, Wageningen Agricultural University.

Snrech, S., with Cour, J.-M., de Lattre, A. and Naudet, J.D., 1994 *West Africa Long Term Perspective Study. Preparing for the future: a vision of West Africa in the year 2020. Summary report.* Paris: Club du Sahel/OECD.

Somerville, D., 1986 *Drought and aid in the Sahel. A decade of development co-operation.* Boulder, CO: Westview Press.

Stamp, L.D., 1940 'The southern margins of the Sahara: comments on some recent studies on the question of desiccation in West Africa.' *The Geographical Review*, 30: 297–300.

Stangel, P.J., 1995 'Nutrient cycling and its importance in sustaining crop-livestock systems in sub-Saharan Africa: an overview.' In: Powell, J.M. *et al.* (eds.): 37–62.

Stebbing, E.P., 1935 'The encroaching Sahara: the threat to the West African colonies.' *The Geographical Journal*, 88: 506–24.

1937 'The threat of the Sahara.' *Journal of the Royal African Society*, Supplement (May).

1953 *The creeping desert in the Sudan and elsewhere in Africa, 15–13 degrees latitude.* Khartoum: McCorqudale.

Stern, R.D., Dennett, M.D. and Larbutt, D.J., 1981 'The start of the rains in West Africa.' *Journal of Climatology*, 1: 59–68.

Stiles, D., 1995 'Desertification is not a myth.' *Desertification Control Bulletin*, 26: 29–36.

Stock, R., 1995 *Africa south of the Sahara. A geographical interpretation.* New York: Guilford Press.

Stocking, M., 1996 'Soil erosion. Breaking new ground.' In: Leach, M. and Mearns, R. (eds.): 140–54.

Stocking, M. and Pain, A., 1983 'Soil life and minimum soil depth for product yields: developing a new concept.' *Discussion Paper* 50. Norwich: School of Development Studies, University of East Anglia.

Sutter, J. W., 1987 'Cattle and inequality: herd size differences and pastoral production among the Fulani of northeastern Senegal.' *Africa*, 57: 196–218.

Swift, Jeremy, 1981 'Labour and subsistence in a pastoral economy.' In: Chambers, R., Longhurst, R. and Pacey, A. (eds.): 80–86.

1996 'Desertification: narratives, winners and losers.' In: Leach, M. and Mearns, R.(eds.): 73–90.

Swindell, K., 1984 'Farmers, traders and labourers: dry season migration from north-west Nigeria, 1900–1933.' *Africa*, 54: 3–19.

Temple, C.L., 1918 *Native races and their rulers.* Capetown (reprinted 1968, London: Frank Cass).

Thomas, D.B., 1991 'Soil erosion.' In: Mortimore, M. (ed.), 'Environmental change and dryland management in Machakos District, Kenya, 1930–90. Environmental profile.' *ODI Working Paper* 53. London: Overseas Development Institute.

Thomas, D. and Middleton, N., 1994 *Desertification: exploding the myth.* Chichester: John Wiley.

Thomas, M.F. and Thorp, M.B., 1993 'Landscape dynamics and surface deposits arising from late Quaternary fluctuations in the forest–savanna boundary.' In: Furley, P.A., Proctor, J. and Ratter, J.A. (eds.), *Nature and dynamics of forest–savanna boundaries*: 215–53. London: Chapman and Hall.

Tiffen, M., 1991 'Environmental change and dryland management in Machakos District, Kenya, 1930–90. Population profile.' *ODI Working Paper* 54. London: Overseas Development Institute.

Tiffen, M., Mortimore, M. and Gichuki, F., 1994 *More people, less erosion: environmental recovery in Kenya.* Chichester: John Wiley.

Tiffen, M. and Mortimore, M., 1994 'Malthus controverted: the role of capital and technology in growth and environmental recovery in Kenya.' *World Development*, 22(7): 997–1010.

Tolba, M.K., 1986 'Desertification.' *WMO Bulletin*, 35: 17–22.

1987 'Ten years after UNCOD.' *Land Use Policy*, 4: 363–70.

Toulmin, C., 1992 *Cattle, women and wells. Managing household survival in the Sahel.* Oxford: The Clarendon Press.

Tucker, Compton J., Dregne, Harold E. and Newcomb, Wilbur W., 1991 'Expansion and contraction of the Sahara Desert from 1980 to 1990.' *Science*, 253: 299–301.

Turner, B., 1984 'Changing land use patterns in the *fadamas* of northern Nigeria.' In: Scott, Earl (ed.), *Life before the drought*: 149–70. London: Allen and Unwin.

1986 'The importance of *dambos* in African agriculture.' *Land Use Policy*, 3: 343–7.

1989 'The role of *fadamas* in land resource management in northern Nigeria.' In: Olofin, E.A. and Patrick, S. (eds.), *Land administration and development in northern Nigeria: case studies.* Kano: Department of Geography, Bayero University.

1990 'Water resources development and irrigation: a case study of the Kafue flats.' In: Wood, A.P., Kean, S.A., Milimo, J.T. and Warren, D.M. (eds.), *The dynamics of agricultural policy and reform in Zambia*: 137–51. Ames: Iowa State University Press.

1996 'Land cover around four villages in north-east Nigeria: methodology and results.' *Soils, Cultivars and Livelihoods in north-east Nigeria – Working Paper No. 5.* Department of Geography, University of Cambridge/Department of Geography, Bayero University, Kano.

Turner, B.L. II, Kates, R.W. and Hyden, G. (eds.), 1993 *Population growth and agricultural change in Africa.* Gainesville: University Press of Florida.

UNDP, 1991 *Human development report, 1991.* Oxford: Oxford University Press.

UNEP, 1977a *Report of the United Nations Conference on Desertification, 29 August – 9 September, 1977.* Nairobi: United Nations Environment Programme.

1977b *United Nations Conference on Desertification, 29 August – 9 September, 1977. World map of desertification, at a scale of 1: 25M.* Nairobi: United Nations Environment Programme.

1992 *World atlas of desertification.* Nairobi: United Nations Environment Programme.

1993 'Good news in the fight against desertification.' *Desertification Control Bulletin*, 22: 3.

UNESCO, 1979 *Carte de la répartition mondiale des régions arides.* Notes Techniques du MAB 7. Paris: United Nations Educational, Scientific and Cultural Organisation.

UNESCO/AETFAT/UNSO (White, F.), 1981 *Vegetation map of Africa, 1: 5M.* Paris: United Nations Educational, Scientific and Cultural Organisation.

Union of South Africa, 1923 *Final Report of the Drought Investigation Commission.* Capetown: Government of South Africa.

1951 *Report of the Desert Encroachment Committee.* Pretoria: Government Printer.

USAID, 1972 *Desert encroachment on arable lands: significance, causes and control.* Washington, DC: United States Agency for International Development.

de Waal, A., 1989 *The famine that kills. Darfur, Sudan, 1984–1985.* Oxford: The Clarendon Press.

Walker, B.H., Ludwig, D., Holling, C.S. and Peterman, R.M., 1981 'Stability of semi-arid savanna grazing systems.' *Journal of Ecology,* 69: 473–98.

Walker, J. and Rowntree, P.R., 1977 'The effect of soil moisture on circulation and rainfall in a tropical model.' *Quarterly Journal of the Royal Meteorological Society,* 103: 29–46.

Wallace, J.S. *et al.,* 1994 *Hapex-Sahel southern super-site report. An overview of the Hapex-Sahel southern super-site and the experimental programme during the intensive observation period in 1992.* Wallingford: Institute of Hydrology.

Warren, A. and Khogali, M., 1992 *Assessment of desertification and drought in the Sudano-Sahelian region, 1985–1991.* New York: United Nations Sudano-Sahelian Office.

Watts, M., 1983a *Silent violence. Food, famine and the peasantry in northern Nigeria.* University of California Press.

1983b 'On the poverty of theory: natural hazards research in context.' In: Hewitt, K. (ed.): 231–62.

Western, D., 1982 'The environment and ecology of pastoralism in arid savannas.' *Development and Change,* 13: 183–211.

White, C., 1987 'Food shortages and seasonality in WoDaaBe communities in Niger.' *IDS Bulletin,* 17: 19–26.

1990 'Changing animal ownership and access to land among the WoDaaBe (Fulani) of central Niger.' In: Baxter, P.T.W. and Hogg, R. (eds.), *Property, poverty and people: changing rights in property and problems of pastoral development:* 240–74. Manchester: Manchester University Press.

de Wilde, J.C., assisted by McLoughlin, P.F.M., Guinard, A., Scudder, T. and Maubouche, R., 1967 *Experiences with agricultural development in tropical Africa. Vol. 2. The case studies.* Baltimore: The Johns Hopkins University Press.

Williams, M.A.J. and Balling, R.C., 1995 'Interactions of desertification and climate: an overview.' *Desertification Control Bulletin,* 26: 8–16.

de Wispelaere, G. and Peyre de Fabregues, B., 1986 *Action de recherche méthodologique sur l'évaluation des ressources forragères par télédétection dans la région du Sud-Tamesna (Niger). Rapport de seconde année.* Maisons-Alfort: Institut d'Elevage et de Médicine Vétérinaire des Pays Tropicaux.

Wynne, B. and Sackley, S., 1994 'Environmental models – truth machine or social heuristics.' *The Globe* (UK Global Environmental Research Office), 21: 6–8.

Yusuf, M., 1996 'The farming system of Tumbau, Kano State, Nigeria.' *Soils, Cultivars and Livelihoods in North-east Nigeria. Working paper* No 1. Kano: Department of Geography, Bayero University.

Index

214